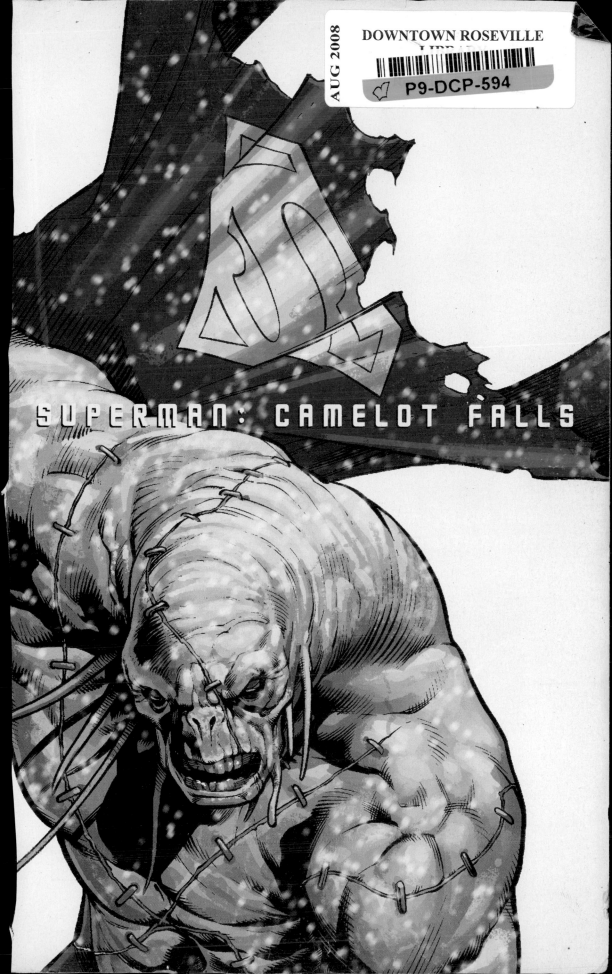

SUPERMAN: CAMELOT FALLS

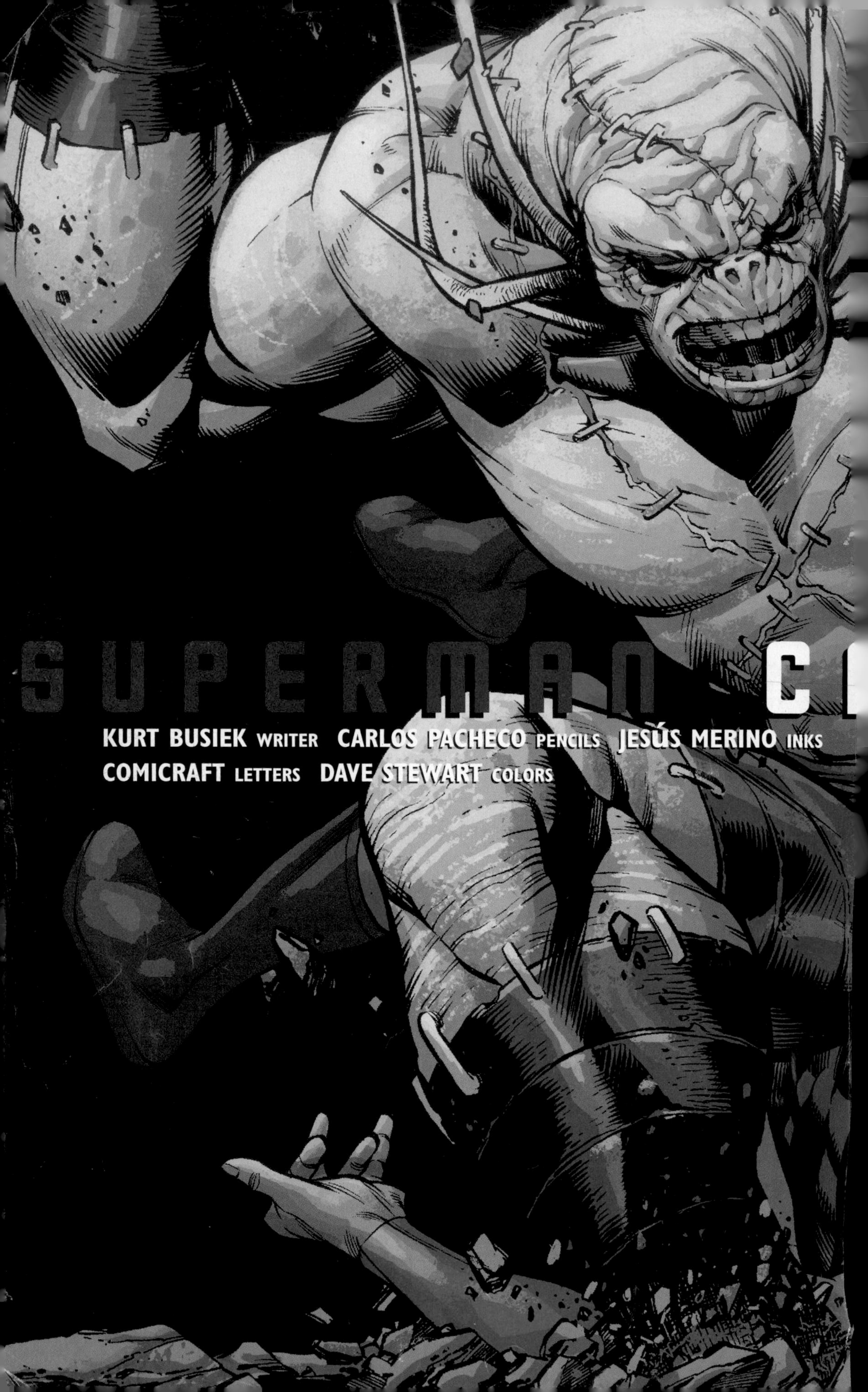
SUPERMAN C
KURT BUSIEK WRITER CARLOS PACHECO PENCILS JESÚS MERINO INKS
COMICRAFT LETTERS DAVE STEWART COLORS

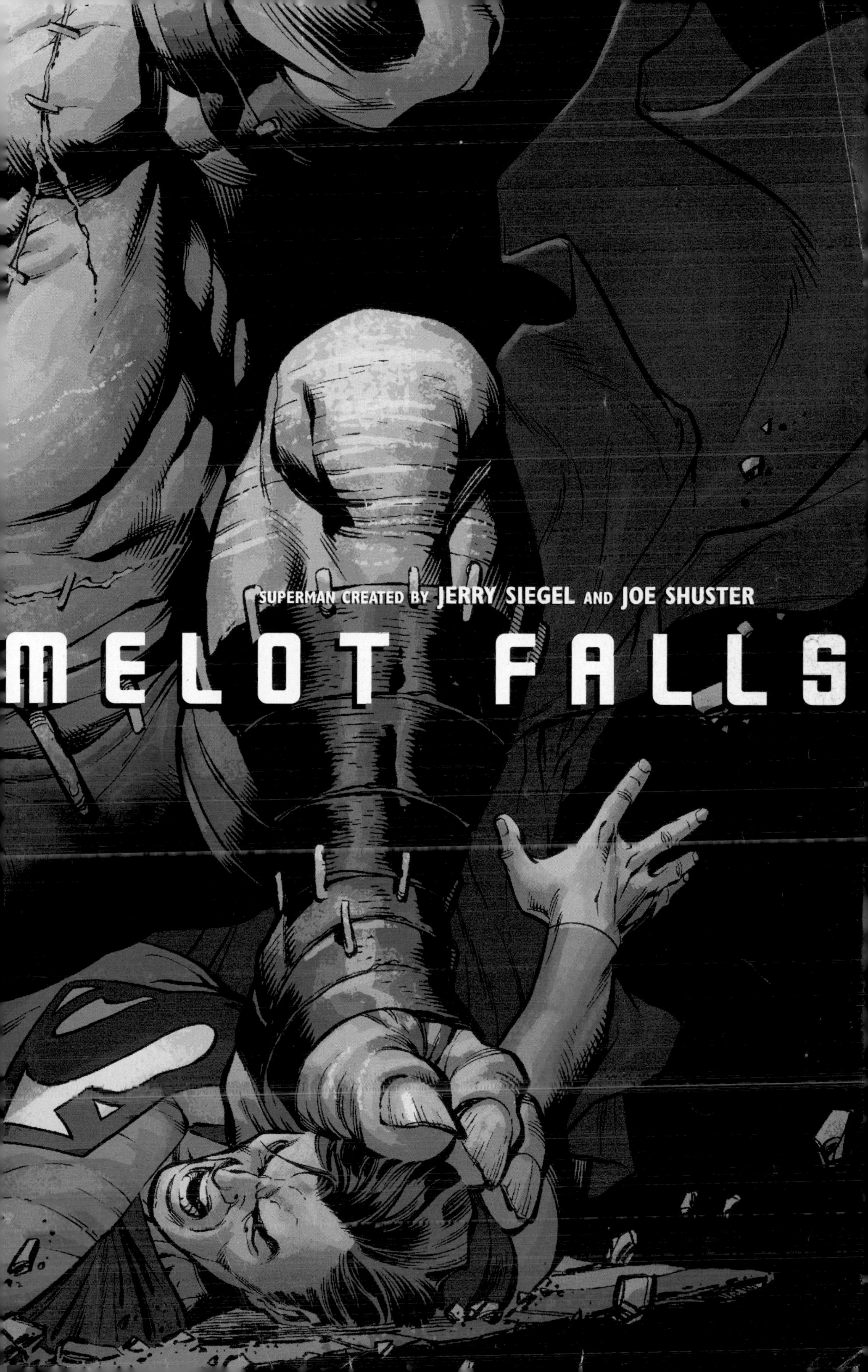
SUPERMAN CREATED BY JERRY SIEGEL AND JOE SHUSTER
MELOT FALLS

Dan DiDio
Senior VP-Executive Editor

Matt Idelson
Editor-original series

Nachie Castro
Associate editor-original series

Bob Harras
Group Editor-collected edition

Robbin Brosterman
Senior Art Director

Paul Levitz
President & Publisher

Georg Brewer
VP-Design & DC Direct Creative

Richard Bruning
Senior VP-Creative Director

Patrick Caldon
Executive VP-Finance & Operations

Chris Caramalis
VP-Finance

John Cunningham
VP-Marketing

Terri Cunningham
VP-Managing Editor

Stephanie Fierman
Senior VP-Sales & Marketing

Alison Gill
VP-Manufacturing

Hank Kanalz
VP-General Manager, WildStorm

Jim Lee
Editorial Director-WildStorm

Paula Lowitt
Senior VP-Business & Legal Affairs

MaryEllen McLaughlin
VP-Advertising & Custom Publishing

John Nee
VP-Business Development

Gregory Noveck
Senior VP-Creative Affairs

Cheryl Rubin
Senior VP-Brand Management

Jeff Trojan
VP-Business Development, DC Direct

Bob Wayne
VP-Sales

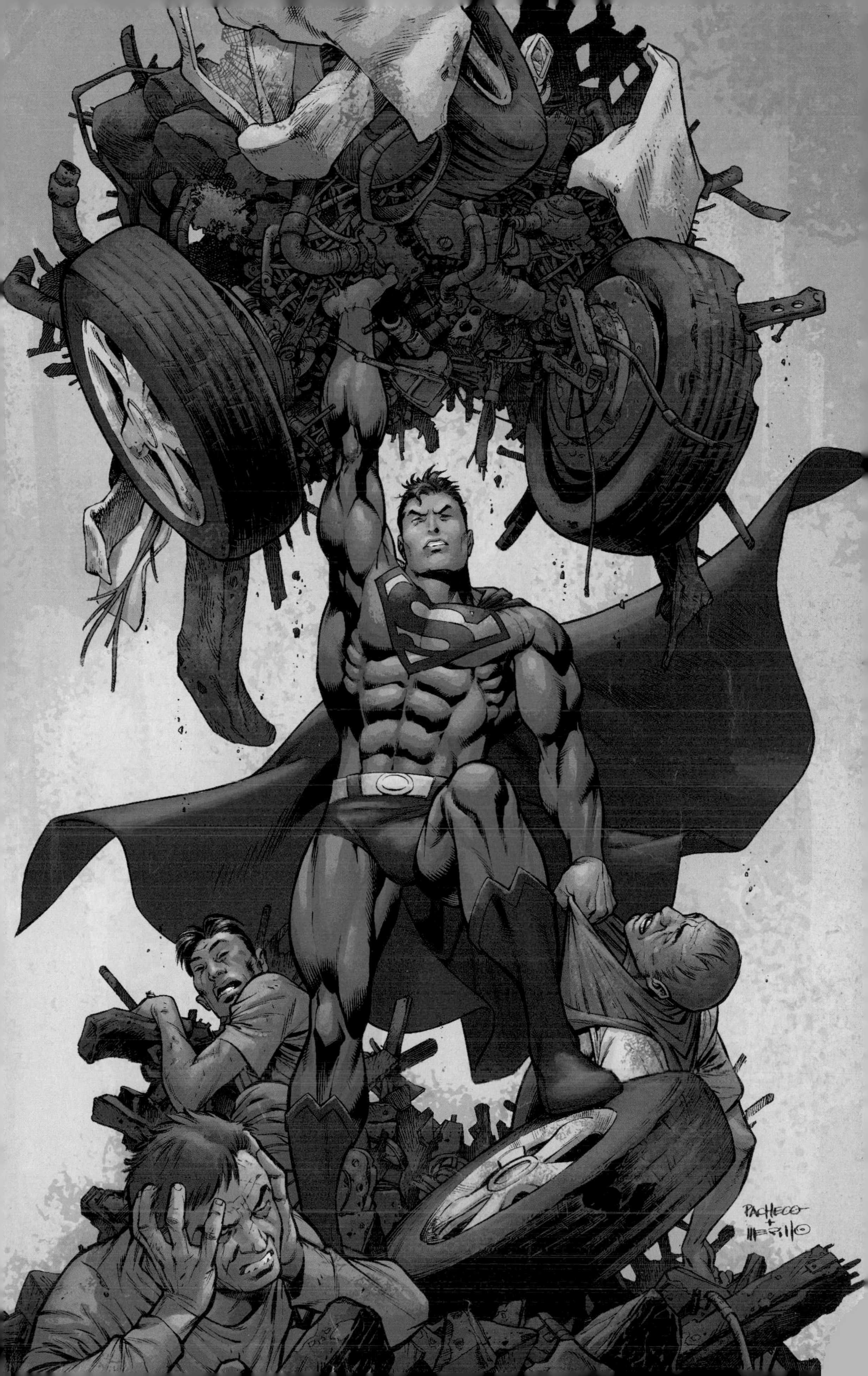
PACHECO
+
MERINO

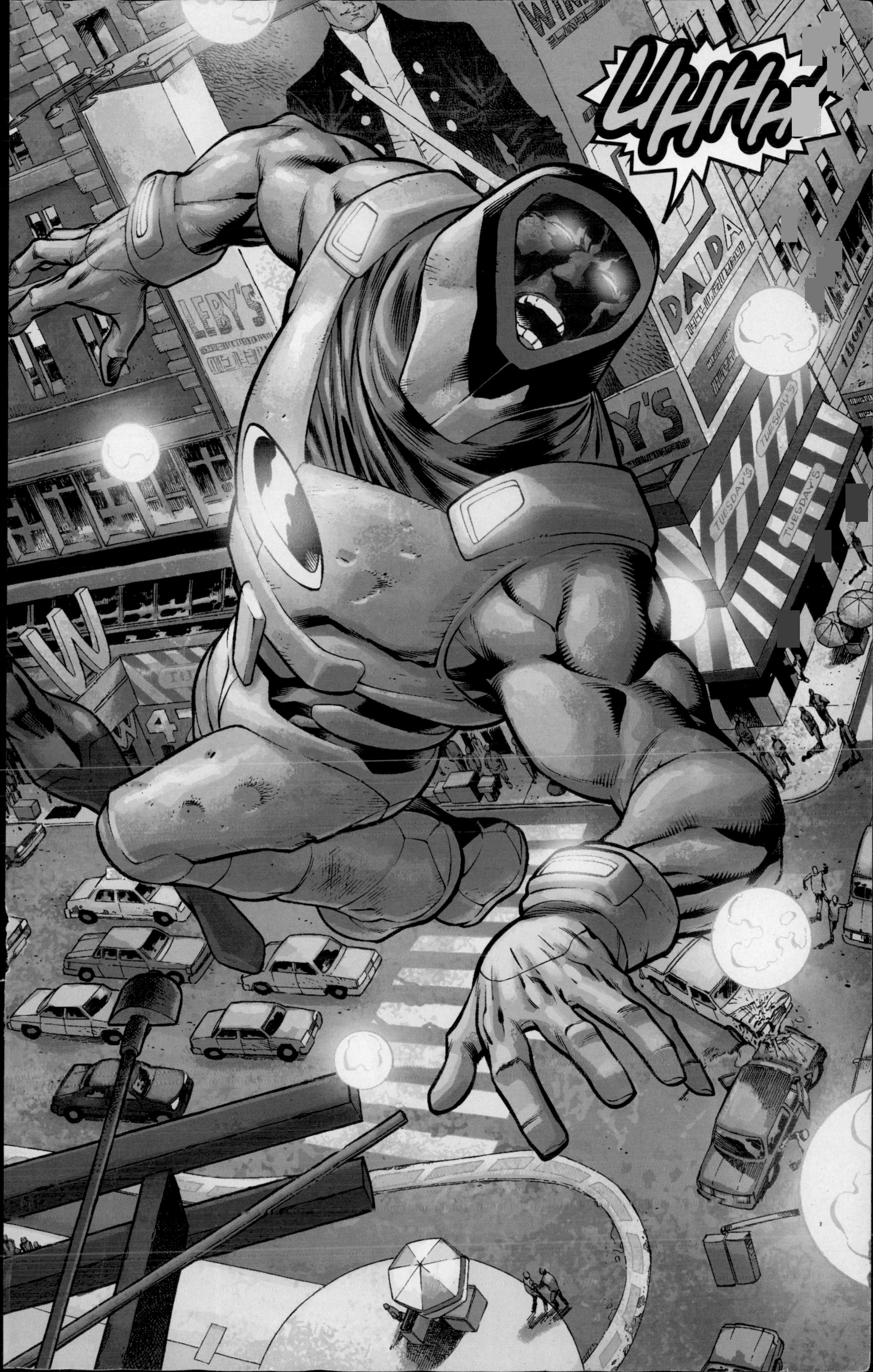
UHHH
LEBY'S
DAIDA
TUESDAY'S
TUESDAY'S
TUESDAY'S

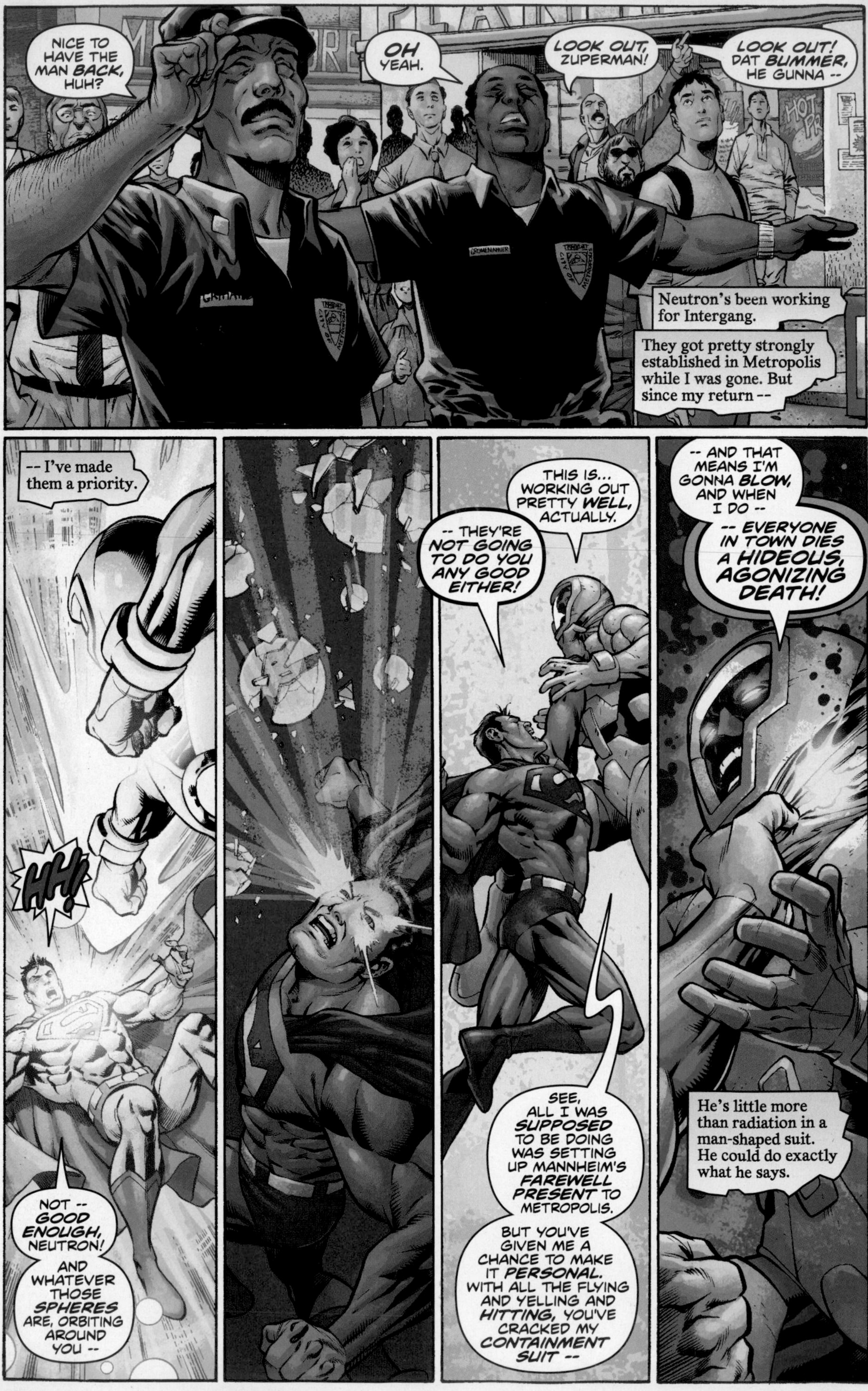
NICE TO HAVE THE MAN BACK, HUH?
OH YEAH.
LOOK OUT, ZUPERMAN!
LOOK OUT! DAT BUMMER, HE GUNNA --
Neutron's been working for Intergang.
They got pretty strongly established in Metropolis while I was gone. But since my return --
-- I've made them a priority.
HH!
NOT -- GOOD ENOUGH, NEUTRON!
AND WHATEVER THOSE SPHERES ARE, ORBITING AROUND YOU --
-- THEY'RE NOT GOING TO DO YOU ANY GOOD EITHER!
THIS IS... WORKING OUT PRETTY WELL, ACTUALLY.
SEE, ALL I WAS SUPPOSED TO BE DOING WAS SETTING UP MANNHEIM'S FAREWELL PRESENT TO METROPOLIS.
BUT YOU'VE GIVEN ME A CHANCE TO MAKE IT PERSONAL. WITH ALL THE FLYING AND YELLING AND HITTING, YOU'VE CRACKED MY CONTAINMENT SUIT --
-- AND THAT MEANS I'M GONNA BLOW, AND WHEN I DO --
-- EVERYONE IN TOWN DIES A HIDEOUS, AGONIZING DEATH!
He's little more than radiation in a man-shaped suit. He could do exactly what he says.

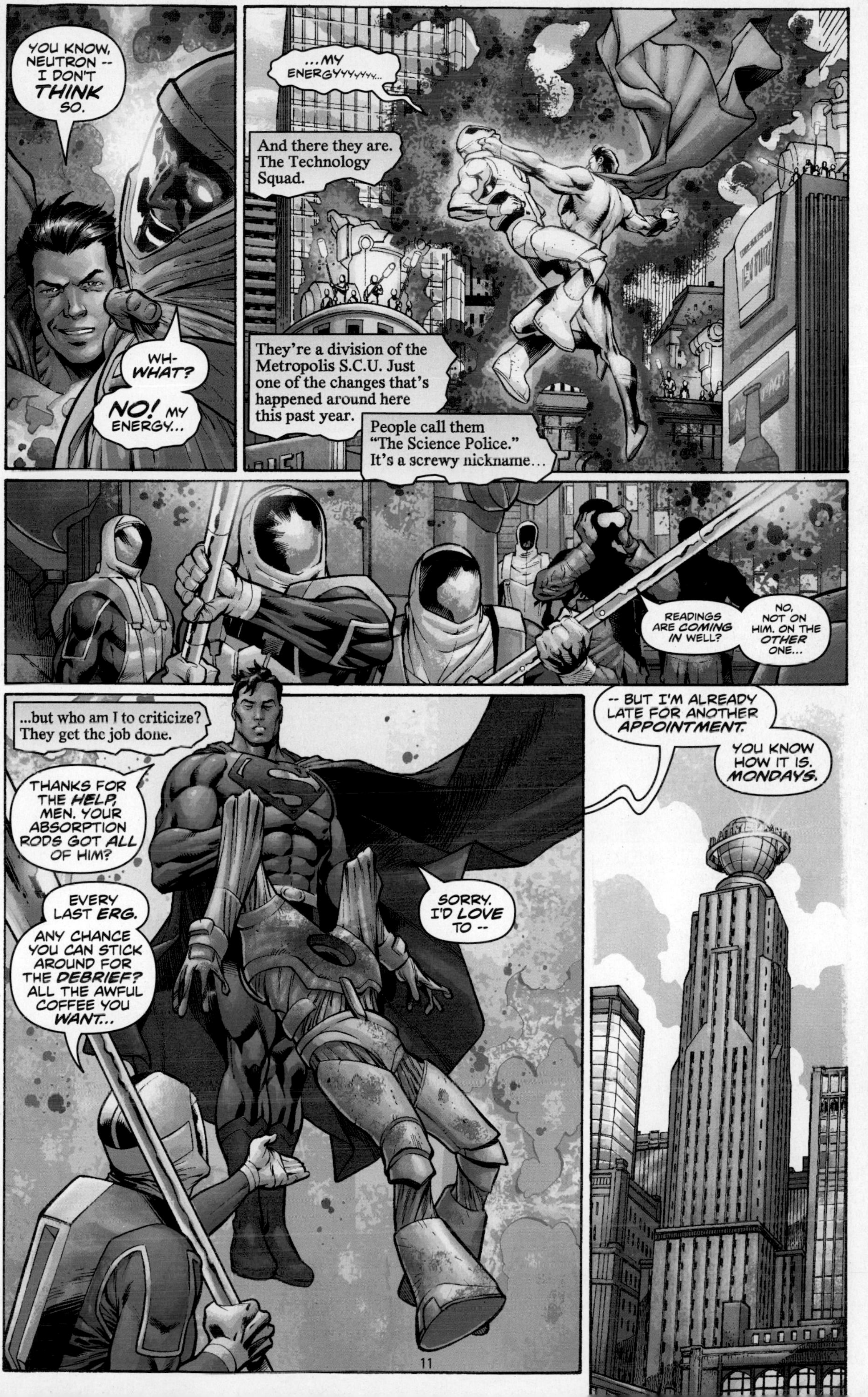
YOU KNOW, NEUTRON -- I DON'T THINK SO.
WH- WHAT?
NO! MY ENERGY...
...MY ENERGYYYYYYY...
And there they are. The Technology Squad.
They're a division of the Metropolis S.C.U. Just one of the changes that's happened around here this past year.
People call them "The Science Police." It's a screwy nickname...
READINGS ARE COMING IN WELL?
NO, NOT ON HIM. ON THE OTHER ONE...
...but who am I to criticize? They get the job done.
THANKS FOR THE HELP, MEN. YOUR ABSORPTION RODS GOT ALL OF HIM?
EVERY LAST ERG.
ANY CHANCE YOU CAN STICK AROUND FOR THE DEBRIEF? ALL THE AWFUL COFFEE YOU WANT...
SORRY. I'D LOVE TO --
-- BUT I'M ALREADY LATE FOR ANOTHER APPOINTMENT.
YOU KNOW HOW IT IS. MONDAYS.

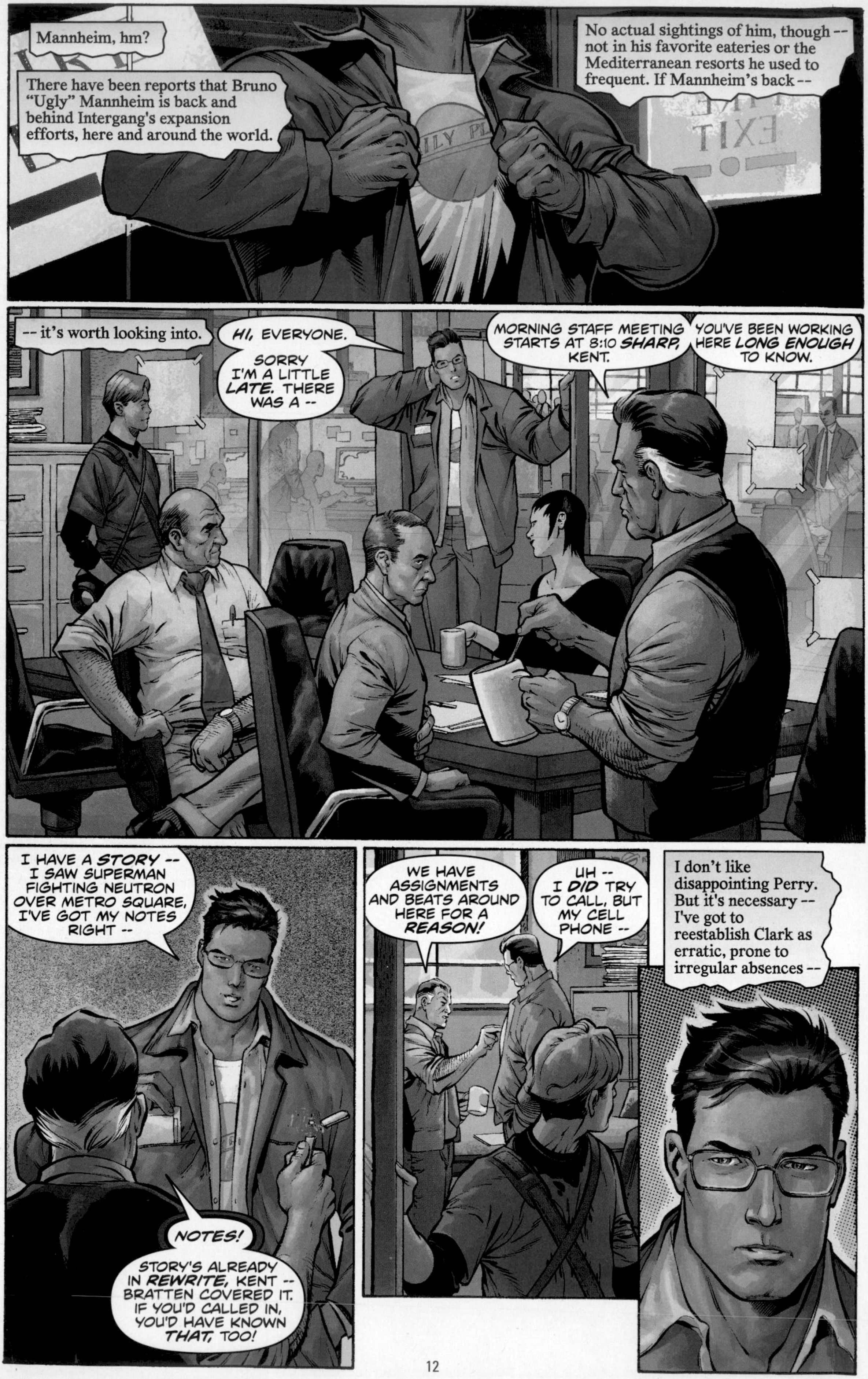

Mannheim, hm?
There have been reports that Bruno "Ugly" Mannheim is back and behind Intergang's expansion efforts, here and around the world.
No actual sightings of him, though -- not in his favorite eateries or the Mediterranean resorts he used to frequent. If Mannheim's back --
EXIT
-- it's worth looking into.
HI, EVERYONE.
SORRY I'M A LITTLE LATE. THERE WAS A --
MORNING STAFF MEETING STARTS AT 8:10 SHARP, KENT.
YOU'VE BEEN WORKING HERE LONG ENOUGH TO KNOW.
I HAVE A STORY -- I SAW SUPERMAN FIGHTING NEUTRON OVER METRO SQUARE, I'VE GOT MY NOTES RIGHT --
NOTES!
STORY'S ALREADY IN REWRITE, KENT -- BRATTEN COVERED IT. IF YOU'D CALLED IN, YOU'D HAVE KNOWN THAT, TOO!
WE HAVE ASSIGNMENTS AND BEATS AROUND HERE FOR A REASON!
UH -- I DID TRY TO CALL, BUT MY CELL PHONE --
I don't like disappointing Perry. But it's necessary -- I've got to reestablish Clark as erratic, prone to irregular absences --

I'M *SORRY*, PERRY. DIDN'T THINK IT THROUGH.

YOU REALLY *SHOULD* HAVE BEEN HERE, TOO. A COUPLE OF OLD *GIRLFRIENDS* OF YOURS HAVE POPPED UP IN THE NEWS.

OH?

LEXCORP WILL BE ANNOUNCING THEIR NEW *C.E.O.* TOMORROW, NOW THAT THEY'VE FORMALLY OUSTED LUTHOR. YOU MAY *RECOGNIZE* THE NAME --

-- I BELIEVE YOU TOOK HER TO THE *PROM.*

LANA LANG

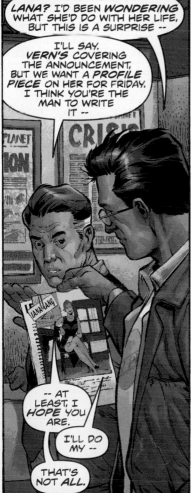

LANA? I'D BEEN *WONDERING* WHAT SHE'D DO WITH HER LIFE, BUT THIS IS A SURPRISE --

I'LL SAY. VERN'S COVERING THE ANNOUNCEMENT, BUT WE WANT A *PROFILE PIECE* ON HER FOR FRIDAY. I THINK YOU'RE THE MAN TO WRITE IT --

-- AT LEAST, I *HOPE* YOU ARE.

I'LL DO MY --

THAT'S NOT *ALL.*

LANA LANG

CAN YOU TELL ME WHY DR. CAROLYN LLEWELLYN, THE WORLD'S FOREMOST *ARCANOBIOLOGIST* --

-- WOULD ASK SPECIFICALLY FOR *YOU* TO BE THE PLANET REPORTER SENT TO COVER A BIG *HUSH-HUSH* PROJECT SHE'S WORKING ON IN KAZAKHSTAN?

CALLIE? NO, I --

"CALLIE"?

UH --

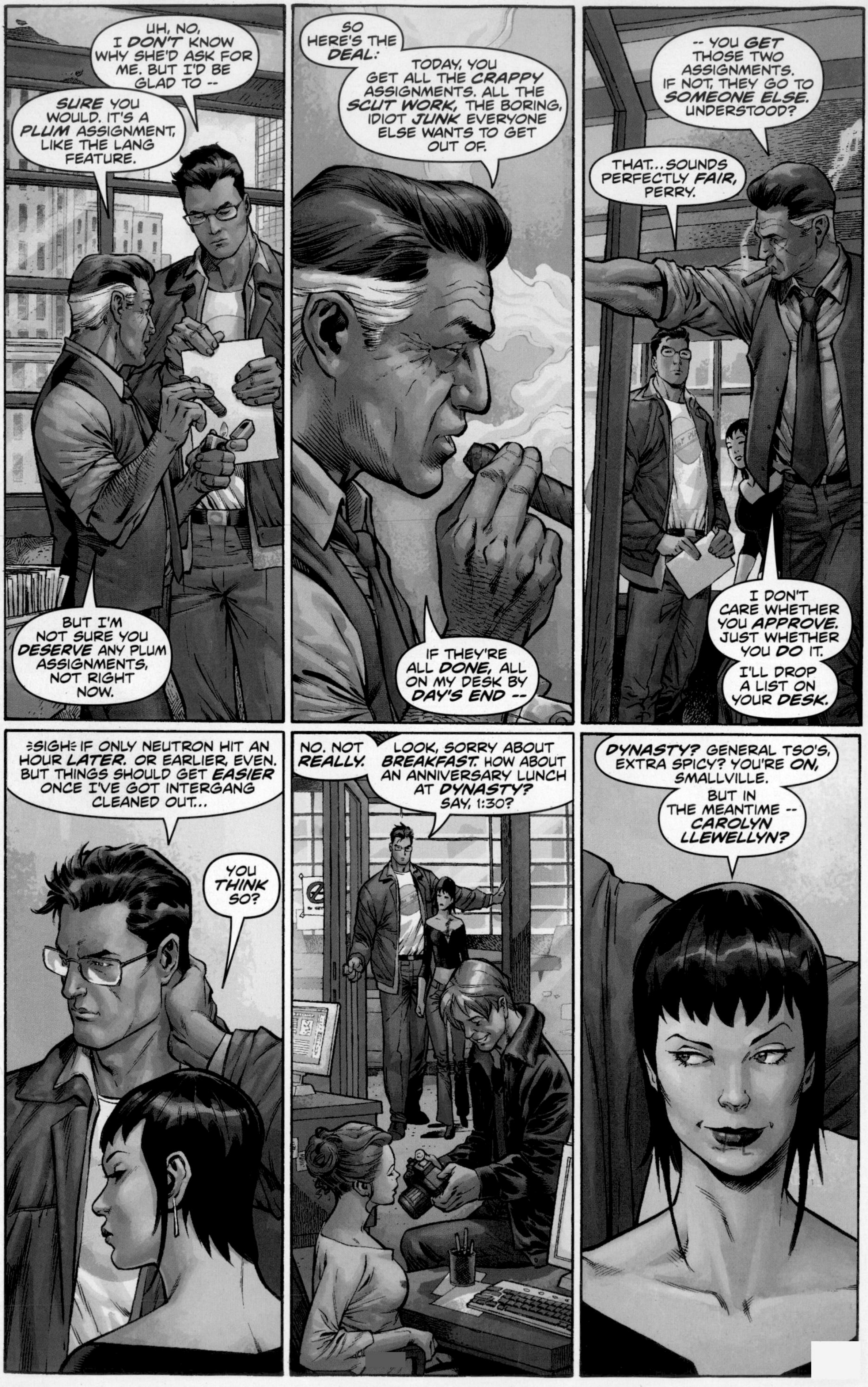
UH, NO, I DON'T KNOW WHY SHE'D ASK FOR ME. BUT I'D BE GLAD TO --
SURE YOU WOULD. IT'S A PLUM ASSIGNMENT, LIKE THE LANG FEATURE.
BUT I'M NOT SURE YOU DESERVE ANY PLUM ASSIGNMENTS, NOT RIGHT NOW.
SO HERE'S THE DEAL:
TODAY, YOU GET ALL THE CRAPPY ASSIGNMENTS. ALL THE SCUT WORK, THE BORING, IDIOT JUNK EVERYONE ELSE WANTS TO GET OUT OF.
IF THEY'RE ALL DONE, ALL ON MY DESK BY DAY'S END --
-- YOU GET THOSE TWO ASSIGNMENTS. IF NOT, THEY GO TO SOMEONE ELSE. UNDERSTOOD?
THAT... SOUNDS PERFECTLY FAIR, PERRY.
I DON'T CARE WHETHER YOU APPROVE. JUST WHETHER YOU DO IT.
I'LL DROP A LIST ON YOUR DESK.
=SIGH= IF ONLY NEUTRON HIT AN HOUR LATER. OR EARLIER, EVEN. BUT THINGS SHOULD GET EASIER ONCE I'VE GOT INTERGANG CLEANED OUT...
YOU THINK SO?
NO. NOT REALLY.
LOOK, SORRY ABOUT BREAKFAST. HOW ABOUT AN ANNIVERSARY LUNCH AT DYNASTY? SAY, 1:30?
DYNASTY? GENERAL TSO'S, EXTRA SPICY? YOU'RE ON, SMALLVILLE.
BUT IN THE MEANTIME -- CAROLYN LLEWELLYN?

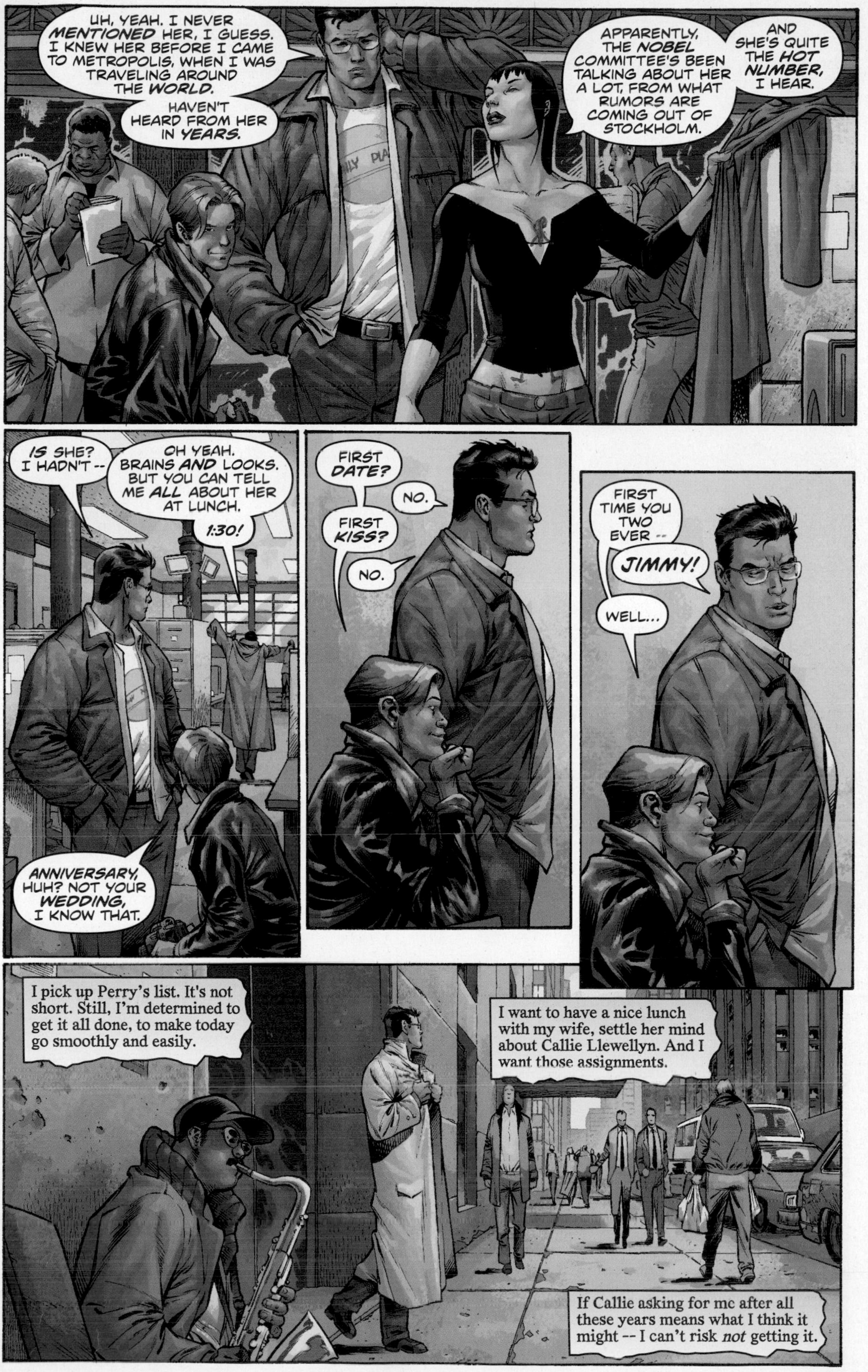

UH, YEAH. I NEVER MENTIONED HER, I GUESS. I KNEW HER BEFORE I CAME TO METROPOLIS, WHEN I WAS TRAVELING AROUND THE WORLD.
HAVEN'T HEARD FROM HER IN YEARS.
APPARENTLY, THE NOBEL COMMITTEE'S BEEN TALKING ABOUT HER A LOT, FROM WHAT RUMORS ARE COMING OUT OF STOCKHOLM.
AND SHE'S QUITE THE HOT NUMBER, I HEAR.
IS SHE? I HADN'T --
OH YEAH. BRAINS AND LOOKS. BUT YOU CAN TELL ME ALL ABOUT HER AT LUNCH.
1:30!
ANNIVERSARY, HUH? NOT YOUR WEDDING, I KNOW THAT.
FIRST DATE?
NO.
FIRST KISS?
NO.
FIRST TIME YOU TWO EVER --
JIMMY!
WELL...
I pick up Perry's list. It's not short. Still, I'm determined to get it all done, to make today go smoothly and easily.
I want to have a nice lunch with my wife, settle her mind about Callie Llewellyn. And I want those assignments.
If Callie asking for me after all these years means what I think it might -- I can't risk *not* getting it.

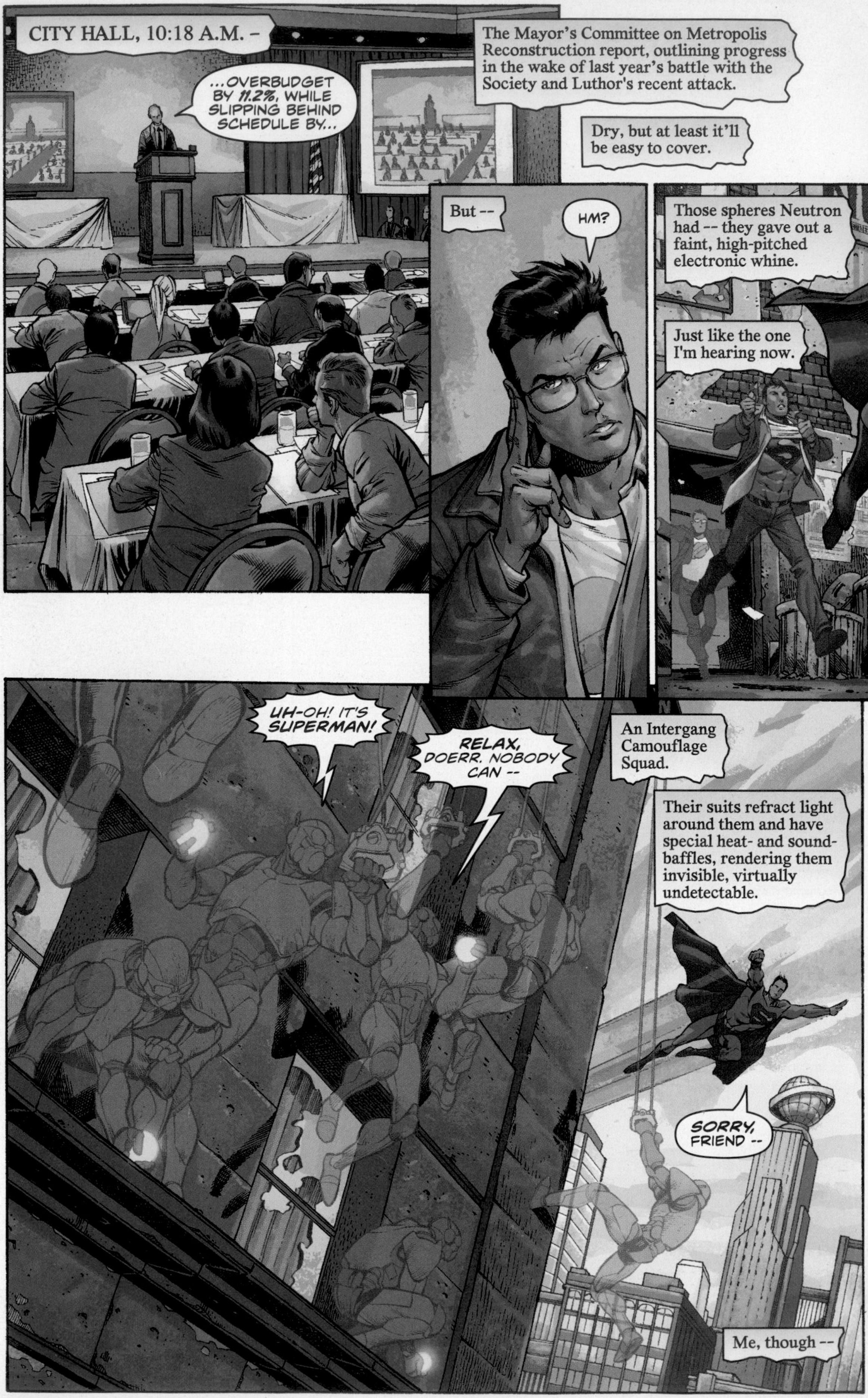
CITY HALL, 10:18 A.M. –
The Mayor's Committee on Metropolis Reconstruction report, outlining progress in the wake of last year's battle with the Society and Luthor's recent attack.
...OVERBUDGET BY 11.2%, WHILE SLIPPING BEHIND SCHEDULE BY...
Dry, but at least it'll be easy to cover.
But --
HM?
Those spheres Neutron had -- they gave out a faint, high-pitched electronic whine.
Just like the one I'm hearing now.
UH-OH! IT'S SUPERMAN!
RELAX, DOERR. NOBODY CAN --
An Intergang Camouflage Squad.
Their suits refract light around them and have special heat- and sound-baffles, rendering them invisible, virtually undetectable.
SORRY, FRIEND --
Me, though --

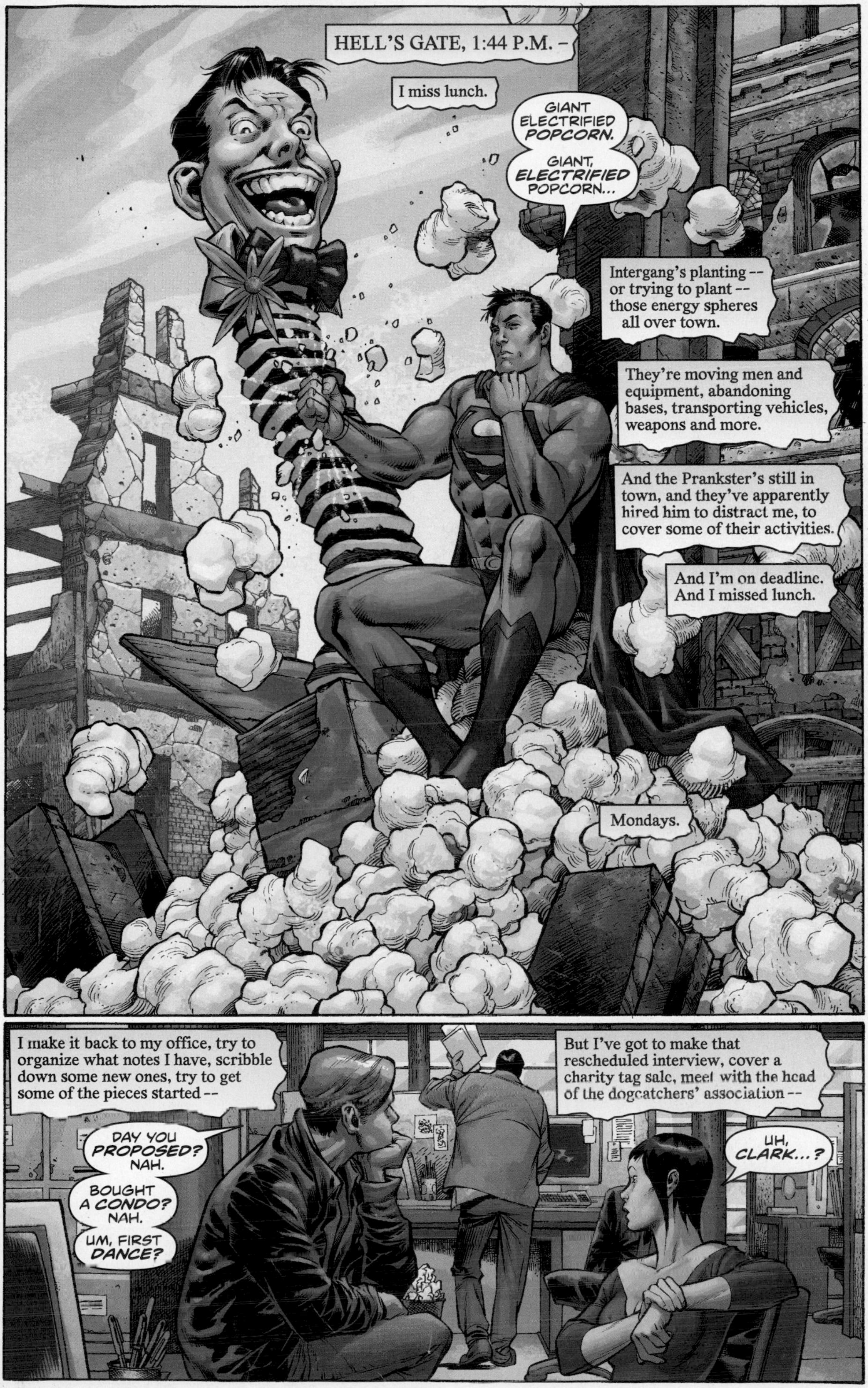
HELL'S GATE, 1:44 P.M. –
I miss lunch.
GIANT ELECTRIFIED POPCORN.
GIANT, ELECTRIFIED POPCORN...
Intergang's planting -- or trying to plant -- those energy spheres all over town.
They're moving men and equipment, abandoning bases, transporting vehicles, weapons and more.
And the Prankster's still in town, and they've apparently hired him to distract me, to cover some of their activities.
And I'm on deadline. And I missed lunch.
Mondays.
I make it back to my office, try to organize what notes I have, scribble down some new ones, try to get some of the pieces started --
But I've got to make that rescheduled interview, cover a charity tag sale, meet with the head of the dogcatchers' association --
DAY YOU PROPOSED? NAH.
BOUGHT A CONDO? NAH.
UM, FIRST DANCE?
UH, CLARK...?

SORRY, LOIS -- I'LL THINK OF SOMETHING TO MAKE UP FOR LUNCH.

I'VE GOT TO RUN...

HNH. NOT DOING SO WELL TODAY, IS HE?

I focus my hearing forward. I don't think I want to hear Lois's answer.

CENTRAL BUSINESS DISTRICT, 3:03 P.M. --

I'm almost done with the dogcatchers when I realize something. That hum the spheres make, there's a pattern to it. I mentally slow it down.

It's a pulse. Deep, slow, mild arrhythmia. It's "Ugly" Mannheim's pulse. I make my excuses and leave.

And I start listening. Hard.

I pick up the sound, but it's slower now. Deeper. It's coming from Suicide Slum.

The building's shielded with an energy field that gives off the spectrographic signature of lead paint.

I could have flown past a hundred times and not seen a thing.

And that "pulse" -- it's slowing further, almost at normal speed now --

Looks like the right place.

ZAK

ZKAM

NOBODY MOVE! I'M TAKING YOU ALL --

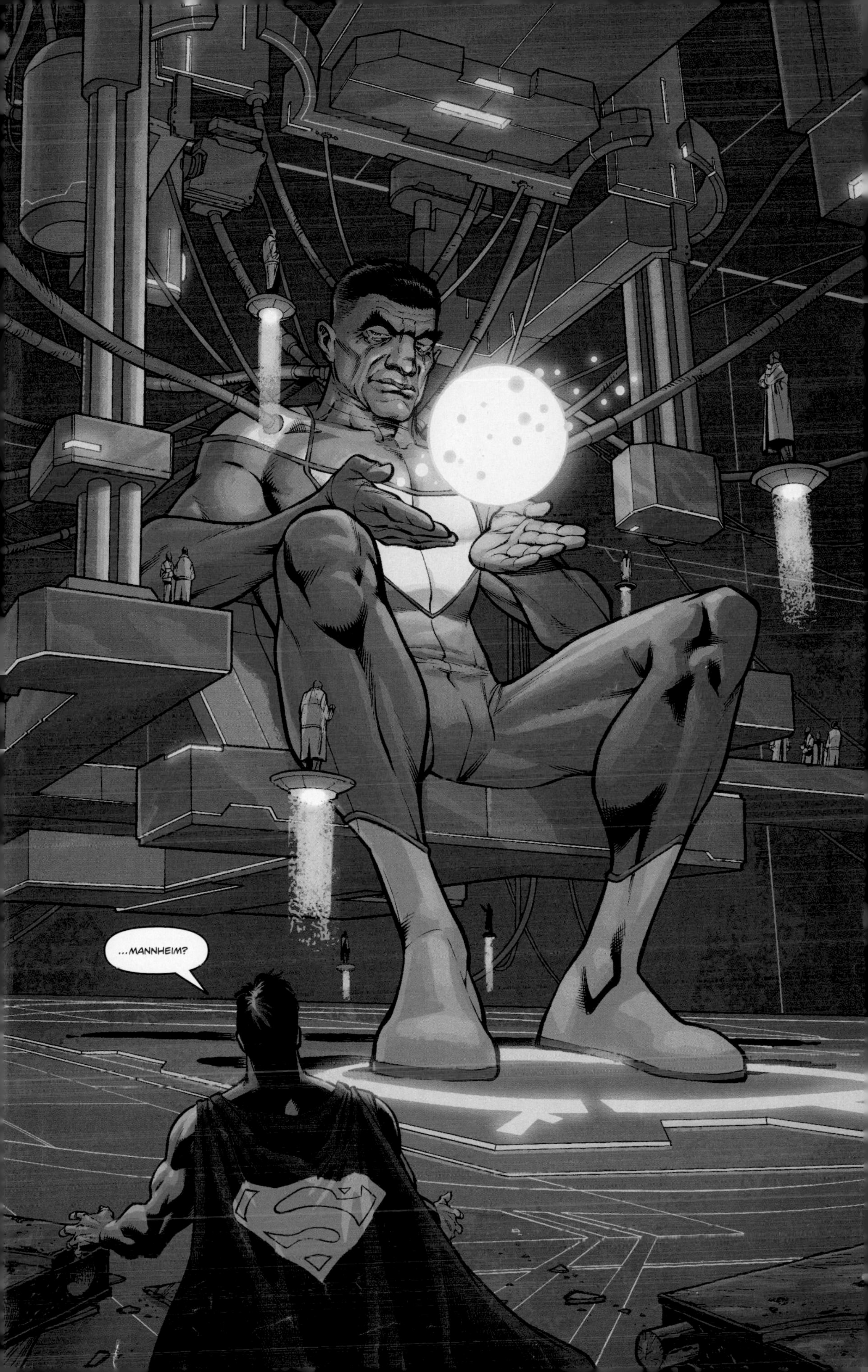
...MANNHEIM?

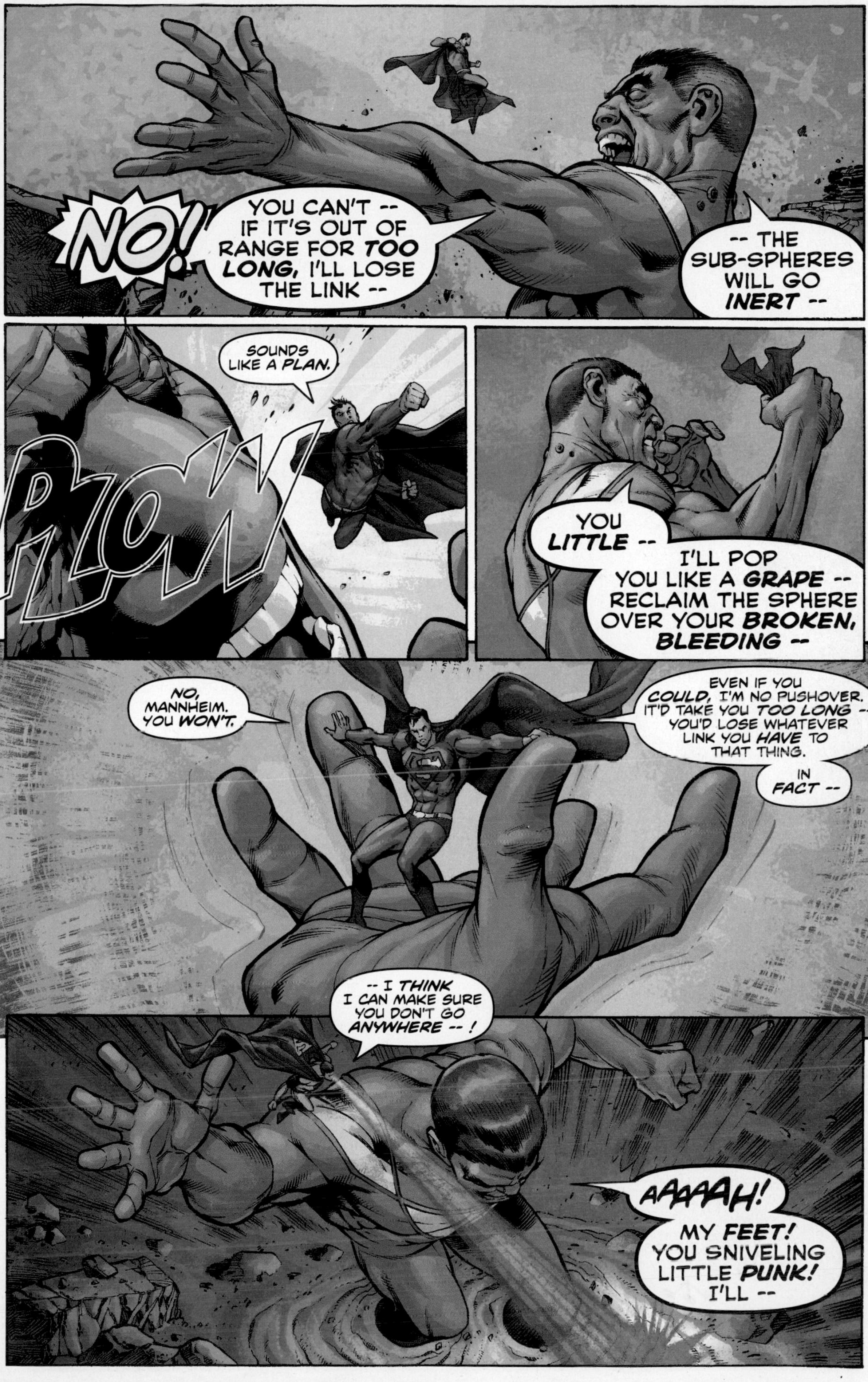
NO!
YOU CAN'T -- IF IT'S OUT OF RANGE FOR TOO LONG, I'LL LOSE THE LINK --
-- THE SUB-SPHERES WILL GO INERT --
SOUNDS LIKE A PLAN.
POW
YOU LITTLE --
I'LL POP YOU LIKE A GRAPE -- RECLAIM THE SPHERE OVER YOUR BROKEN, BLEEDING --
NO, MANNHEIM. YOU WON'T.
EVEN IF YOU COULD, I'M NO PUSHOVER. IT'D TAKE YOU TOO LONG -- YOU'D LOSE WHATEVER LINK YOU HAVE TO THAT THING.
IN FACT --
-- I THINK I CAN MAKE SURE YOU DON'T GO ANYWHERE -- !
AAAAAH!
MY FEET! YOU SNIVELING LITTLE PUNK! I'LL --

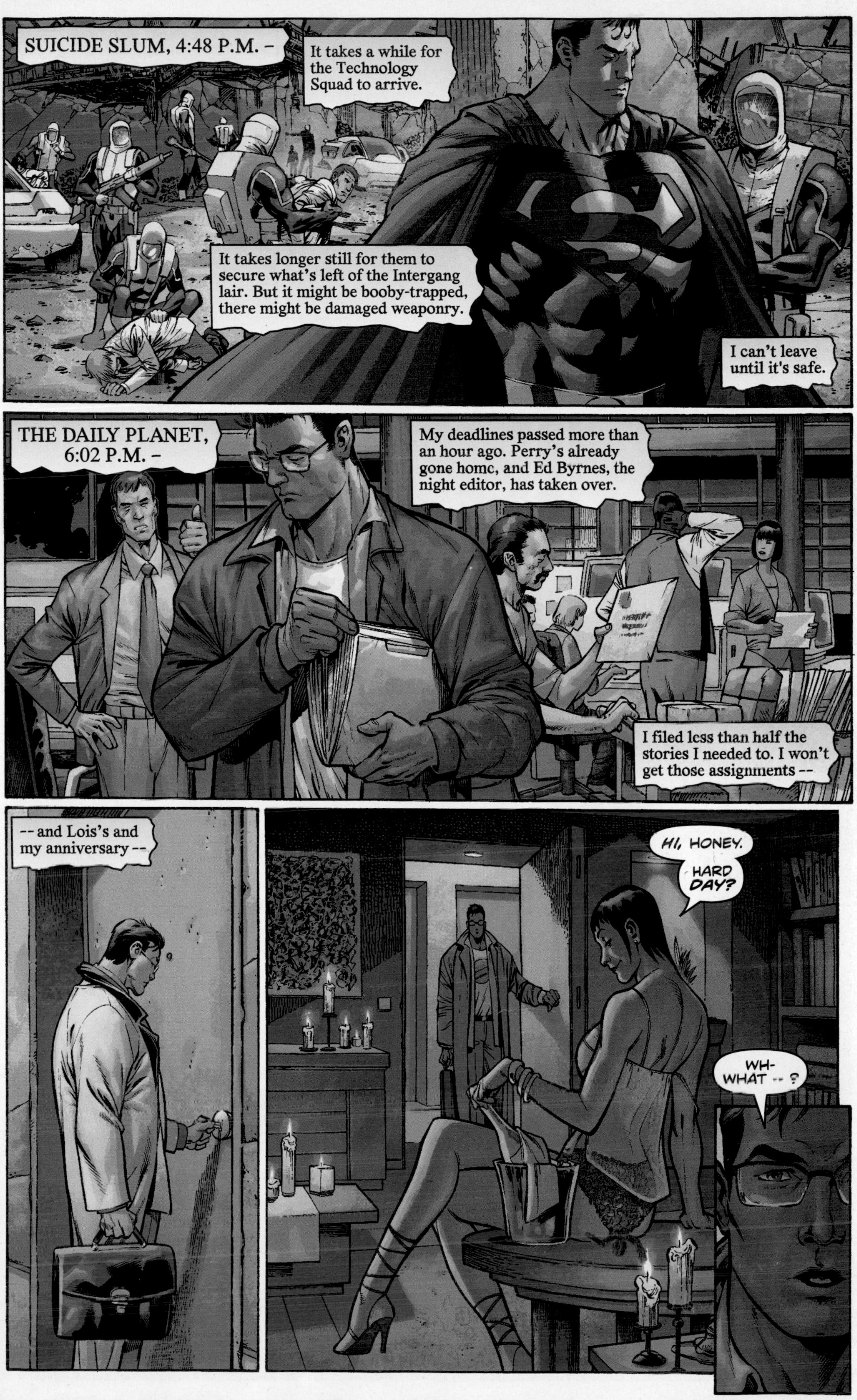
SUICIDE SLUM, 4:48 P.M. –
It takes a while for the Technology Squad to arrive.
It takes longer still for them to secure what's left of the Intergang lair. But it might be booby-trapped, there might be damaged weaponry.
I can't leave until it's safe.
THE DAILY PLANET, 6:02 P.M. –
My deadlines passed more than an hour ago. Perry's already gone home, and Ed Byrnes, the night editor, has taken over.
I filed less than half the stories I needed to. I won't get those assignments --
-- and Lois's and my anniversary --
HI, HONEY.
HARD DAY?
WH- WHAT -- ?

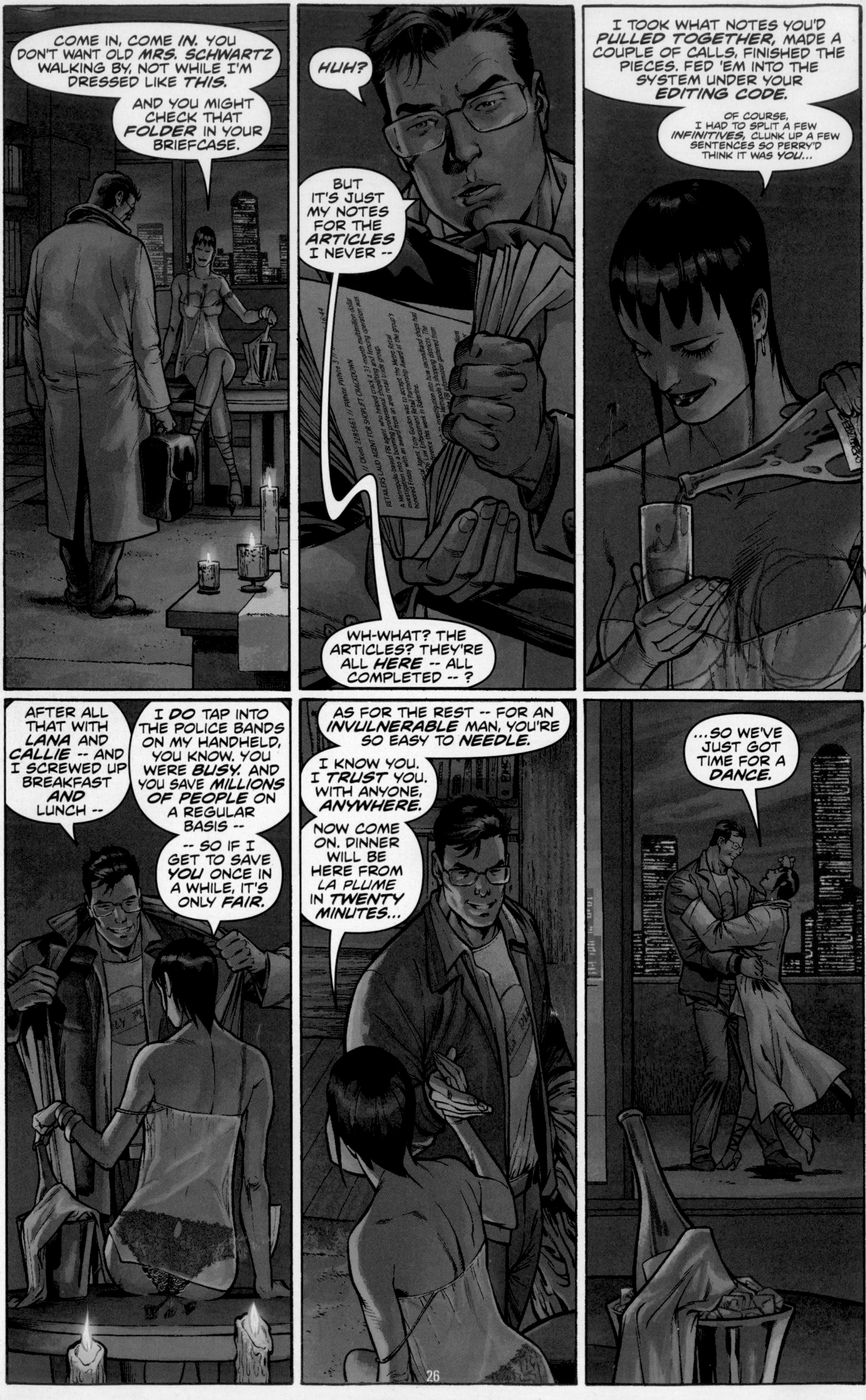
COME IN, COME IN. YOU DON'T WANT OLD MRS. SCHWARTZ WALKING BY, NOT WHILE I'M DRESSED LIKE THIS.
AND YOU MIGHT CHECK THAT FOLDER IN YOUR BRIEFCASE.
HUH?
BUT IT'S JUST MY NOTES FOR THE ARTICLES I NEVER --
WH-WHAT? THE ARTICLES? THEY'RE ALL HERE -- ALL COMPLETED -- ?
I TOOK WHAT NOTES YOU'D PULLED TOGETHER, MADE A COUPLE OF CALLS, FINISHED THE PIECES. FED 'EM INTO THE SYSTEM UNDER YOUR EDITING CODE.
OF COURSE, I HAD TO SPLIT A FEW INFINITIVES, CLUNK UP A FEW SENTENCES SO PERRY'D THINK IT WAS YOU...
AFTER ALL THAT WITH LANA AND CALLIE -- AND I SCREWED UP BREAKFAST AND LUNCH --
I DO TAP INTO THE POLICE BANDS ON MY HANDHELD, YOU KNOW. YOU WERE BUSY. AND YOU SAVE MILLIONS OF PEOPLE ON A REGULAR BASIS --
-- SO IF I GET TO SAVE YOU ONCE IN A WHILE, IT'S ONLY FAIR.
AS FOR THE REST -- FOR AN INVULNERABLE MAN, YOU'RE SO EASY TO NEEDLE.
I KNOW YOU. I TRUST YOU. WITH ANYONE, ANYWHERE.
NOW COME ON. DINNER WILL BE HERE FROM LA PLUME IN TWENTY MINUTES...
...SO WE'VE JUST GOT TIME FOR A DANCE.

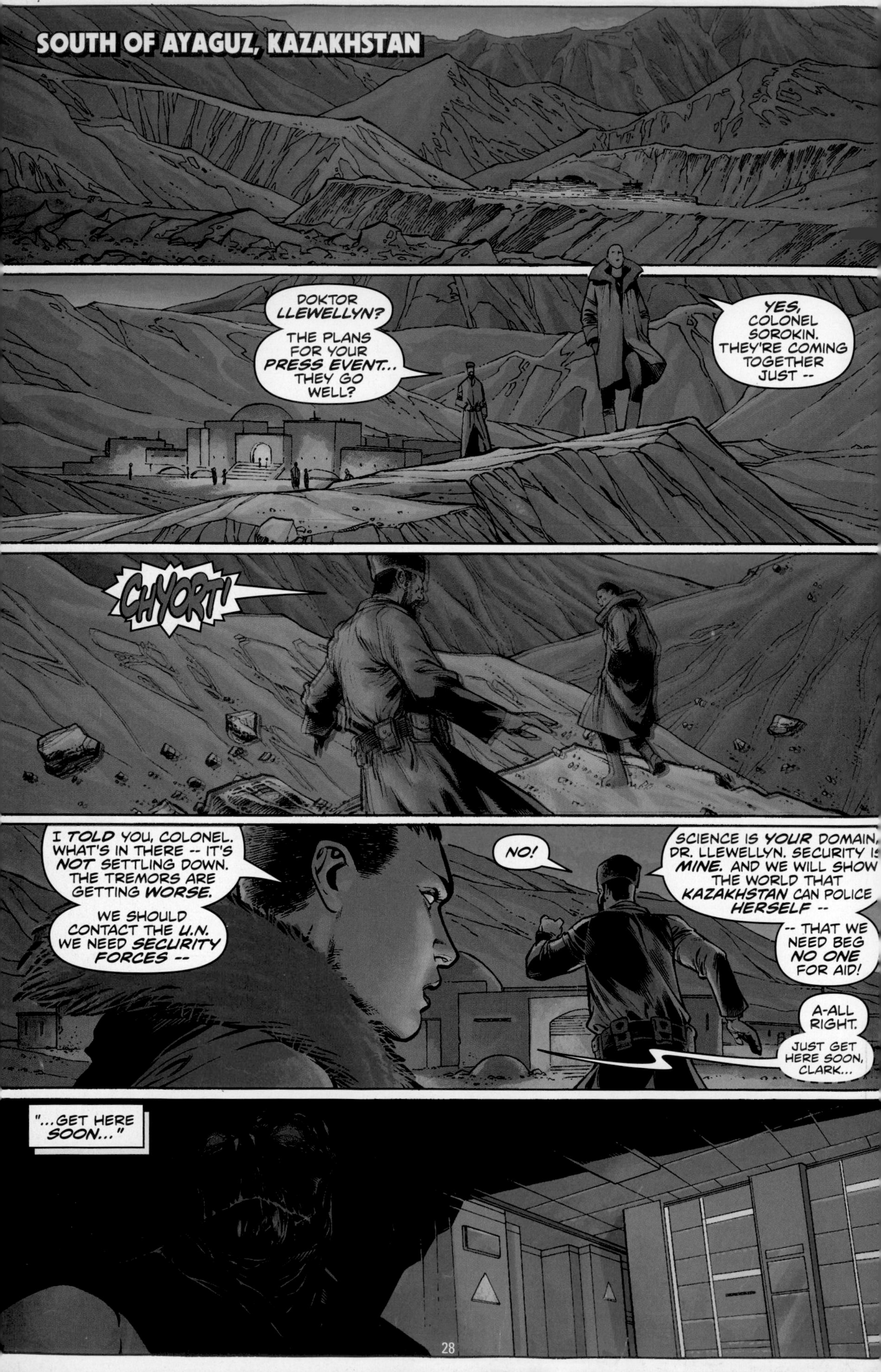
SOUTH OF AYAGUZ, KAZAKHSTAN
DOKTOR LLEWELLYN?
THE PLANS FOR YOUR PRESS EVENT... THEY GO WELL?
YES, COLONEL SOROKIN. THEY'RE COMING TOGETHER JUST --
CHYORT!
I TOLD YOU, COLONEL. WHAT'S IN THERE -- IT'S NOT SETTLING DOWN. THE TREMORS ARE GETTING WORSE.
WE SHOULD CONTACT THE U.N. WE NEED SECURITY FORCES --
NO!
SCIENCE IS YOUR DOMAIN, DR. LLEWELLYN. SECURITY IS MINE. AND WE WILL SHOW THE WORLD THAT KAZAKHSTAN CAN POLICE HERSELF --
-- THAT WE NEED BEG NO ONE FOR AID!
A-ALL RIGHT.
JUST GET HERE SOON, CLARK...
"...GET HERE SOON..."

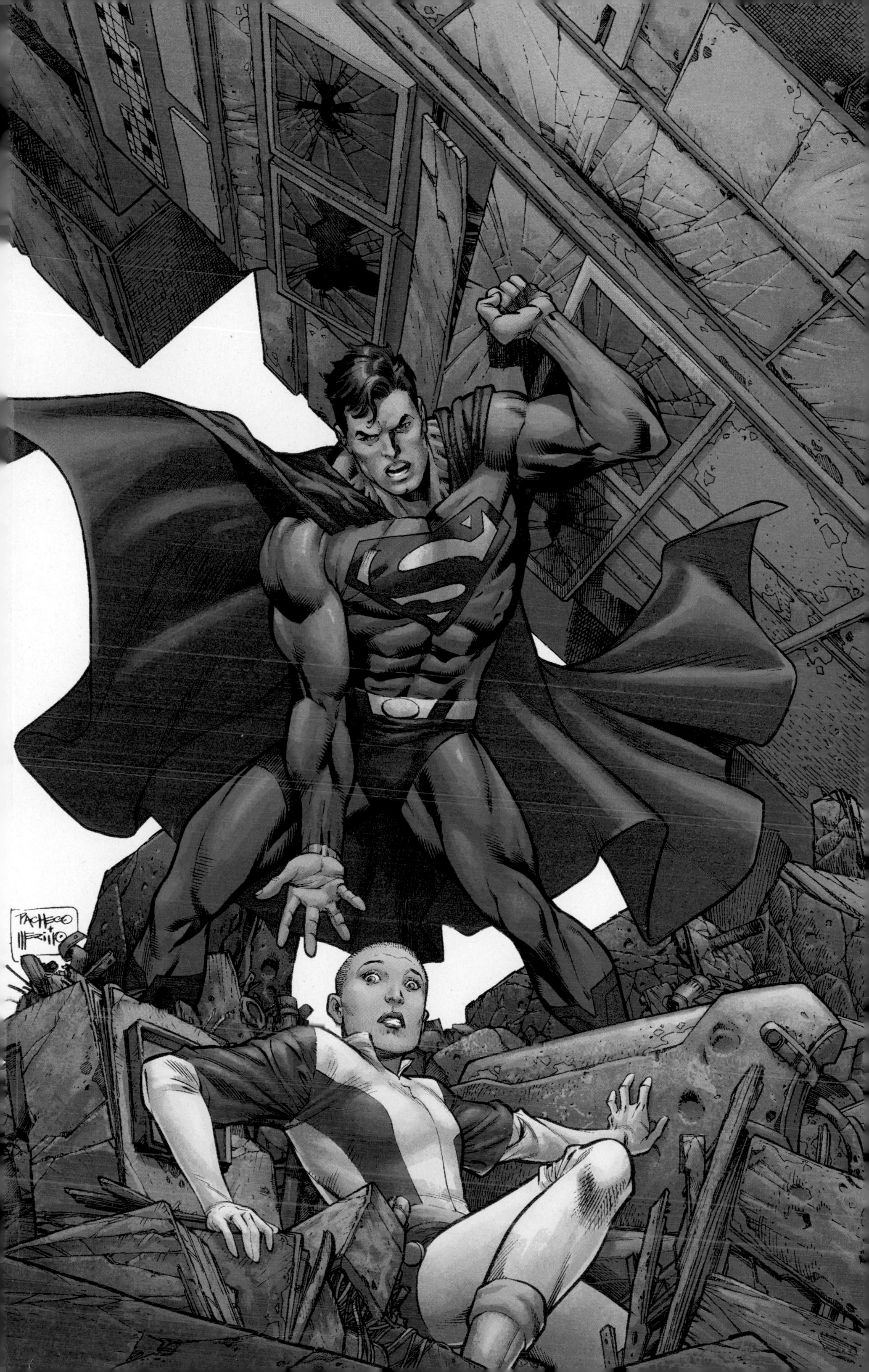
PACHECO + MERINO

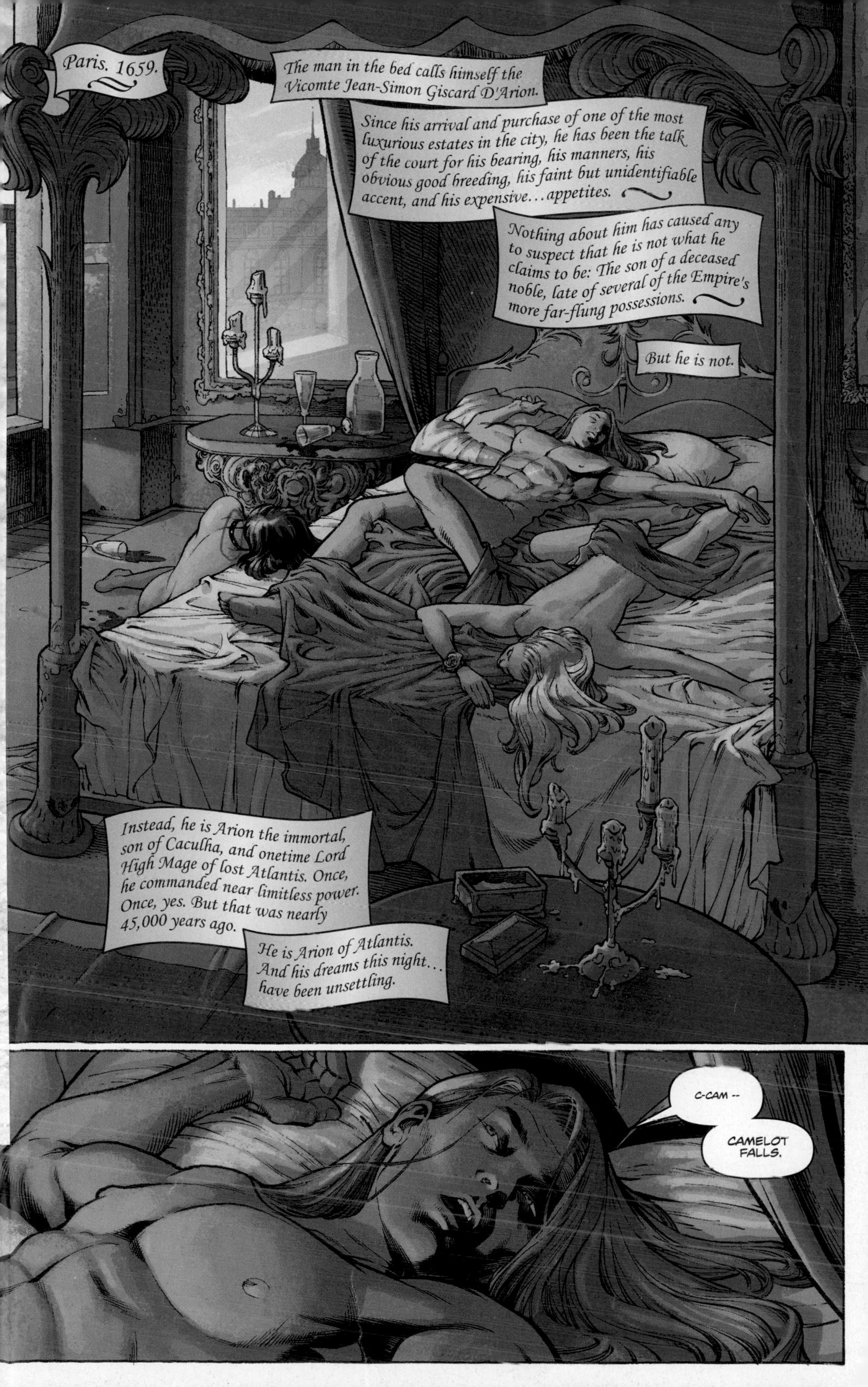
Paris. 1659.
The man in the bed calls himself the Vicomte Jean-Simon Giscard D'Arion.
Since his arrival and purchase of one of the most luxurious estates in the city, he has been the talk of the court for his bearing, his manners, his obvious good breeding, his faint but unidentifiable accent, and his expensive... appetites.
Nothing about him has caused any to suspect that he is not what he claims to be: The son of a deceased noble, late of several of the Empire's more far-flung possessions.
But he is not.
Instead, he is Arion the immortal, son of Caculha, and onetime Lord High Mage of lost Atlantis. Once, he commanded near limitless power. Once, yes. But that was nearly 45,000 years ago.
He is Arion of Atlantis. And his dreams this night... have been unsettling.
C-CAM --
CAMELOT FALLS.

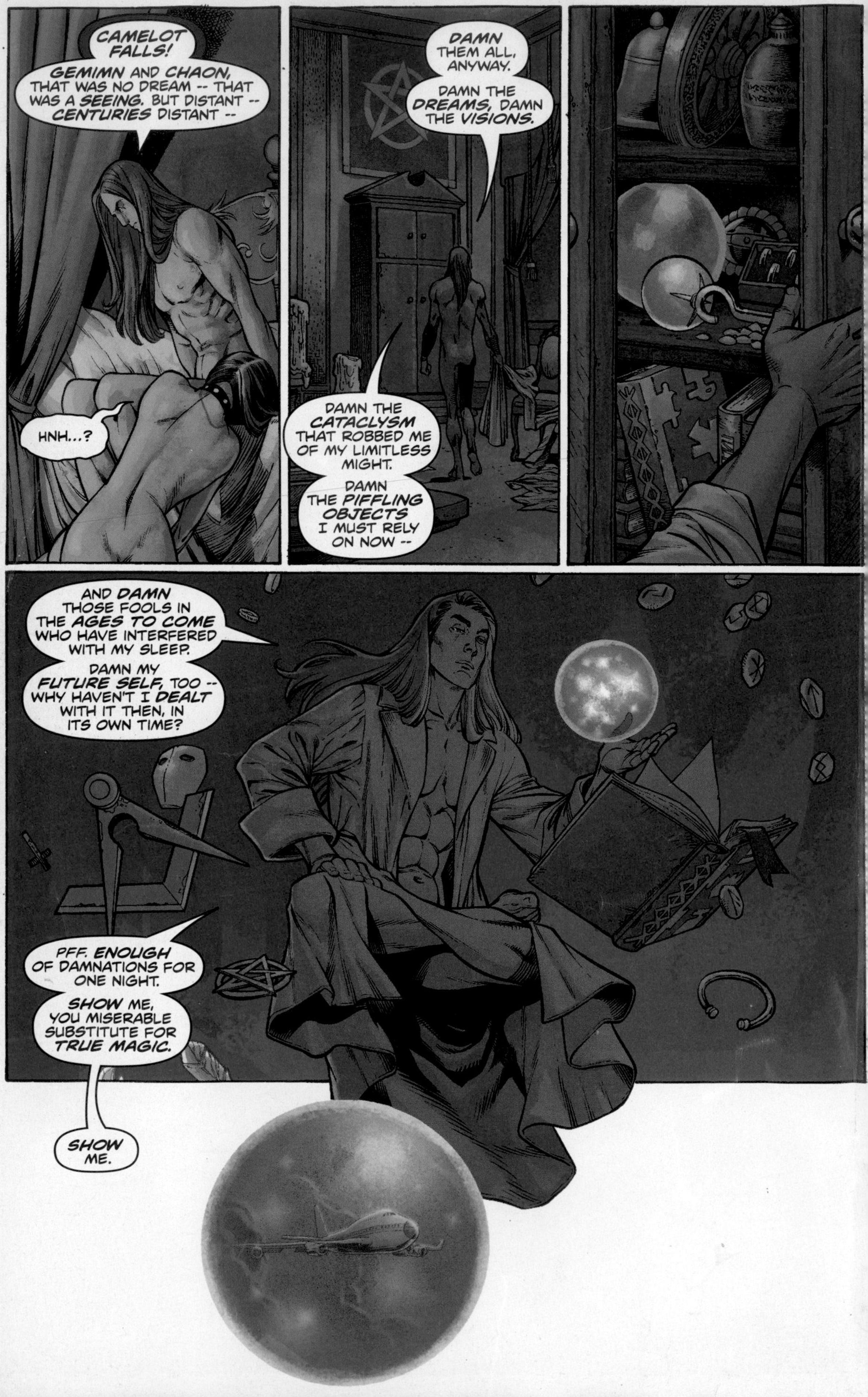
CAMELOT FALLS!
GEMIMN AND CHAON, THAT WAS NO DREAM -- THAT WAS A SEEING. BUT DISTANT -- CENTURIES DISTANT --
HNH...?
DAMN THEM ALL, ANYWAY.
DAMN THE DREAMS, DAMN THE VISIONS.
DAMN THE CATACLYSM THAT ROBBED ME OF MY LIMITLESS MIGHT.
DAMN THE PIFFLING OBJECTS I MUST RELY ON NOW --
AND DAMN THOSE FOOLS IN THE AGES TO COME WHO HAVE INTERFERED WITH MY SLEEP.
DAMN MY FUTURE SELF, TOO -- WHY HAVEN'T I DEALT WITH IT THEN, IN ITS OWN TIME?
PFF. ENOUGH OF DAMNATIONS FOR ONE NIGHT.
SHOW ME, YOU MISERABLE SUBSTITUTE FOR TRUE MAGIC.
SHOW ME.

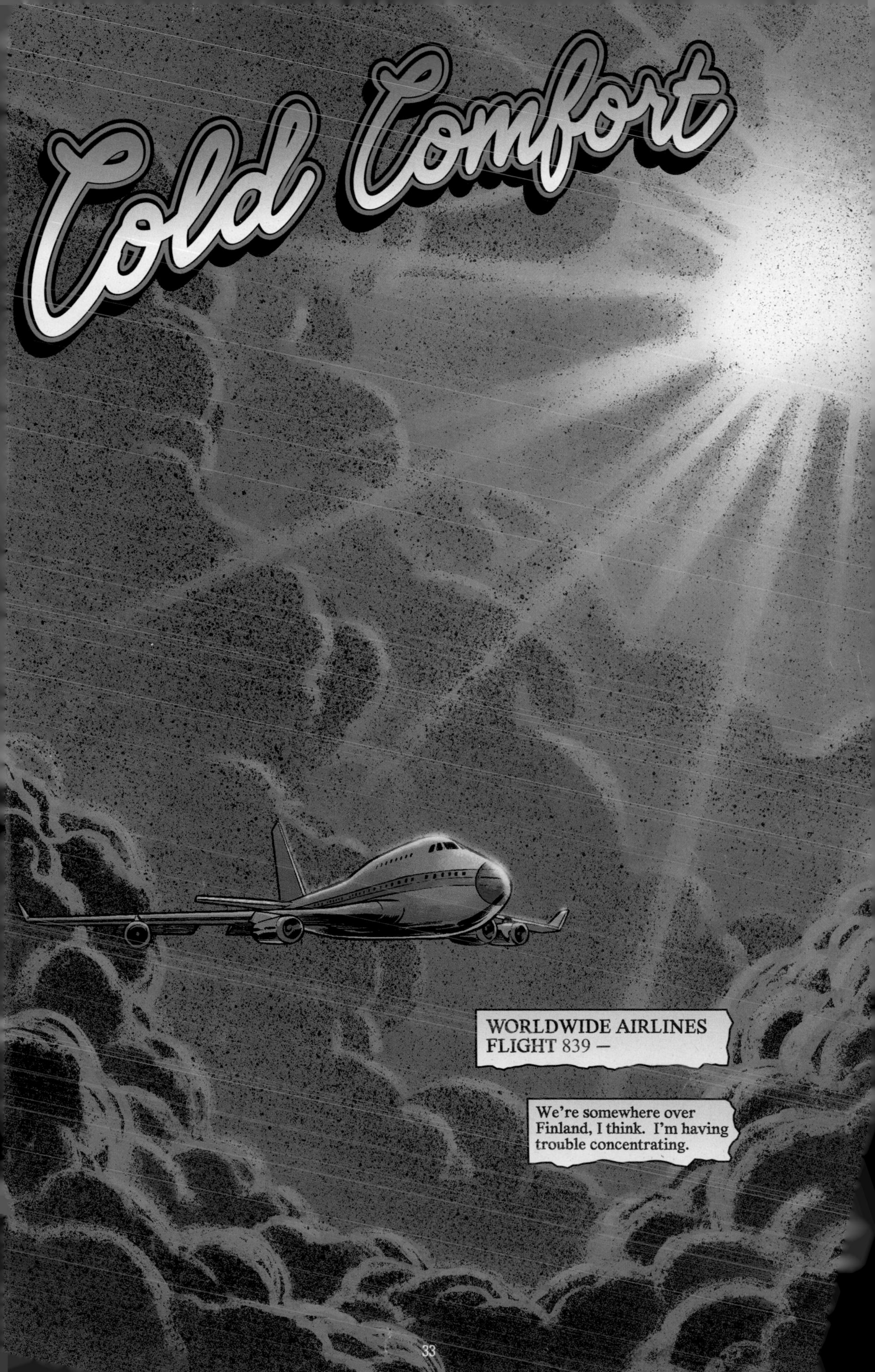
Cold Comfort
WORLDWIDE AIRLINES FLIGHT 839 –
We're somewhere over Finland, I think. I'm having trouble concentrating.

I'm reading the latest John Sandford novel, or pretending to. It's not bad — there's a central conceit he doesn't quite sell, though it moves well enough — but I'm only half paying attention.

When my powers returned recently, my mental faculties improved — my mind sped up, my memory became phenomenal.

That's something I shouldn't just ignore.

Every page of the book, I've implanted microdots into a few periods.

And each microdot holds the complete text of a book — science, history, philosophy, current issues — that I commit to memory.

You never know when you're going to need it.

Right now, I'm slogging my way through a textbook on the lifecycle of anaerobic organisms, and their effect on the world around them.

"And I came to a conclusion, which no doubt you want me to pass along to you for free, as a bennie for all this valuable

KENT? HEY, KENT!

HM?

THOUGHT THAT WAS YOU. TAKE OUT THIS PLANE, Y'KNOW, YOU'D WIPE OUT HALF THE REPORTERS ON THE EASTERN SEABOARD, HUH?

DEATHWATCH BY

I'M JEFFRIES. LOWELL JEFFRIES, OF ACTION BULLETIN NEWS, "YOUR DAILY NEWS BULLET"?

MAYBE YOU SEEN MY WORK...

I GOT THE FRONT PAGE ON THIS ONE. "HE'S BACK, BUT IS HE A FRAUD?"

ACTION BULLETIN NEWS

HE'S BACK, BUT IS HE A FRAUD

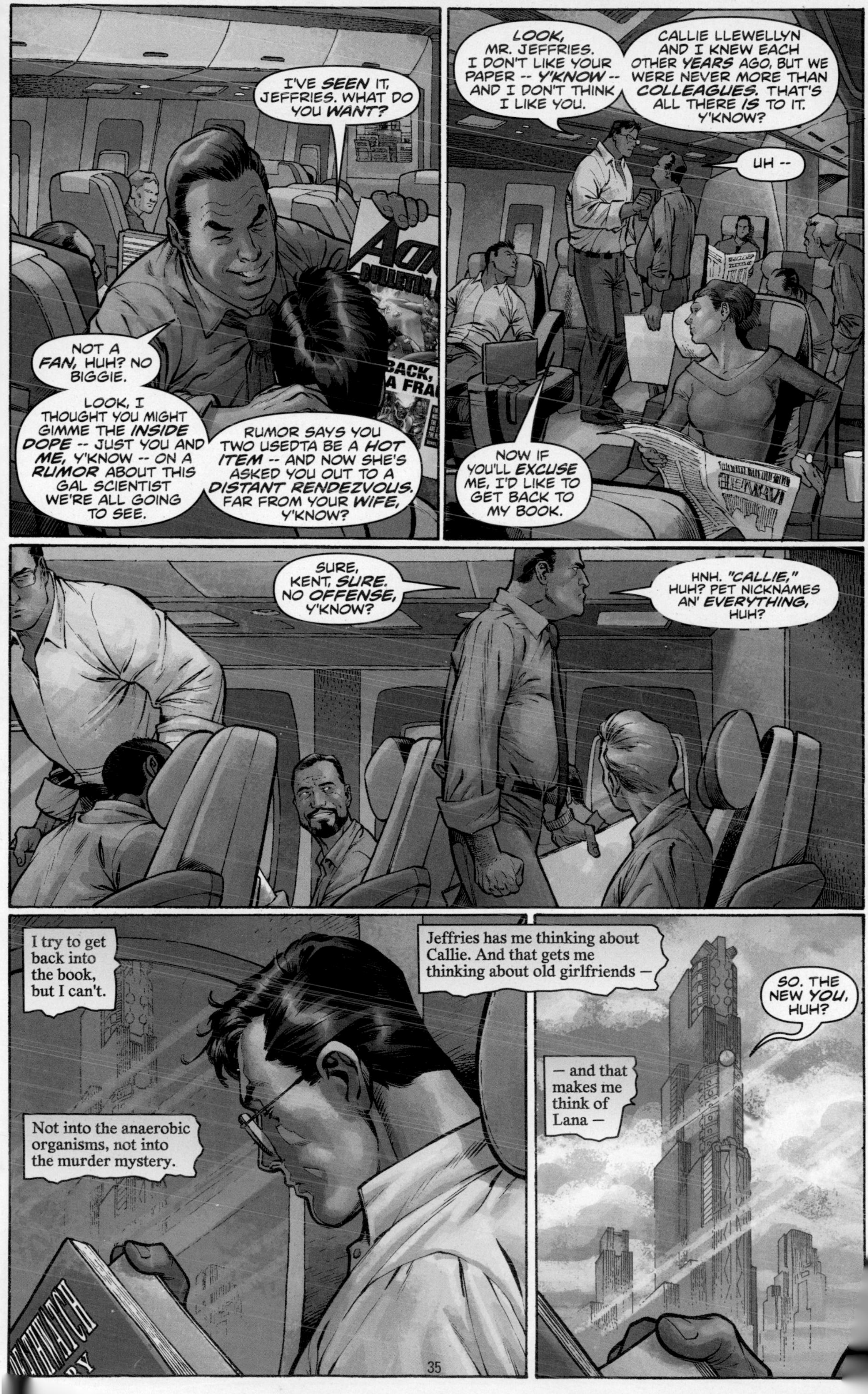
I'VE SEEN IT, JEFFRIES. WHAT DO YOU WANT?
NOT A FAN, HUH? NO BIGGIE.
LOOK, I THOUGHT YOU MIGHT GIMME THE INSIDE DOPE -- JUST YOU AND ME, Y'KNOW -- ON A RUMOR ABOUT THIS GAL SCIENTIST WE'RE ALL GOING TO SEE.
RUMOR SAYS YOU TWO USEDTA BE A HOT ITEM -- AND NOW SHE'S ASKED YOU OUT TO A DISTANT RENDEZVOUS. FAR FROM YOUR WIFE, Y'KNOW?
LOOK, MR. JEFFRIES. I DON'T LIKE YOUR PAPER -- Y'KNOW -- AND I DON'T THINK I LIKE YOU.
CALLIE LLEWELLYN AND I KNEW EACH OTHER YEARS AGO, BUT WE WERE NEVER MORE THAN COLLEAGUES. THAT'S ALL THERE IS TO IT. Y'KNOW?
UH --
NOW IF YOU'LL EXCUSE ME, I'D LIKE TO GET BACK TO MY BOOK.
SURE, KENT, SURE. NO OFFENSE, Y'KNOW?
HNH. "CALLIE," HUH? PET NICKNAMES AN' EVERYTHING, HUH?
I try to get back into the book, but I can't.
Not into the anaerobic organisms, not into the murder mystery.
Jeffries has me thinking about Callie. And that gets me thinking about old girlfriends —
— and that makes me think of Lana —
SO. THE NEW YOU, HUH?

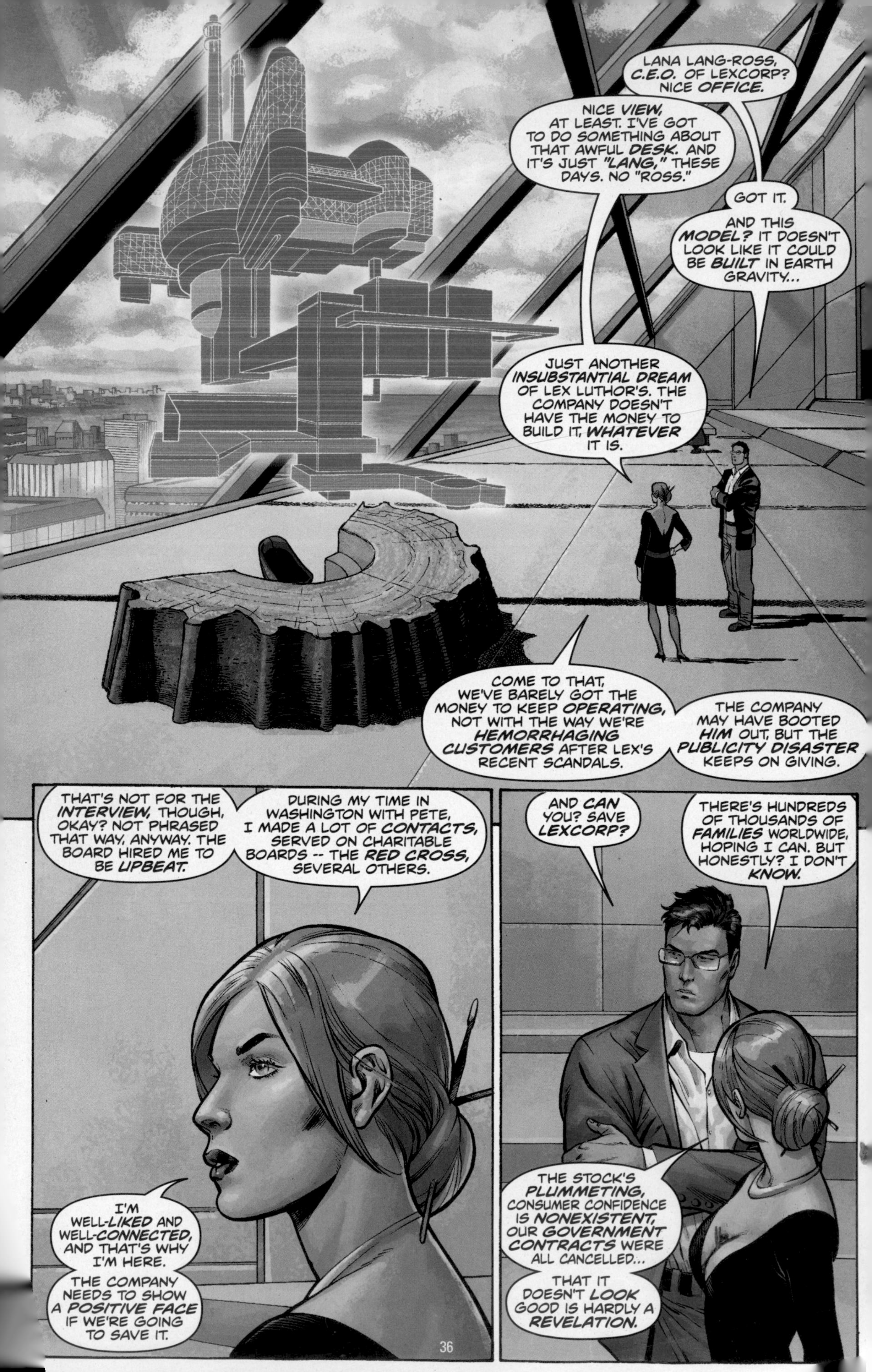
LANA LANG-ROSS, C.E.O. OF LEXCORP? NICE OFFICE.
NICE VIEW, AT LEAST. I'VE GOT TO DO SOMETHING ABOUT THAT AWFUL DESK. AND IT'S JUST "LANG," THESE DAYS. NO "ROSS."
GOT IT.
AND THIS MODEL? IT DOESN'T LOOK LIKE IT COULD BE BUILT IN EARTH GRAVITY...
JUST ANOTHER INSUBSTANTIAL DREAM OF LEX LUTHOR'S. THE COMPANY DOESN'T HAVE THE MONEY TO BUILD IT, WHATEVER IT IS.
COME TO THAT, WE'VE BARELY GOT THE MONEY TO KEEP OPERATING, NOT WITH THE WAY WE'RE HEMORRHAGING CUSTOMERS AFTER LEX'S RECENT SCANDALS.
THE COMPANY MAY HAVE BOOTED HIM OUT, BUT THE PUBLICITY DISASTER KEEPS ON GIVING.
THAT'S NOT FOR THE INTERVIEW, THOUGH, OKAY? NOT PHRASED THAT WAY, ANYWAY. THE BOARD HIRED ME TO BE UPBEAT.
DURING MY TIME IN WASHINGTON WITH PETE, I MADE A LOT OF CONTACTS, SERVED ON CHARITABLE BOARDS -- THE RED CROSS, SEVERAL OTHERS.
I'M WELL-LIKED AND WELL-CONNECTED, AND THAT'S WHY I'M HERE.
THE COMPANY NEEDS TO SHOW A POSITIVE FACE IF WE'RE GOING TO SAVE IT.
AND CAN YOU? SAVE LEXCORP?
THERE'S HUNDREDS OF THOUSANDS OF FAMILIES WORLDWIDE, HOPING I CAN. BUT HONESTLY? I DON'T KNOW.
THE STOCK'S PLUMMETING, CONSUMER CONFIDENCE IS NONEXISTENT, OUR GOVERNMENT CONTRACTS WERE ALL CANCELLED...
THAT IT DOESN'T LOOK GOOD IS HARDLY A REVELATION.

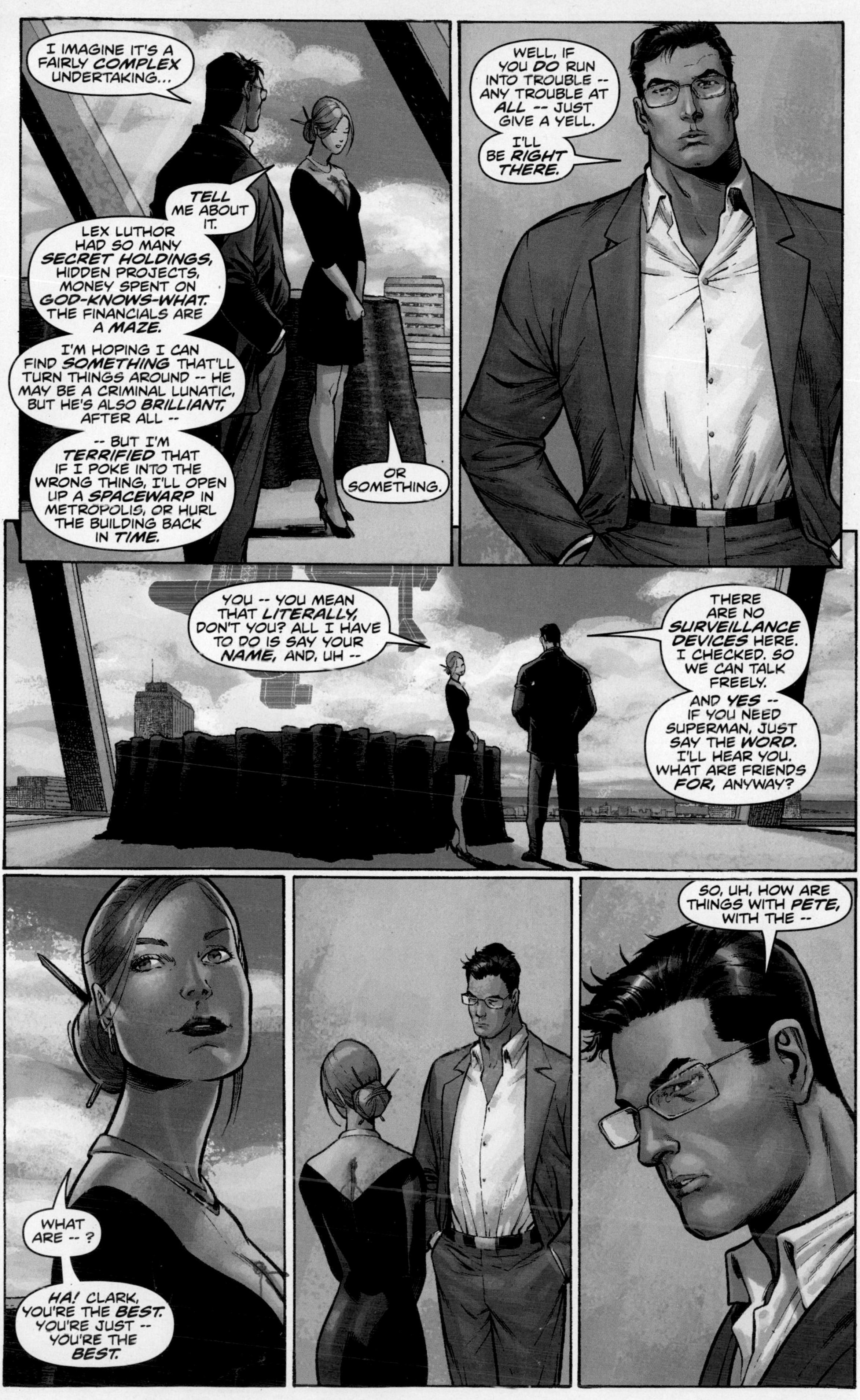
I IMAGINE IT'S A FAIRLY COMPLEX UNDERTAKING...
TELL ME ABOUT IT.
LEX LUTHOR HAD SO MANY SECRET HOLDINGS, HIDDEN PROJECTS, MONEY SPENT ON GOD-KNOWS-WHAT. THE FINANCIALS ARE A MAZE.
I'M HOPING I CAN FIND SOMETHING THAT'LL TURN THINGS AROUND -- HE MAY BE A CRIMINAL LUNATIC, BUT HE'S ALSO BRILLIANT, AFTER ALL --
-- BUT I'M TERRIFIED THAT IF I POKE INTO THE WRONG THING, I'LL OPEN UP A SPACEWARP IN METROPOLIS, OR HURL THE BUILDING BACK IN TIME.
OR SOMETHING.
WELL, IF YOU DO RUN INTO TROUBLE -- ANY TROUBLE AT ALL -- JUST GIVE A YELL.
I'LL BE RIGHT THERE.
YOU -- YOU MEAN THAT LITERALLY, DON'T YOU? ALL I HAVE TO DO IS SAY YOUR NAME, AND, UH --
THERE ARE NO SURVEILLANCE DEVICES HERE. I CHECKED. SO WE CAN TALK FREELY.
AND YES -- IF YOU NEED SUPERMAN, JUST SAY THE WORD. I'LL HEAR YOU. WHAT ARE FRIENDS FOR, ANYWAY?
WHAT ARE -- ?
HA! CLARK, YOU'RE THE BEST. YOU'RE JUST -- YOU'RE THE BEST.
SO, UH, HOW ARE THINGS WITH PETE, WITH THE --

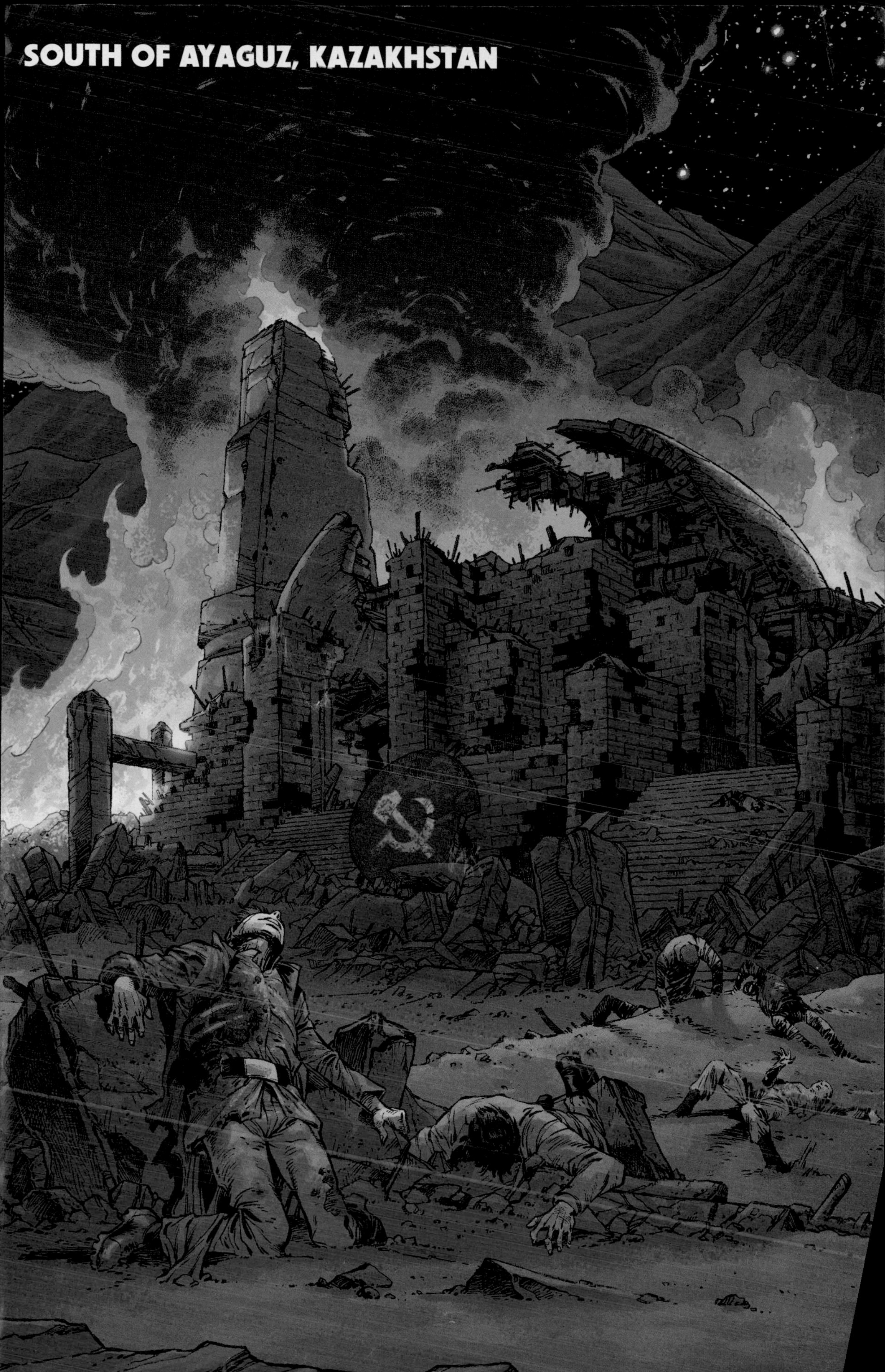
SOUTH OF AYAGUZ, KAZAKHSTAN

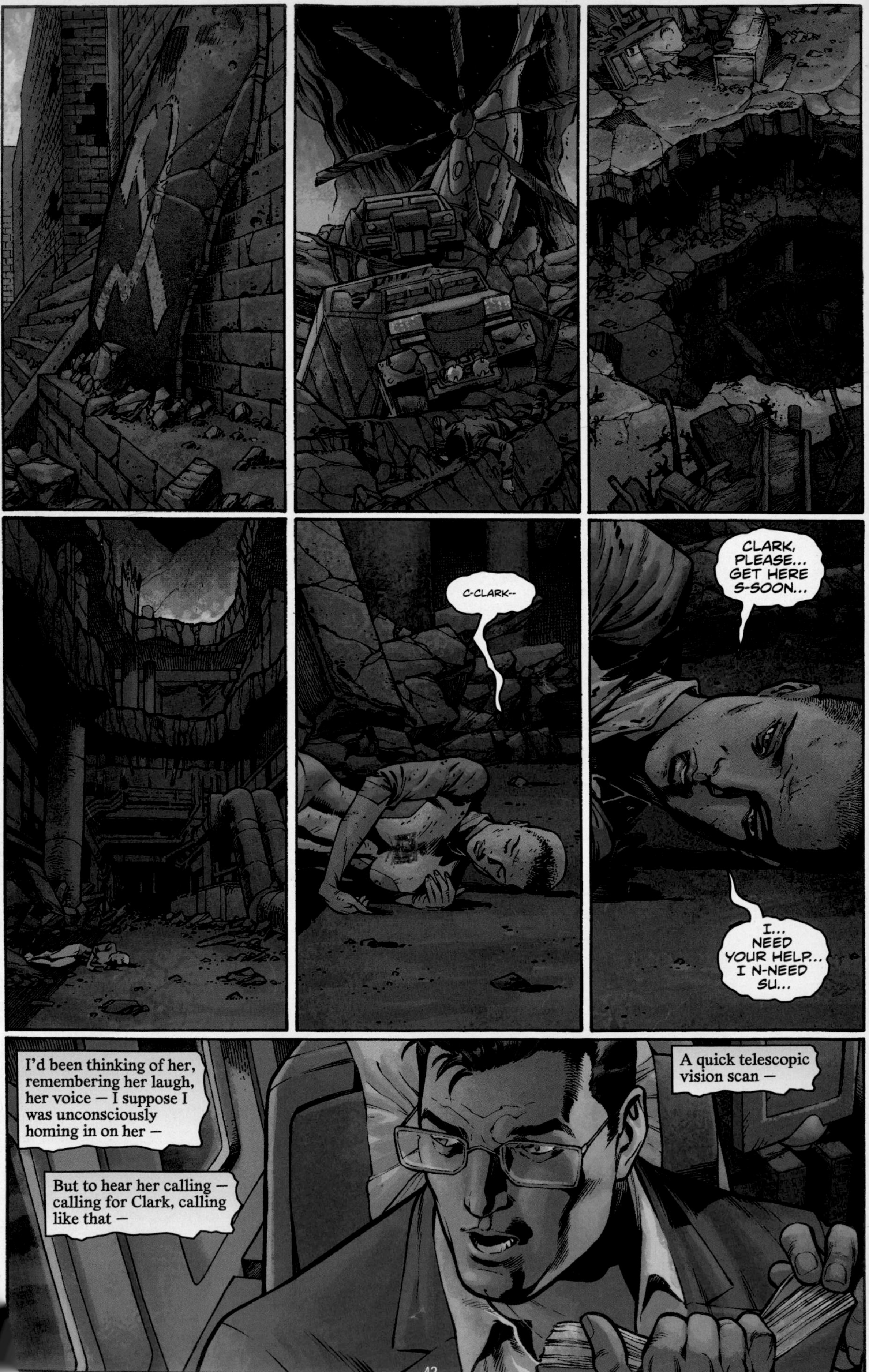

C-CLARK--
CLARK, PLEASE... GET HERE S-SOON...
I... NEED YOUR HELP... I N-NEED SU...
I'd been thinking of her, remembering her laugh, her voice — I suppose I was unconsciously homing in on her —
But to hear her calling — calling for Clark, calling like that —
A quick telescopic vision scan —

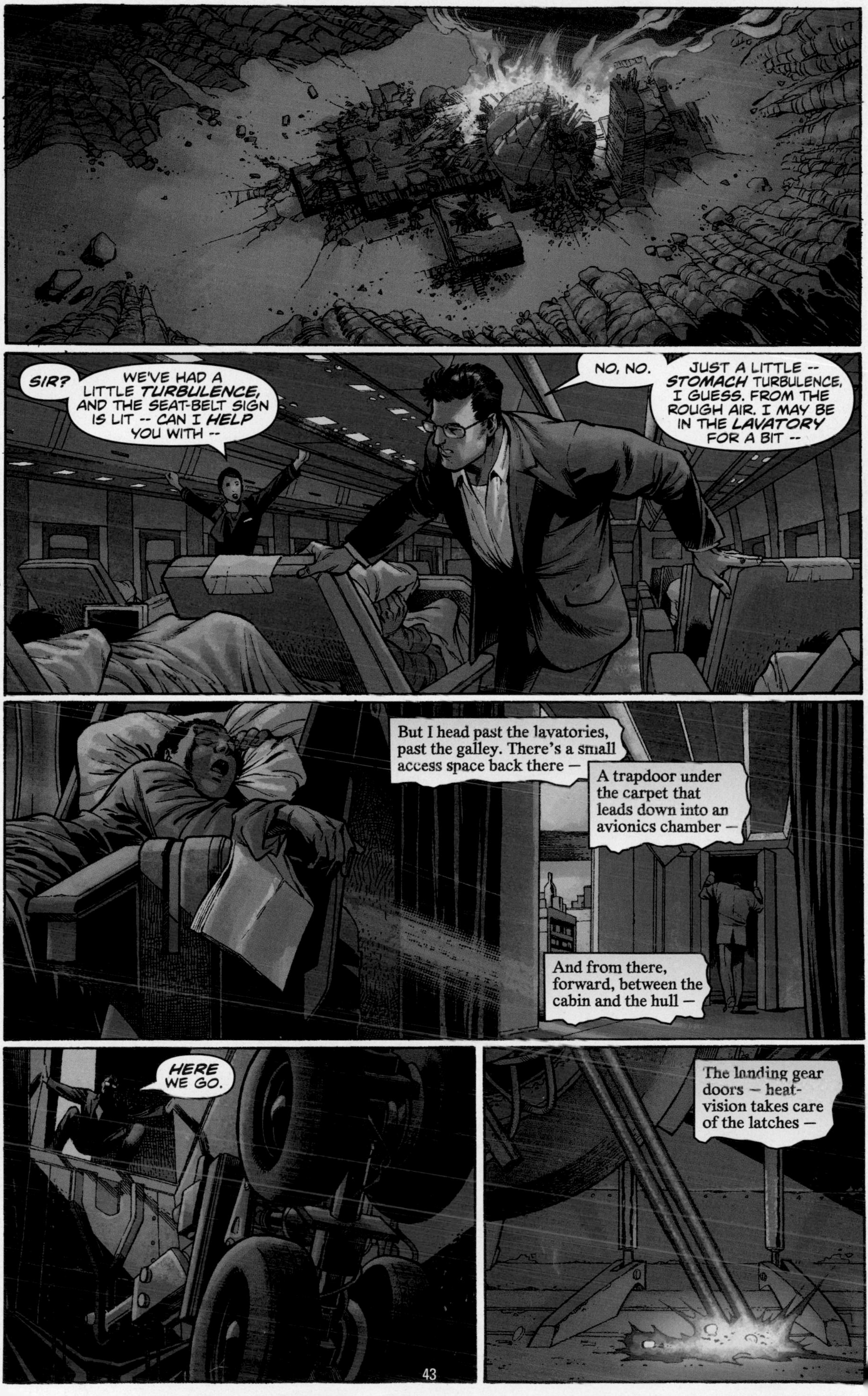
SIR?
WE'VE HAD A LITTLE TURBULENCE, AND THE SEAT-BELT SIGN IS LIT -- CAN I HELP YOU WITH --
NO, NO.
JUST A LITTLE -- STOMACH TURBULENCE, I GUESS. FROM THE ROUGH AIR. I MAY BE IN THE LAVATORY FOR A BIT --
But I head past the lavatories, past the galley. There's a small access space back there —
A trapdoor under the carpet that leads down into an avionics chamber —
And from there, forward, between the cabin and the hull —
HERE WE GO.
The landing gear doors — heat-vision takes care of the latches —

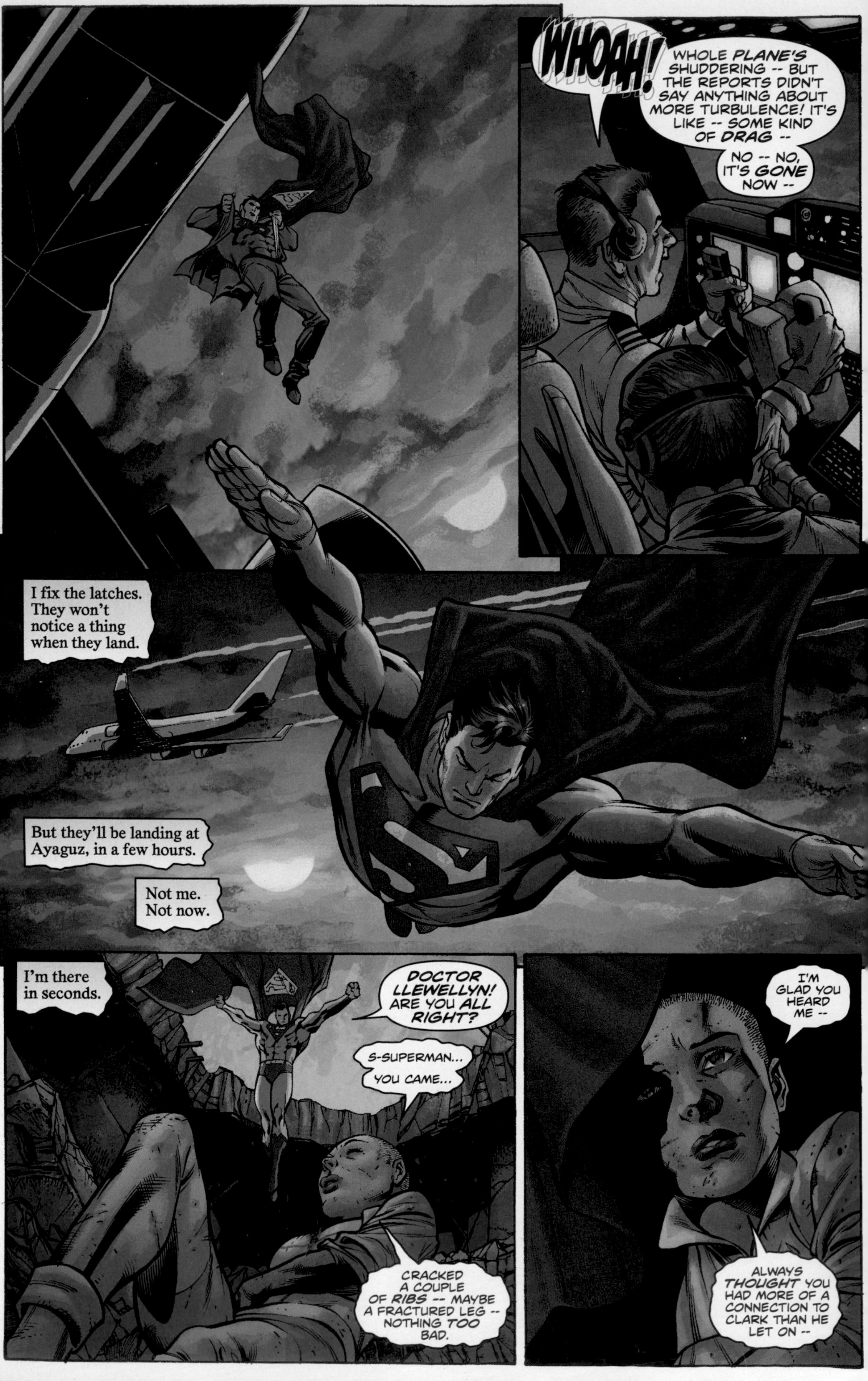
WHOAH!
WHOLE PLANE'S SHUDDERING -- BUT THE REPORTS DIDN'T SAY ANYTHING ABOUT MORE TURBULENCE! IT'S LIKE -- SOME KIND OF DRAG --
NO -- NO, IT'S GONE NOW --
I fix the latches. They won't notice a thing when they land.
But they'll be landing at Ayaguz, in a few hours.
Not me. Not now.
I'm there in seconds.
DOCTOR LLEWELLYN! ARE YOU ALL RIGHT?
S-SUPERMAN...
YOU CAME...
CRACKED A COUPLE OF RIBS -- MAYBE A FRACTURED LEG -- NOTHING TOO BAD.
I'M GLAD YOU HEARD ME --
ALWAYS THOUGHT YOU HAD MORE OF A CONNECTION TO CLARK THAN HE LET ON --

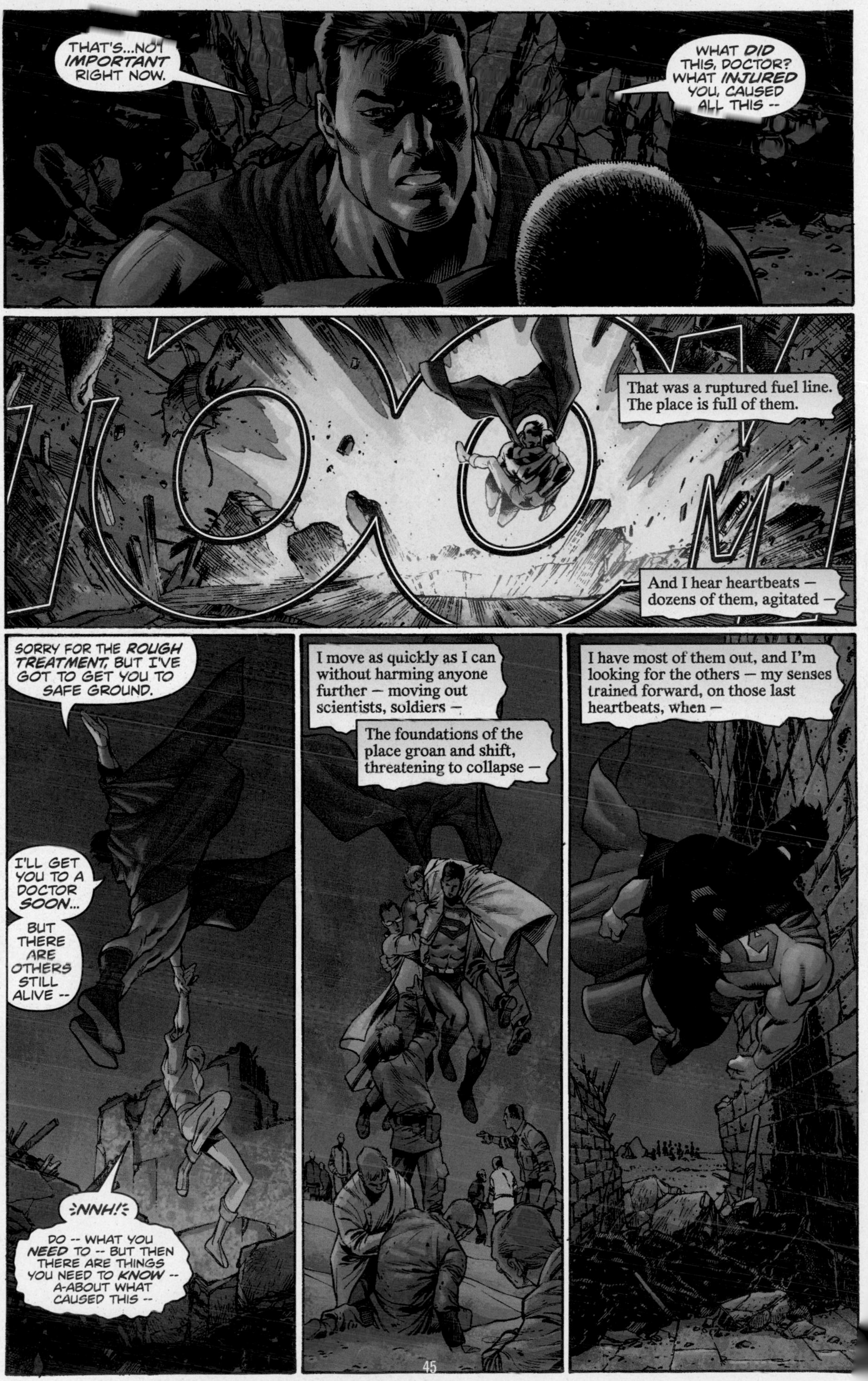
THAT'S...NOT IMPORTANT RIGHT NOW.
WHAT DID THIS, DOCTOR? WHAT INJURED YOU, CAUSED ALL THIS --
That was a ruptured fuel line. The place is full of them.
And I hear heartbeats — dozens of them, agitated —
SORRY FOR THE ROUGH TREATMENT, BUT I'VE GOT TO GET YOU TO SAFE GROUND.
I'LL GET YOU TO A DOCTOR SOON...
BUT THERE ARE OTHERS STILL ALIVE --
NNH!
DO -- WHAT YOU NEED TO -- BUT THEN THERE ARE THINGS YOU NEED TO KNOW -- A-ABOUT WHAT CAUSED THIS --
I move as quickly as I can without harming anyone further — moving out scientists, soldiers —
The foundations of the place groan and shift, threatening to collapse —
I have most of them out, and I'm looking for the others — my senses trained forward, on those last heartbeats, when —

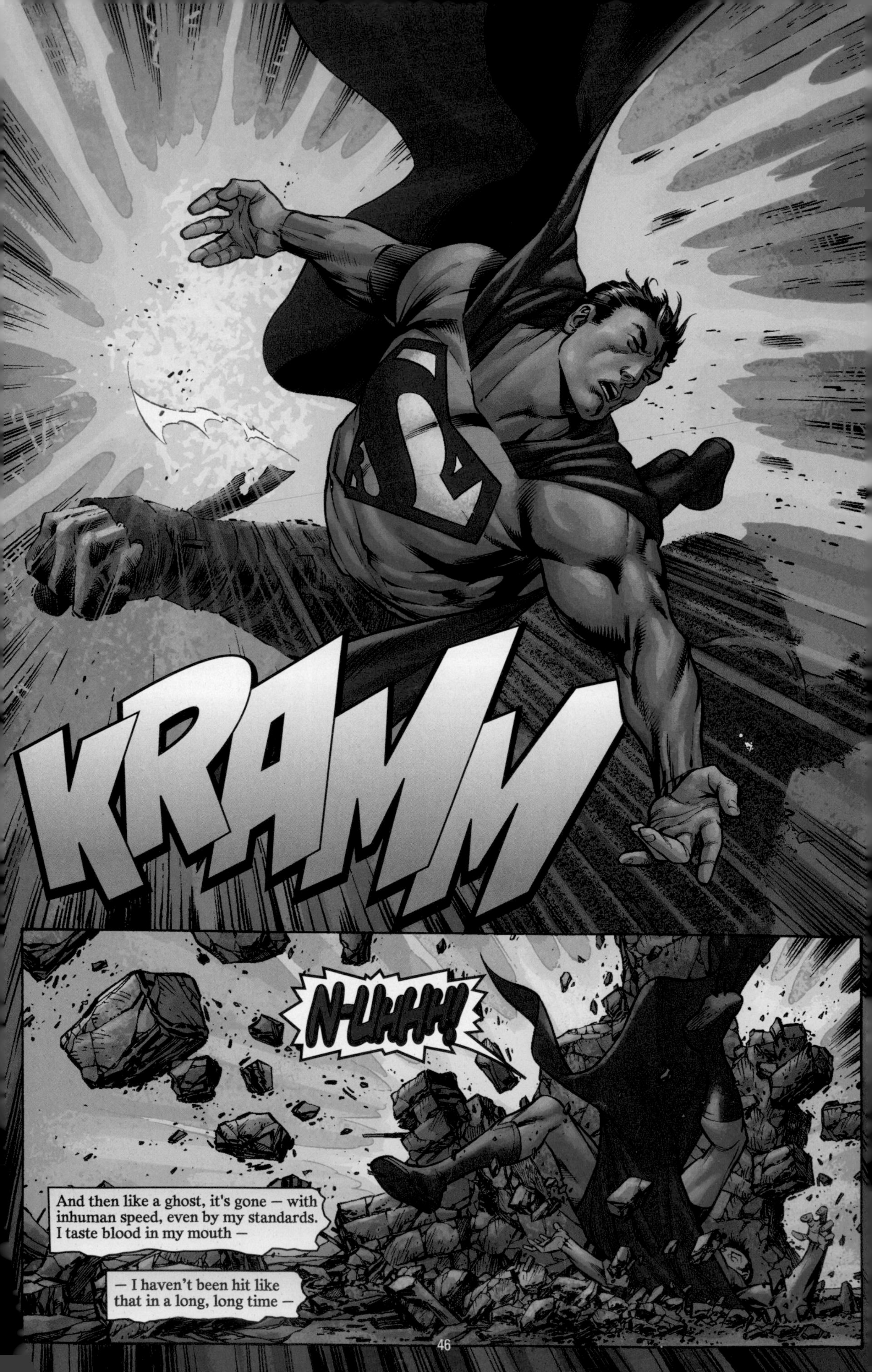
KRAMM
N-UHHH!
And then like a ghost, it's gone — with inhuman speed, even by my standards. I taste blood in my mouth —
— I haven't been hit like that in a long, long time —

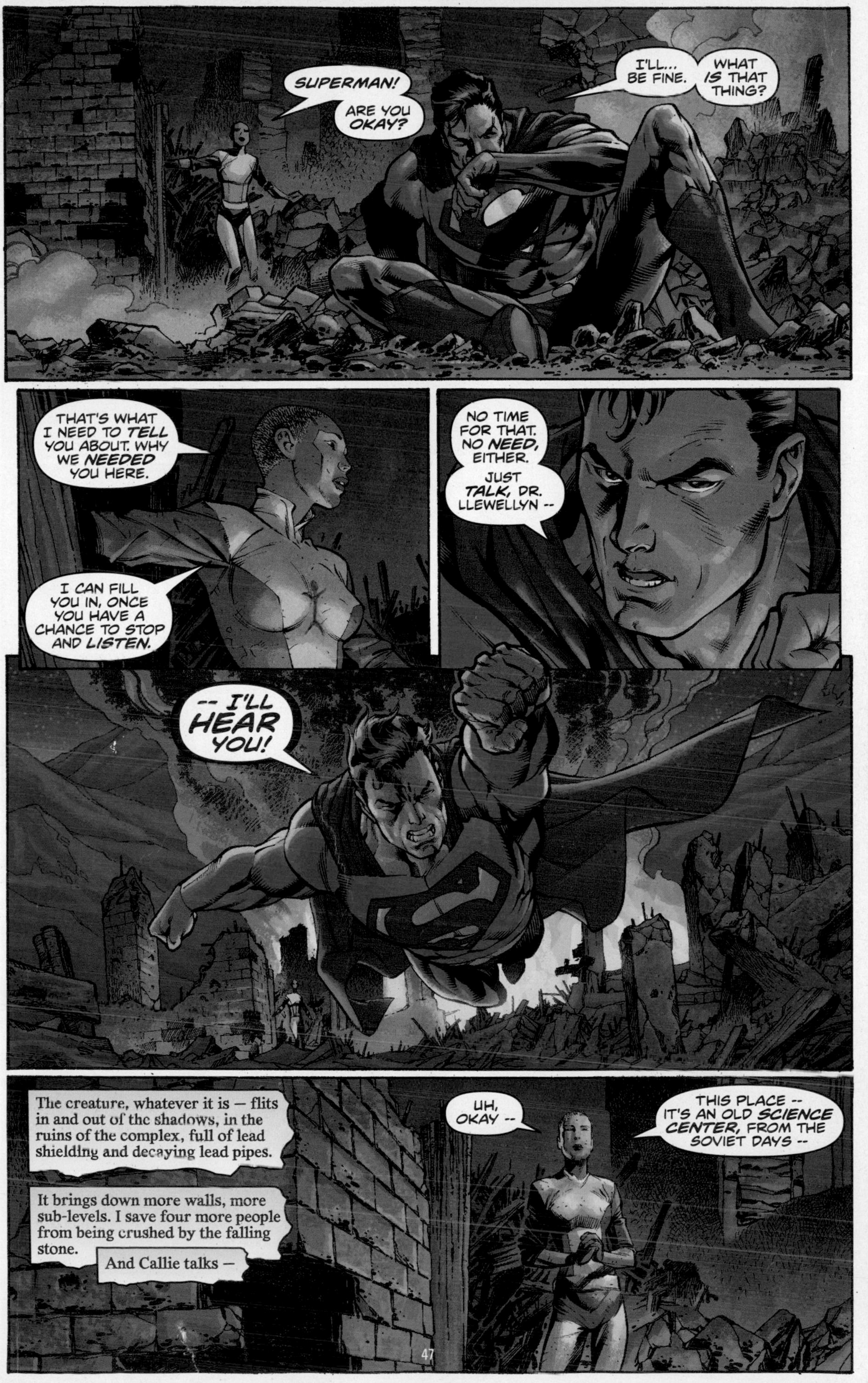
SUPERMAN!
ARE YOU OKAY?
I'LL... BE FINE.
WHAT IS THAT THING?
THAT'S WHAT I NEED TO TELL YOU ABOUT. WHY WE NEEDED YOU HERE.
I CAN FILL YOU IN, ONCE YOU HAVE A CHANCE TO STOP AND LISTEN.
NO TIME FOR THAT. NO NEED, EITHER.
JUST TALK, DR. LLEWELLYN --
-- I'LL HEAR YOU!
The creature, whatever it is — flits in and out of the shadows, in the ruins of the complex, full of lead shielding and decaying lead pipes.
It brings down more walls, more sub-levels. I save four more people from being crushed by the falling stone.
And Callie talks —
UH, OKAY --
THIS PLACE -- IT'S AN OLD SCIENCE CENTER, FROM THE SOVIET DAYS --

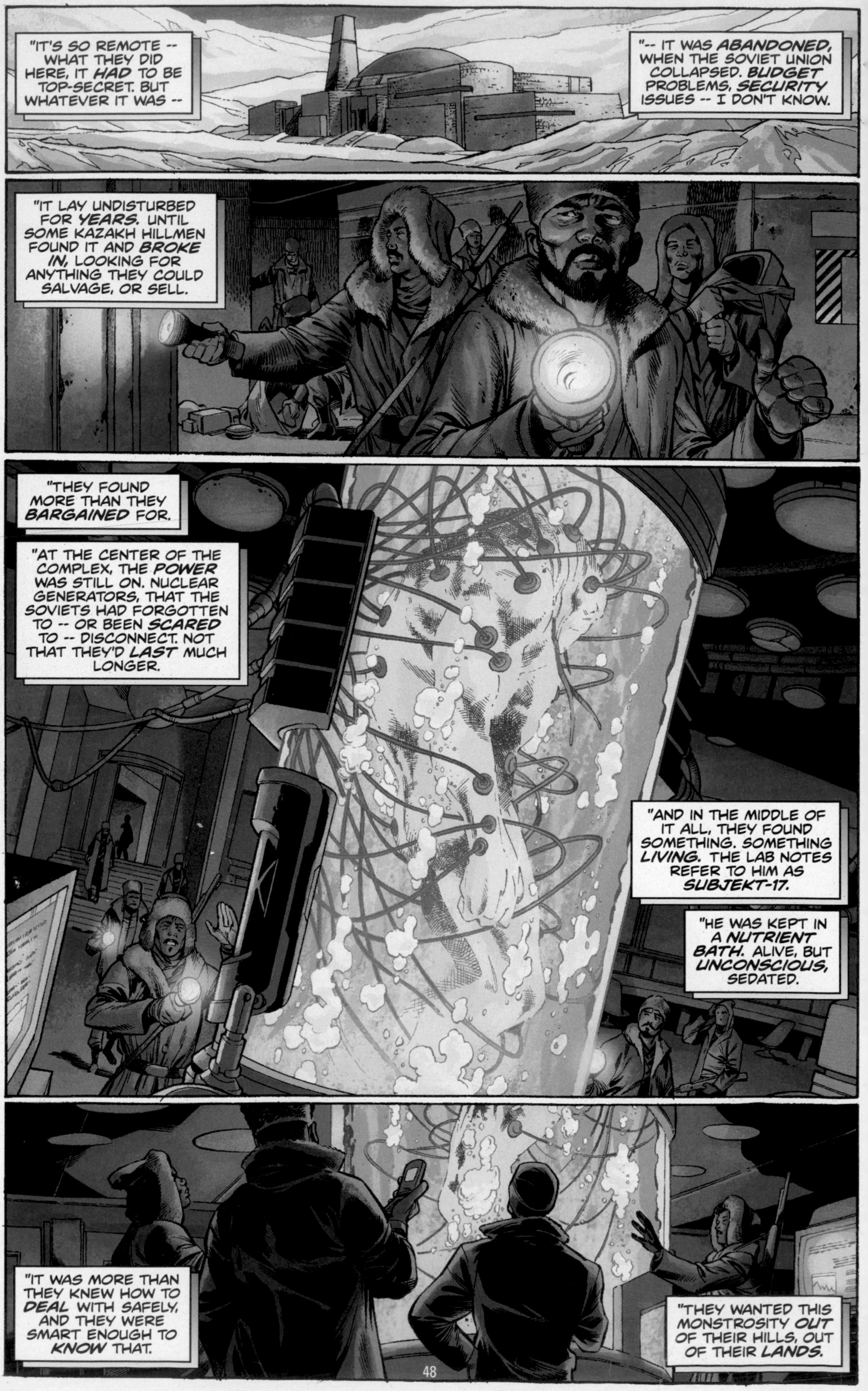
"IT'S SO REMOTE -- WHAT THEY DID HERE, IT HAD TO BE TOP-SECRET. BUT WHATEVER IT WAS --
"-- IT WAS ABANDONED, WHEN THE SOVIET UNION COLLAPSED. BUDGET PROBLEMS, SECURITY ISSUES -- I DON'T KNOW.
"IT LAY UNDISTURBED FOR YEARS. UNTIL SOME KAZAKH HILLMEN FOUND IT AND BROKE IN, LOOKING FOR ANYTHING THEY COULD SALVAGE, OR SELL.
"THEY FOUND MORE THAN THEY BARGAINED FOR.
"AT THE CENTER OF THE COMPLEX, THE POWER WAS STILL ON. NUCLEAR GENERATORS, THAT THE SOVIETS HAD FORGOTTEN TO -- OR BEEN SCARED TO -- DISCONNECT. NOT THAT THEY'D LAST MUCH LONGER.
"AND IN THE MIDDLE OF IT ALL, THEY FOUND SOMETHING. SOMETHING LIVING. THE LAB NOTES REFER TO HIM AS SUBJEKT-17.
"HE WAS KEPT IN A NUTRIENT BATH. ALIVE, BUT UNCONSCIOUS, SEDATED.
"IT WAS MORE THAN THEY KNEW HOW TO DEAL WITH SAFELY, AND THEY WERE SMART ENOUGH TO KNOW THAT.
"THEY WANTED THIS MONSTROSITY OUT OF THEIR HILLS, OUT OF THEIR LANDS.

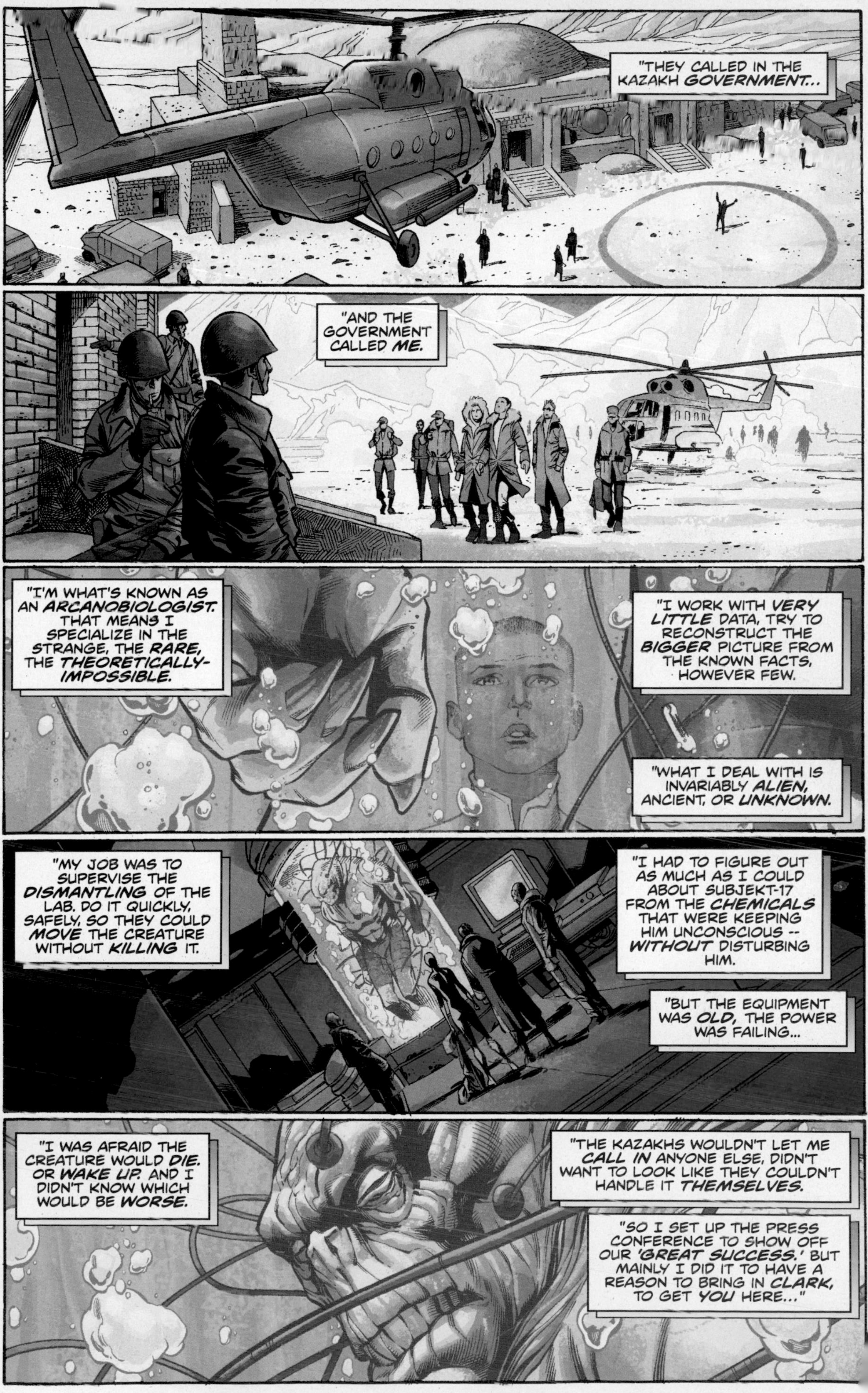
"THEY CALLED IN THE KAZAKH GOVERNMENT...
"AND THE GOVERNMENT CALLED ME.
"I'M WHAT'S KNOWN AS AN ARCANOBIOLOGIST. THAT MEANS I SPECIALIZE IN THE STRANGE, THE RARE, THE THEORETICALLY-IMPOSSIBLE.
"I WORK WITH VERY LITTLE DATA, TRY TO RECONSTRUCT THE BIGGER PICTURE FROM THE KNOWN FACTS, HOWEVER FEW.
"WHAT I DEAL WITH IS INVARIABLY ALIEN, ANCIENT, OR UNKNOWN.
"MY JOB WAS TO SUPERVISE THE DISMANTLING OF THE LAB. DO IT QUICKLY, SAFELY, SO THEY COULD MOVE THE CREATURE WITHOUT KILLING IT.
"I HAD TO FIGURE OUT AS MUCH AS I COULD ABOUT SUBJEKT-17 FROM THE CHEMICALS THAT WERE KEEPING HIM UNCONSCIOUS -- WITHOUT DISTURBING HIM.
"BUT THE EQUIPMENT WAS OLD, THE POWER WAS FAILING...
"I WAS AFRAID THE CREATURE WOULD DIE. OR WAKE UP. AND I DIDN'T KNOW WHICH WOULD BE WORSE.
"THE KAZAKHS WOULDN'T LET ME CALL IN ANYONE ELSE, DIDN'T WANT TO LOOK LIKE THEY COULDN'T HANDLE IT THEMSELVES.
"SO I SET UP THE PRESS CONFERENCE TO SHOW OFF OUR 'GREAT SUCCESS.' BUT MAINLY I DID IT TO HAVE A REASON TO BRING IN CLARK, TO GET YOU HERE..."

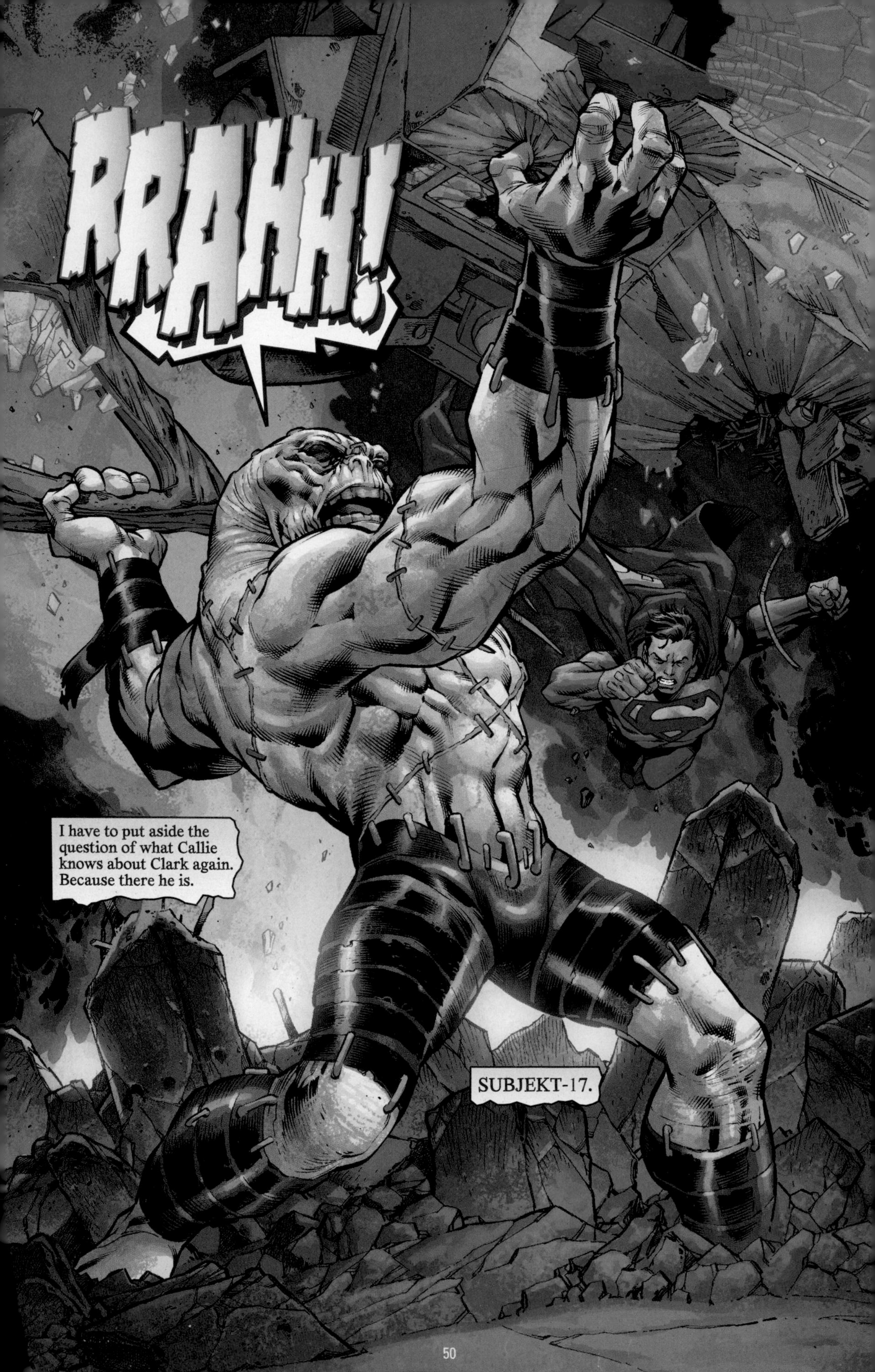
RRAHH!
I have to put aside the question of what Callie knows about Clark again. Because there he is.
SUBJEKT-17.

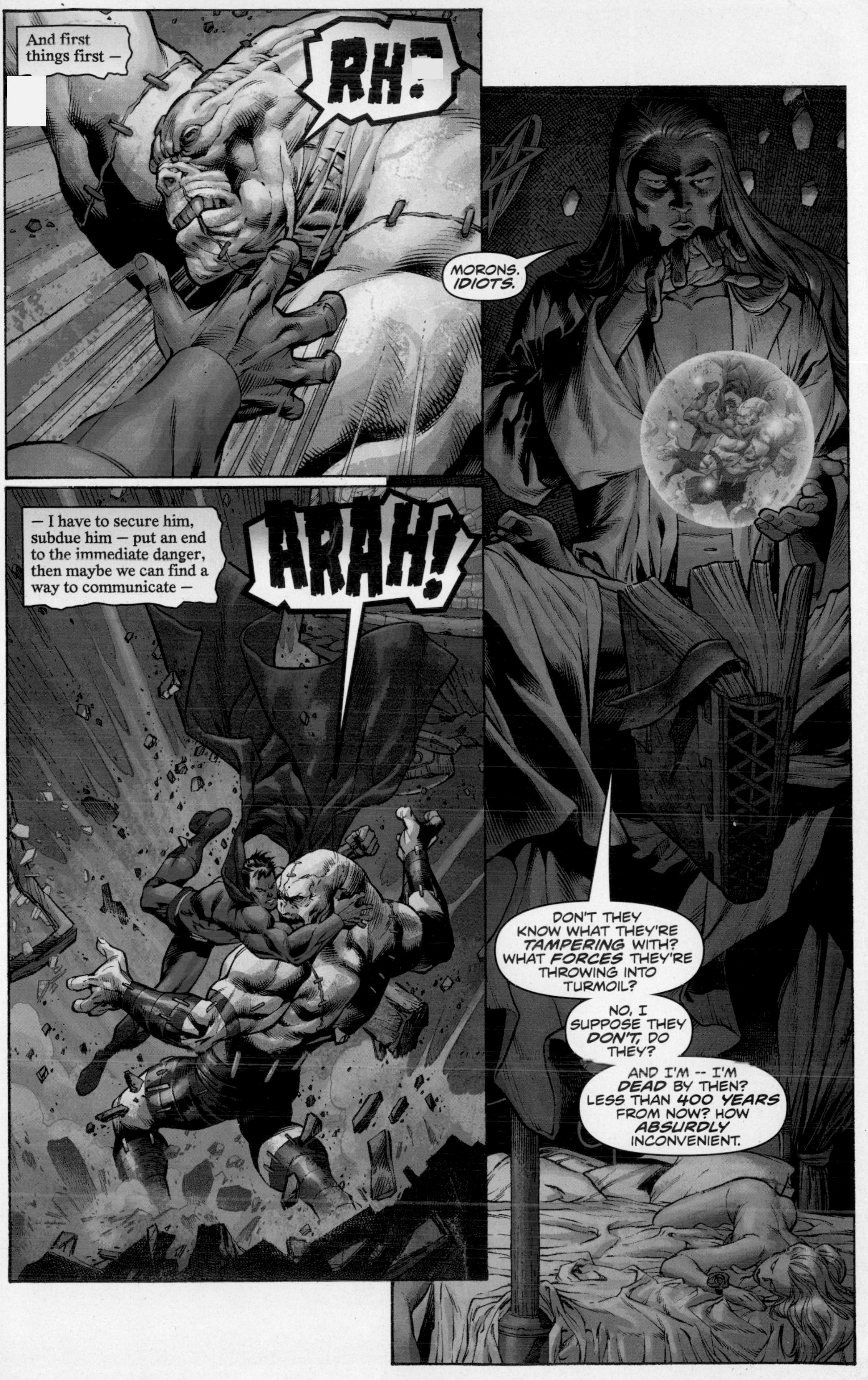
And first things first —
RH
— I have to secure him, subdue him — put an end to the immediate danger, then maybe we can find a way to communicate —
ARAH!
MORONS. IDIOTS.
DON'T THEY KNOW WHAT THEY'RE TAMPERING WITH? WHAT FORCES THEY'RE THROWING INTO TURMOIL?
NO, I SUPPOSE THEY DON'T, DO THEY?
AND I'M -- I'M DEAD BY THEN? LESS THAN 400 YEARS FROM NOW? HOW ABSURDLY INCONVENIENT.

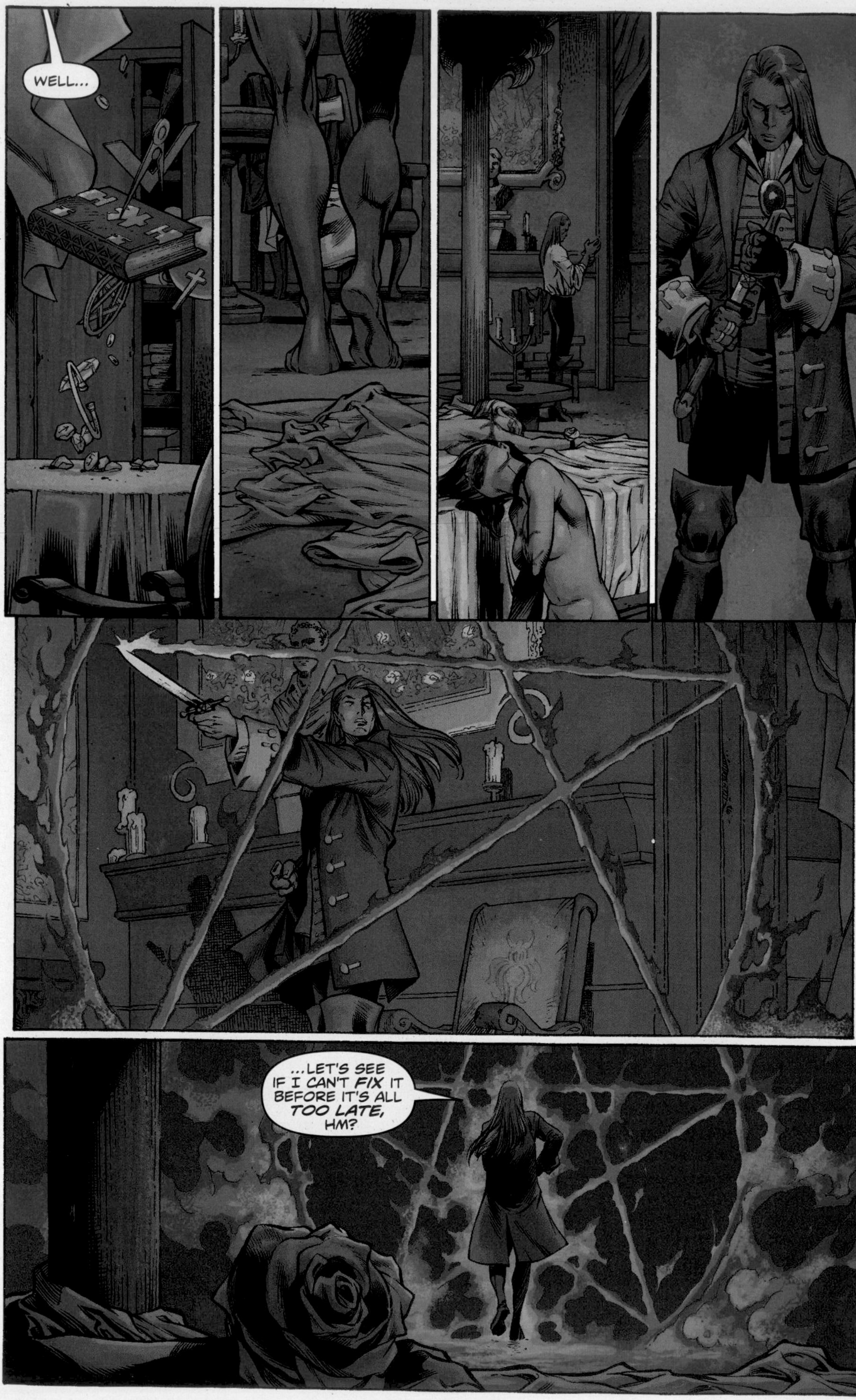
WELL...
...LET'S SEE IF I CAN'T FIX IT BEFORE IT'S ALL TOO LATE, HM?

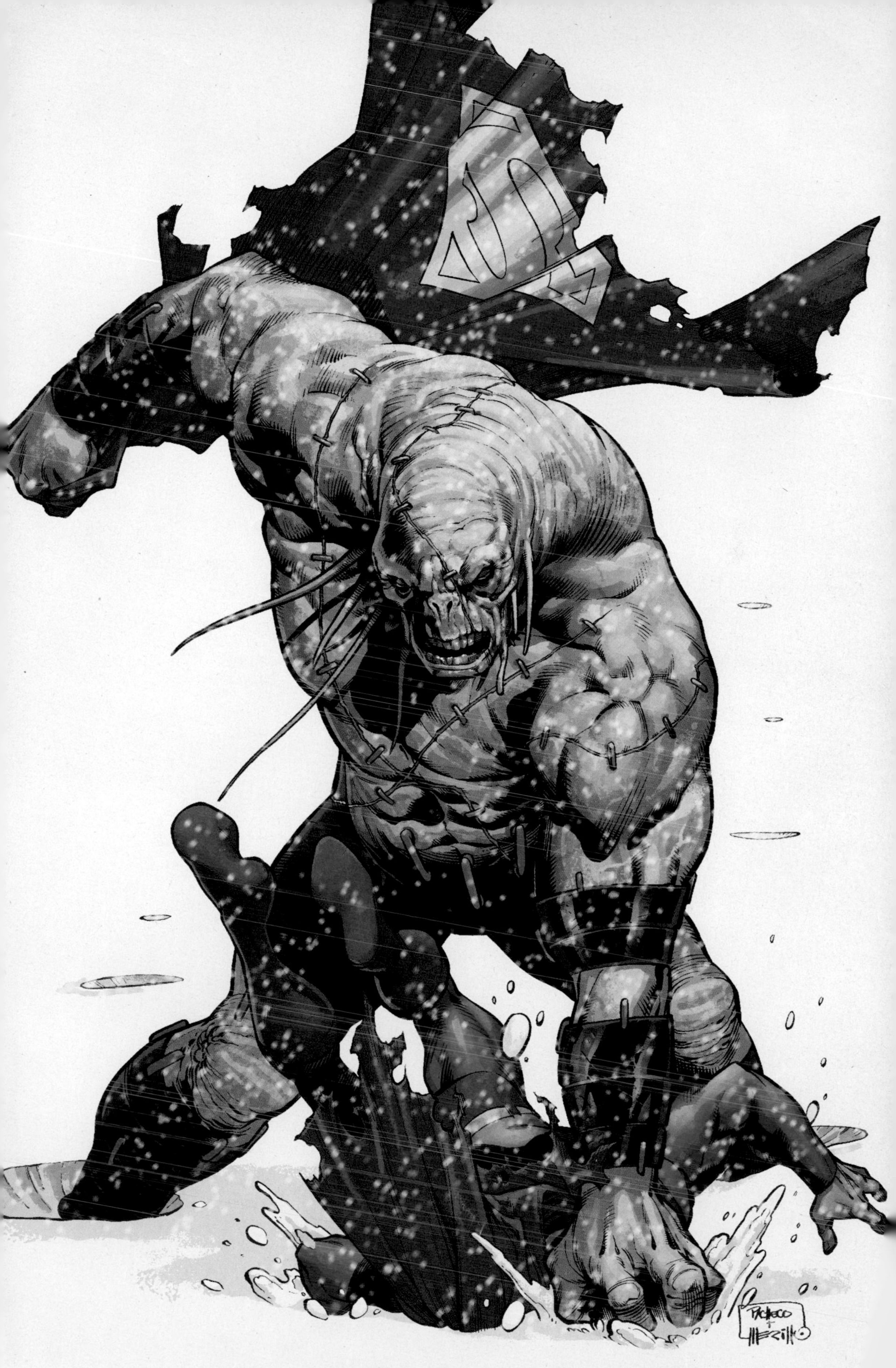

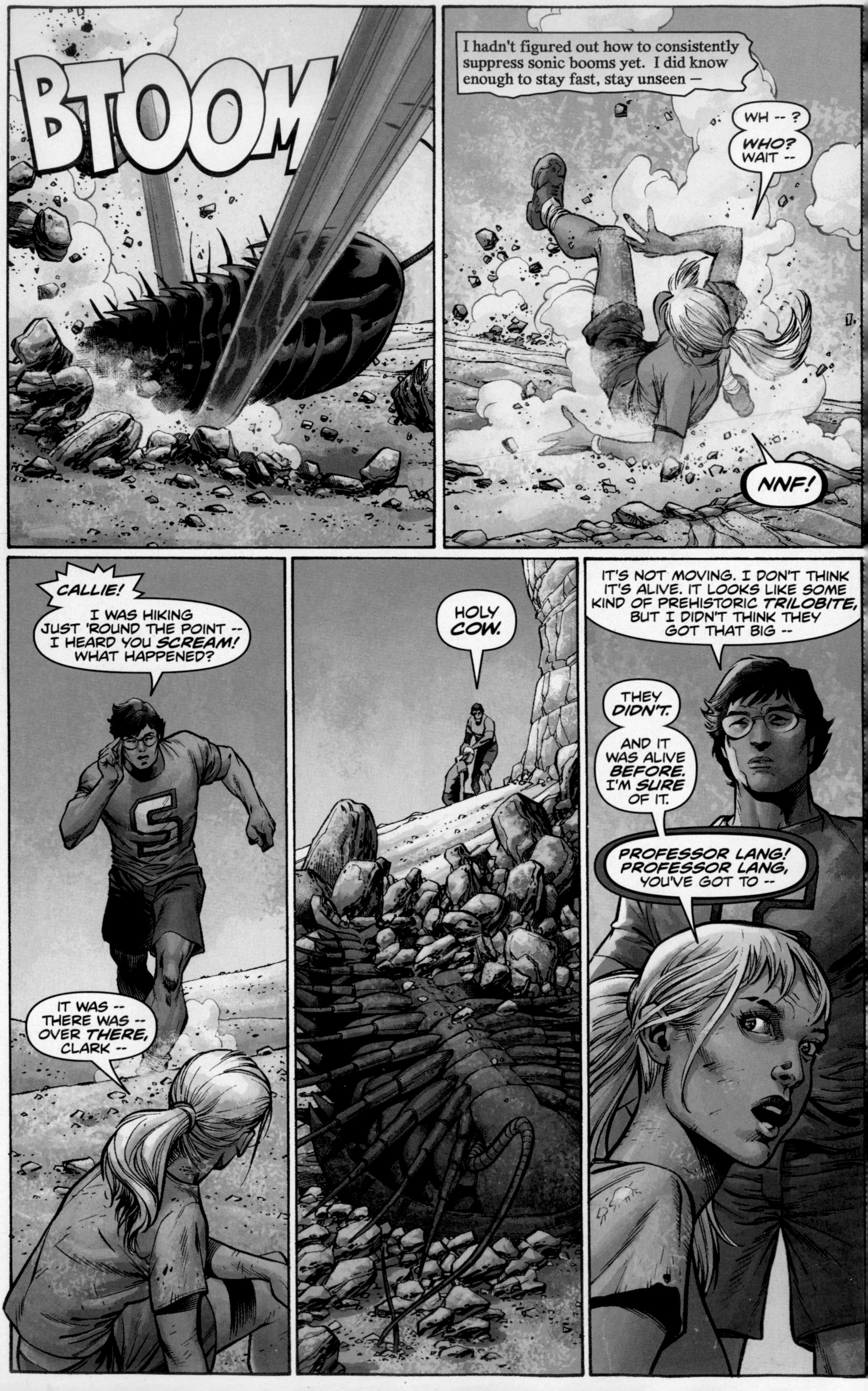
BTOOM
I hadn't figured out how to consistently suppress sonic booms yet. I did know enough to stay fast, stay unseen —
WH -- ? WHO? WAIT --
NNF!
CALLIE!
I WAS HIKING JUST 'ROUND THE POINT -- I HEARD YOU SCREAM! WHAT HAPPENED?
IT WAS -- THERE WAS -- OVER THERE, CLARK --
HOLY COW.
IT'S NOT MOVING. I DON'T THINK IT'S ALIVE. IT LOOKS LIKE SOME KIND OF PREHISTORIC TRILOBITE, BUT I DIDN'T THINK THEY GOT THAT BIG --
THEY DIDN'T.
AND IT WAS ALIVE BEFORE. I'M SURE OF IT.
PROFESSOR LANG! PROFESSOR LANG, YOU'VE GOT TO --

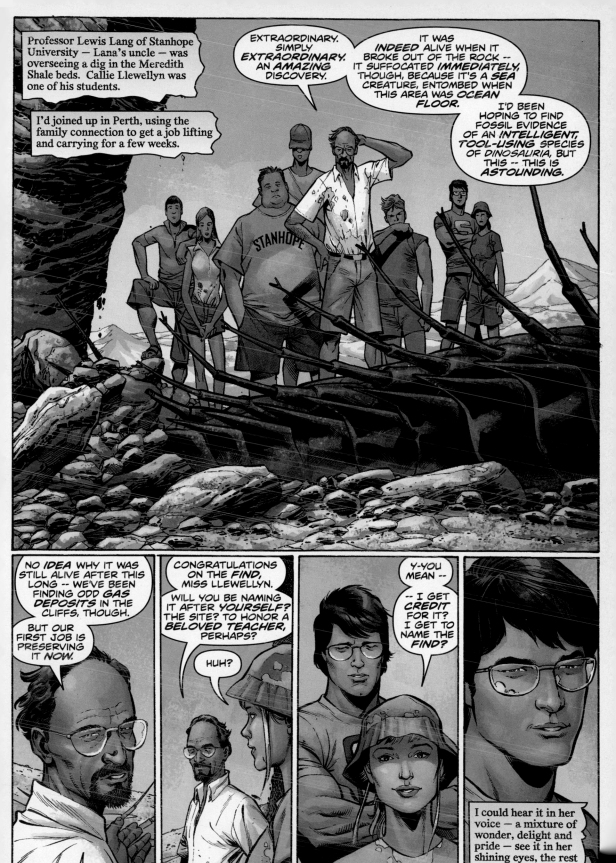

Professor Lewis Lang of Stanhope University — Lana's uncle — was overseeing a dig in the Meredith Shale beds. Callie Llewellyn was one of his students.

I'd joined up in Perth, using the family connection to get a job lifting and carrying for a few weeks.

EXTRAORDINARY. SIMPLY EXTRAORDINARY. AN AMAZING DISCOVERY.

IT WAS INDEED ALIVE WHEN IT BROKE OUT OF THE ROCK -- IT SUFFOCATED IMMEDIATELY, THOUGH, BECAUSE IT'S A SEA CREATURE, ENTOMBED WHEN THIS AREA WAS OCEAN FLOOR.

I'D BEEN HOPING TO FIND FOSSIL EVIDENCE OF AN INTELLIGENT, TOOL-USING SPECIES OF DINOSAURIA, BUT THIS -- THIS IS ASTOUNDING.

NO IDEA WHY IT WAS STILL ALIVE AFTER THIS LONG -- WE'VE BEEN FINDING ODD GAS DEPOSITS IN THE CLIFFS, THOUGH.

BUT OUR FIRST JOB IS PRESERVING IT NOW.

CRICK, HENDLER -- REFLECTIVE BLANKETS, KEEP THE SUN OFF IT. DRYER -- CALL THE UNIVERSITY FOR A VACUUM CHAMBER, TOP-SPEED.

CONGRATULATIONS ON THE FIND, MISS LLEWELLYN.

WILL YOU BE NAMING IT AFTER YOURSELF? THE SITE? TO HONOR A BELOVED TEACHER, PERHAPS?

HUH?

Y-YOU MEAN --

-- I GET CREDIT FOR IT? I GET TO NAME THE FIND?

I could hear it in her voice — a mixture of wonder, delight and pride — see it in her shining eyes, the rest of the trip.

This is where she decided on her life's work, decided on what she was going to be...

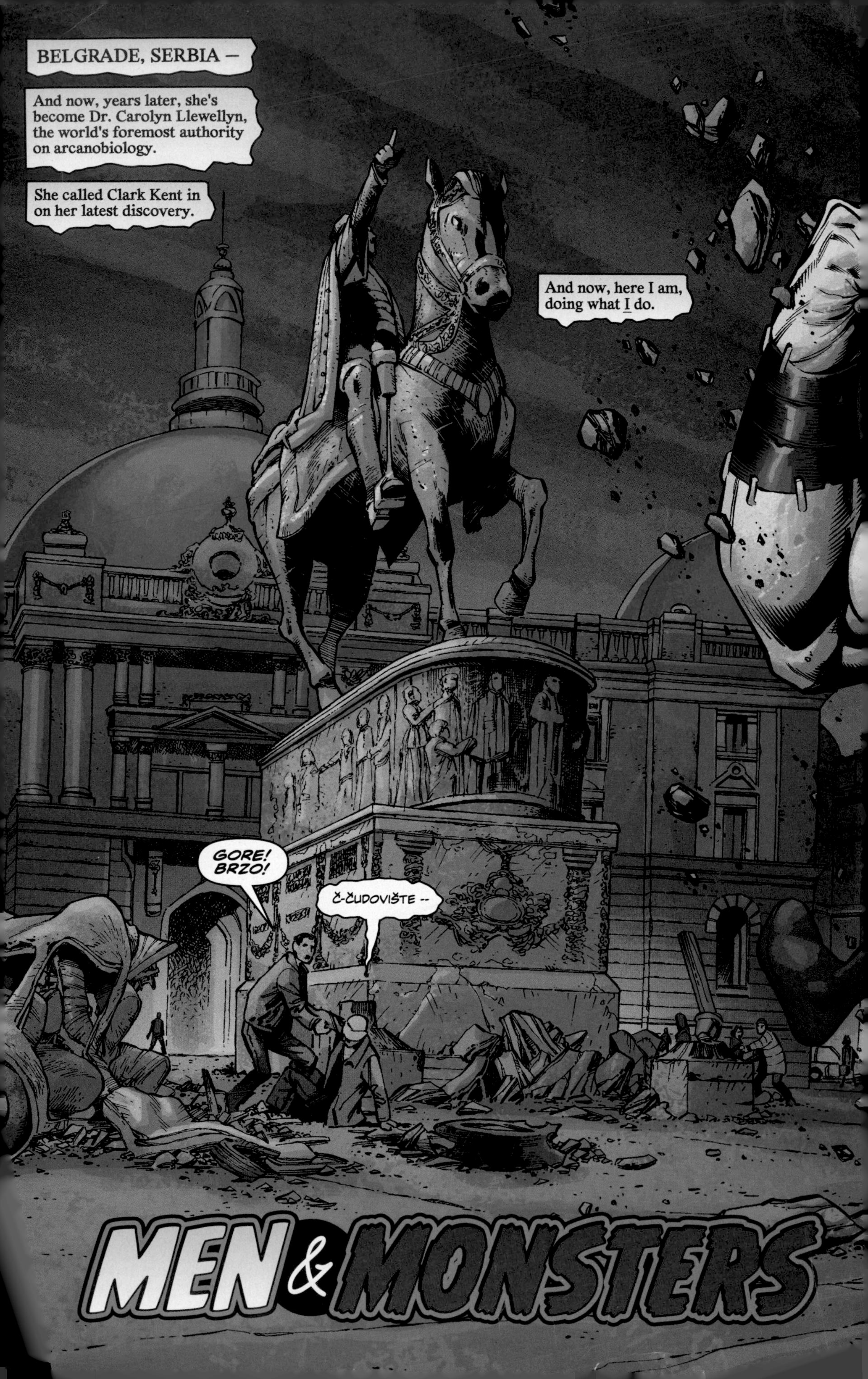
BELGRADE, SERBIA —
And now, years later, she's become Dr. Carolyn Llewellyn, the world's foremost authority on arcanobiology.
She called Clark Kent in on her latest discovery.
And now, here I am, doing what I do.
GORE! BRZO!
Č-ČUDOVIŠTE --
MEN & MONSTERS

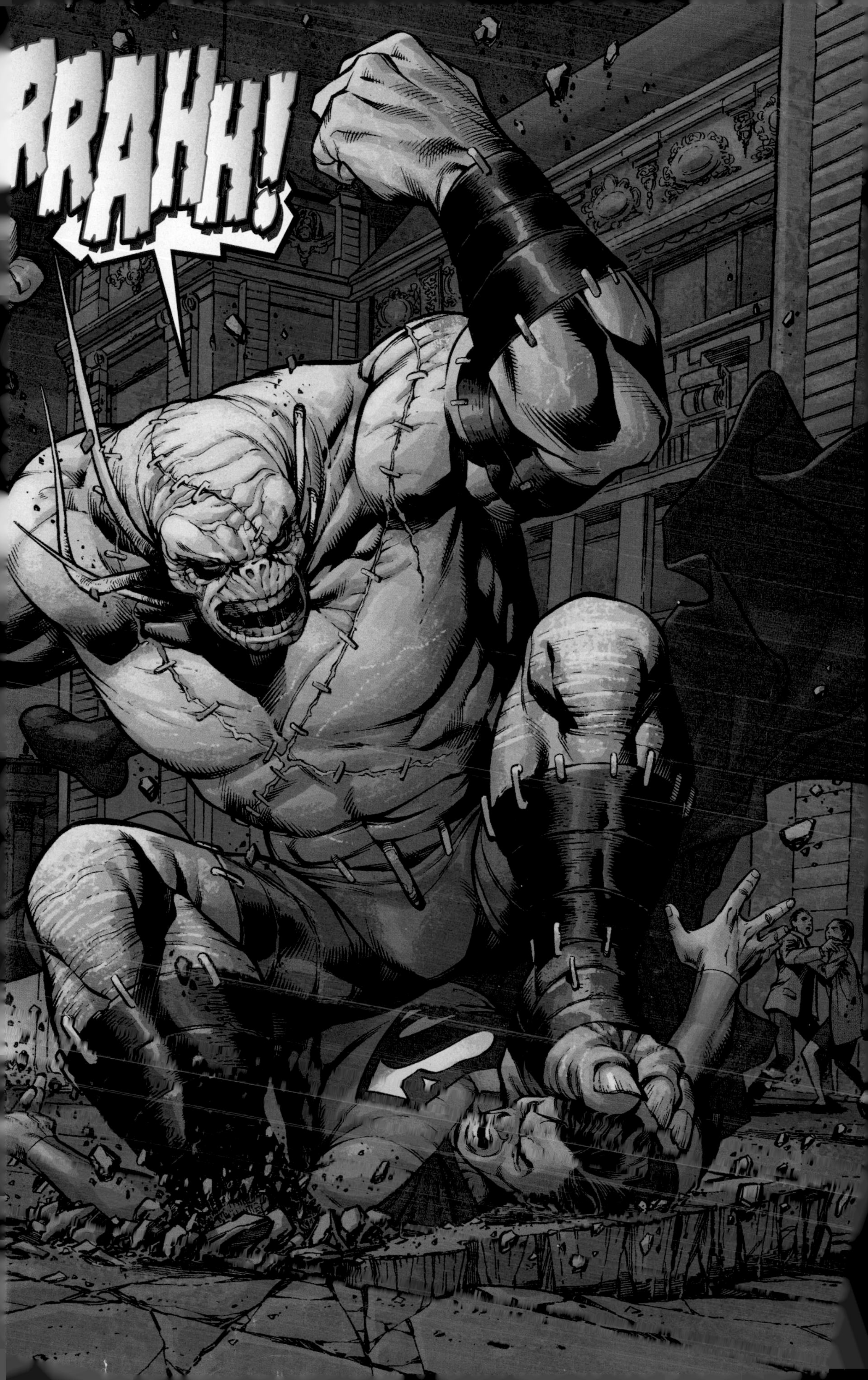
RRAHH!

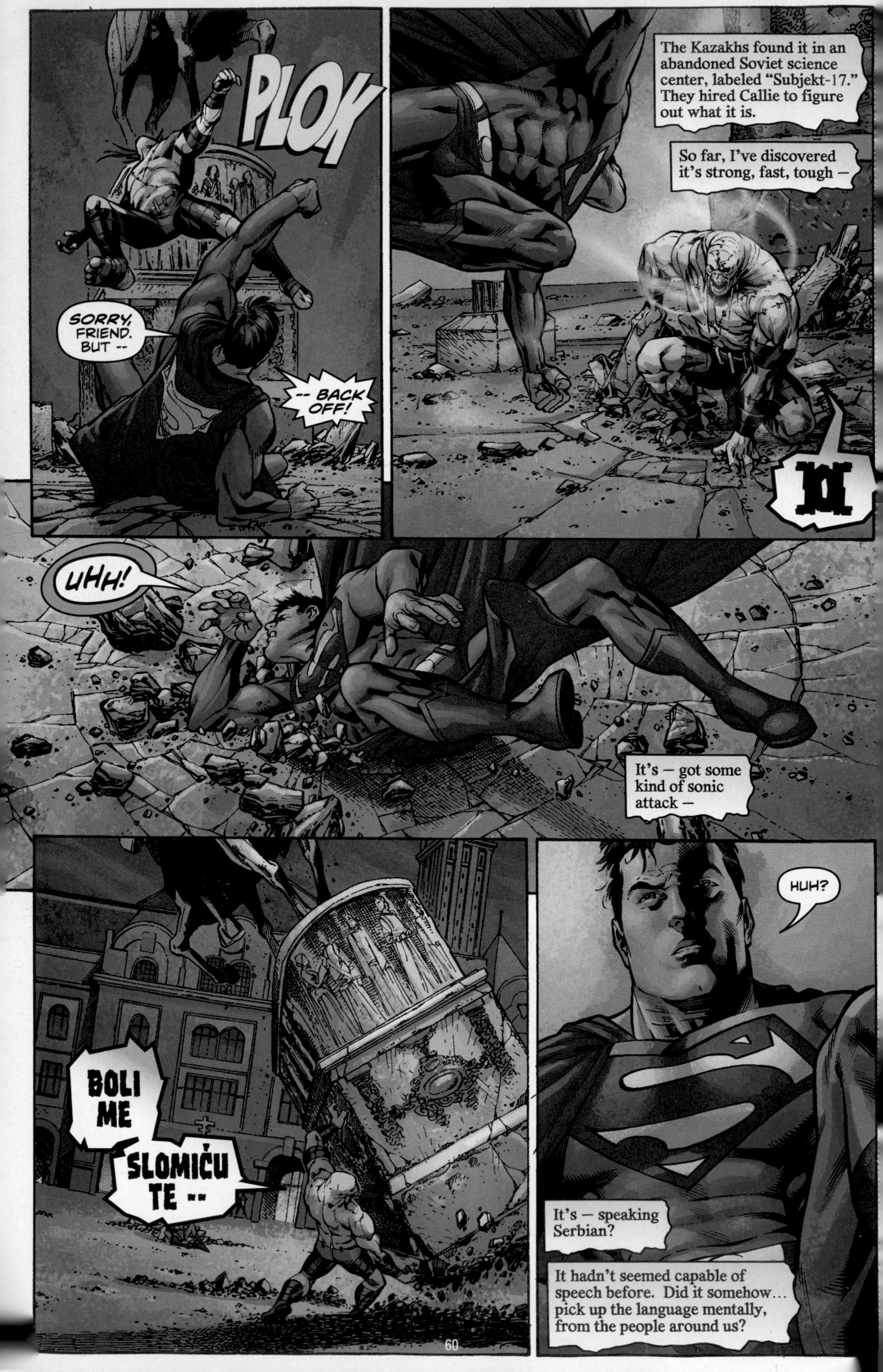
PLOK
SORRY, FRIEND. BUT --
-- BACK OFF!
The Kazakhs found it in an abandoned Soviet science center, labeled "Subjekt-17." They hired Callie to figure out what it is.
So far, I've discovered it's strong, fast, tough —
UHH!
It's — got some kind of sonic attack —
BOLI ME
SLOMIĆU TE --
HUH?
It's — speaking Serbian?
It hadn't seemed capable of speech before. Did it somehow… pick up the language mentally, from the people around us?

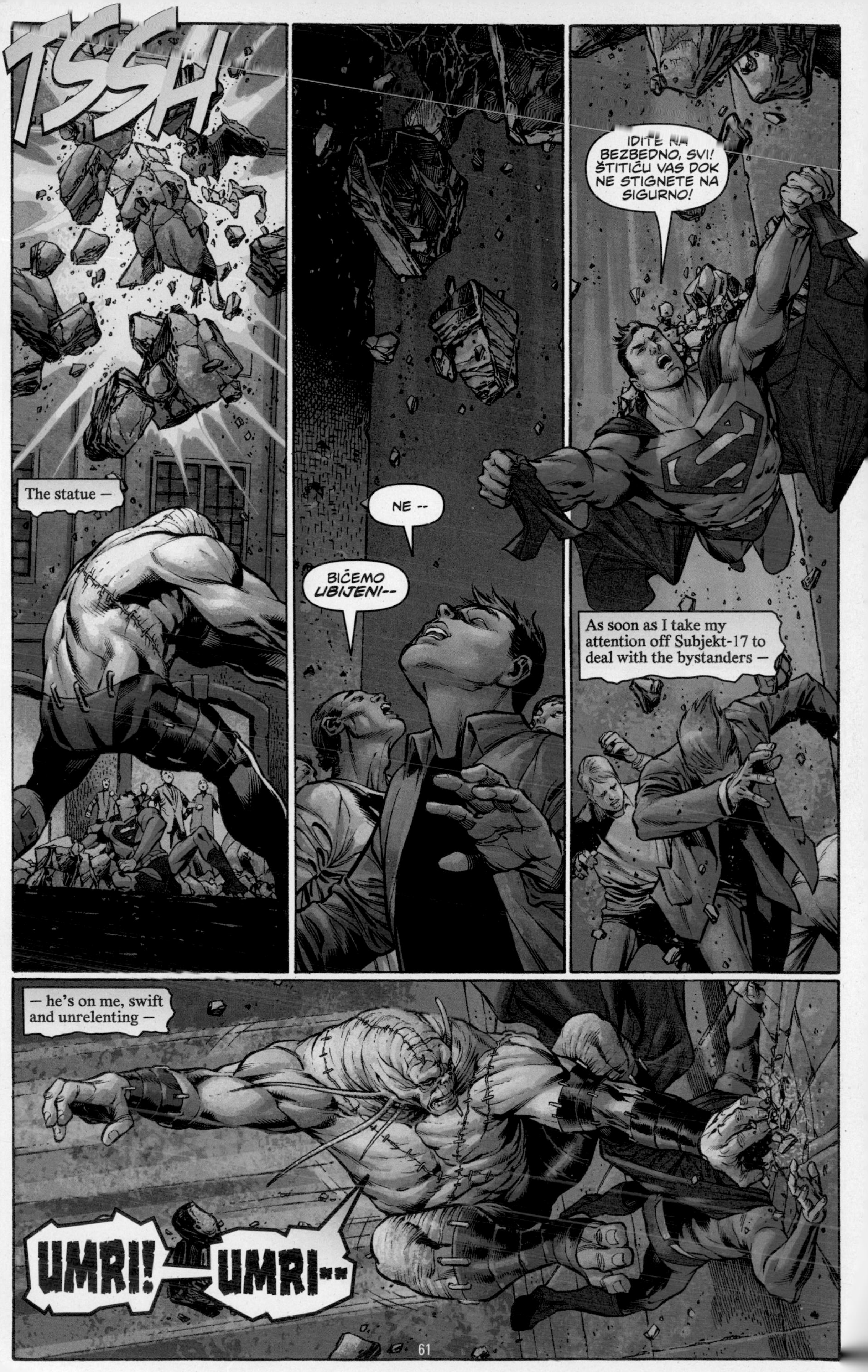
TSSH
The statue —
NE --
BIĆEMO UBIJENI--
IDITE NA BEZBEDNO, SVI! ŠTITIĆU VAS DOK NE STIGNETE NA SIGURNO!
As soon as I take my attention off Subjekt-17 to deal with the bystanders —
— he's on me, swift and unrelenting —
UMRI! UMRI--

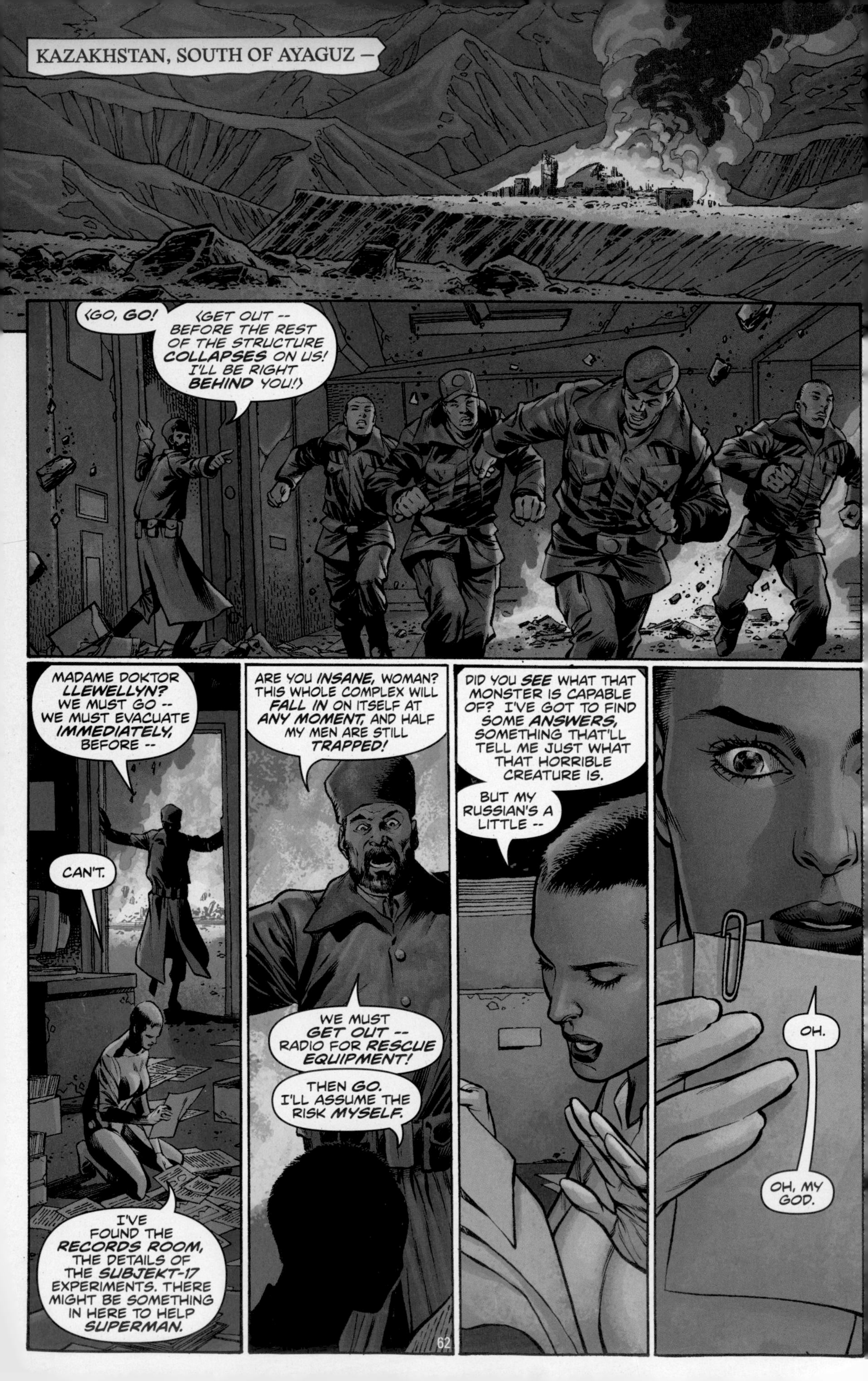
KAZAKHSTAN, SOUTH OF AYAGUZ —
‹GO, GO!
‹GET OUT -- BEFORE THE REST OF THE STRUCTURE COLLAPSES ON US! I'LL BE RIGHT BEHIND YOU!›
MADAME DOKTOR LLEWELLYN? WE MUST GO -- WE MUST EVACUATE IMMEDIATELY, BEFORE --
CAN'T.
I'VE FOUND THE RECORDS ROOM, THE DETAILS OF THE SUBJEKT-17 EXPERIMENTS. THERE MIGHT BE SOMETHING IN HERE TO HELP SUPERMAN.
ARE YOU INSANE, WOMAN? THIS WHOLE COMPLEX WILL FALL IN ON ITSELF AT ANY MOMENT, AND HALF MY MEN ARE STILL TRAPPED!
WE MUST GET OUT -- RADIO FOR RESCUE EQUIPMENT!
THEN GO. I'LL ASSUME THE RISK MYSELF.
DID YOU SEE WHAT THAT MONSTER IS CAPABLE OF? I'VE GOT TO FIND SOME ANSWERS, SOMETHING THAT'LL TELL ME JUST WHAT THAT HORRIBLE CREATURE IS.
BUT MY RUSSIAN'S A LITTLE --
OH.
OH, MY GOD.

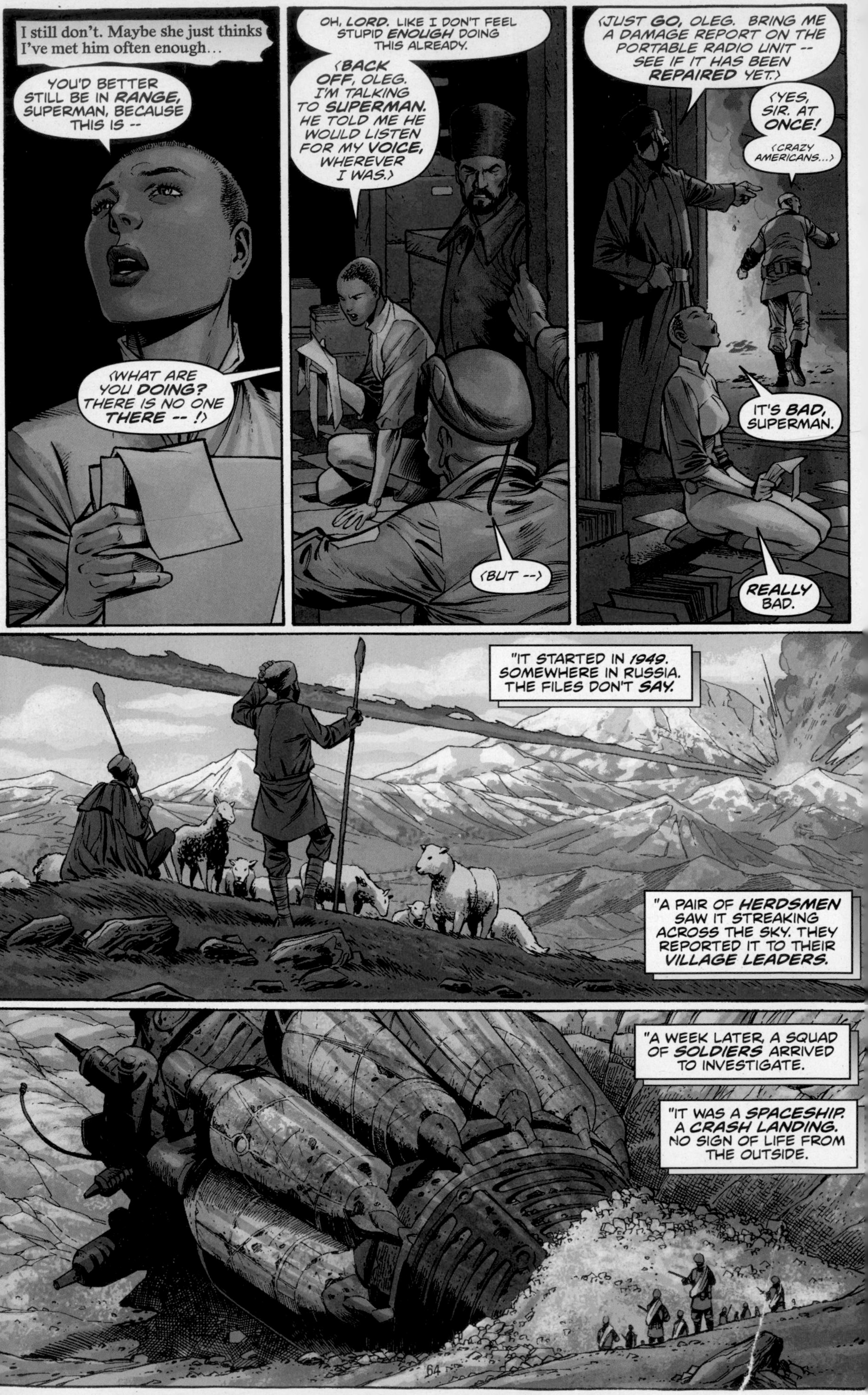
I still don't. Maybe she just thinks I've met him often enough...
YOU'D BETTER STILL BE IN RANGE, SUPERMAN, BECAUSE THIS IS --
‹WHAT ARE YOU DOING? THERE IS NO ONE THERE -- !›
OH, LORD. LIKE I DON'T FEEL STUPID ENOUGH DOING THIS ALREADY.
‹BACK OFF, OLEG. I'M TALKING TO SUPERMAN. HE TOLD ME HE WOULD LISTEN FOR MY VOICE, WHEREVER I WAS.›
‹BUT --›
‹JUST GO, OLEG. BRING ME A DAMAGE REPORT ON THE PORTABLE RADIO UNIT -- SEE IF IT HAS BEEN REPAIRED YET.›
‹YES, SIR. AT ONCE!
‹CRAZY AMERICANS...›
IT'S BAD, SUPERMAN.
REALLY BAD.
"IT STARTED IN 1949. SOMEWHERE IN RUSSIA. THE FILES DON'T SAY.
"A PAIR OF HERDSMEN SAW IT STREAKING ACROSS THE SKY. THEY REPORTED IT TO THEIR VILLAGE LEADERS.
"A WEEK LATER, A SQUAD OF SOLDIERS ARRIVED TO INVESTIGATE.
"IT WAS A SPACESHIP. A CRASH LANDING. NO SIGN OF LIFE FROM THE OUTSIDE.

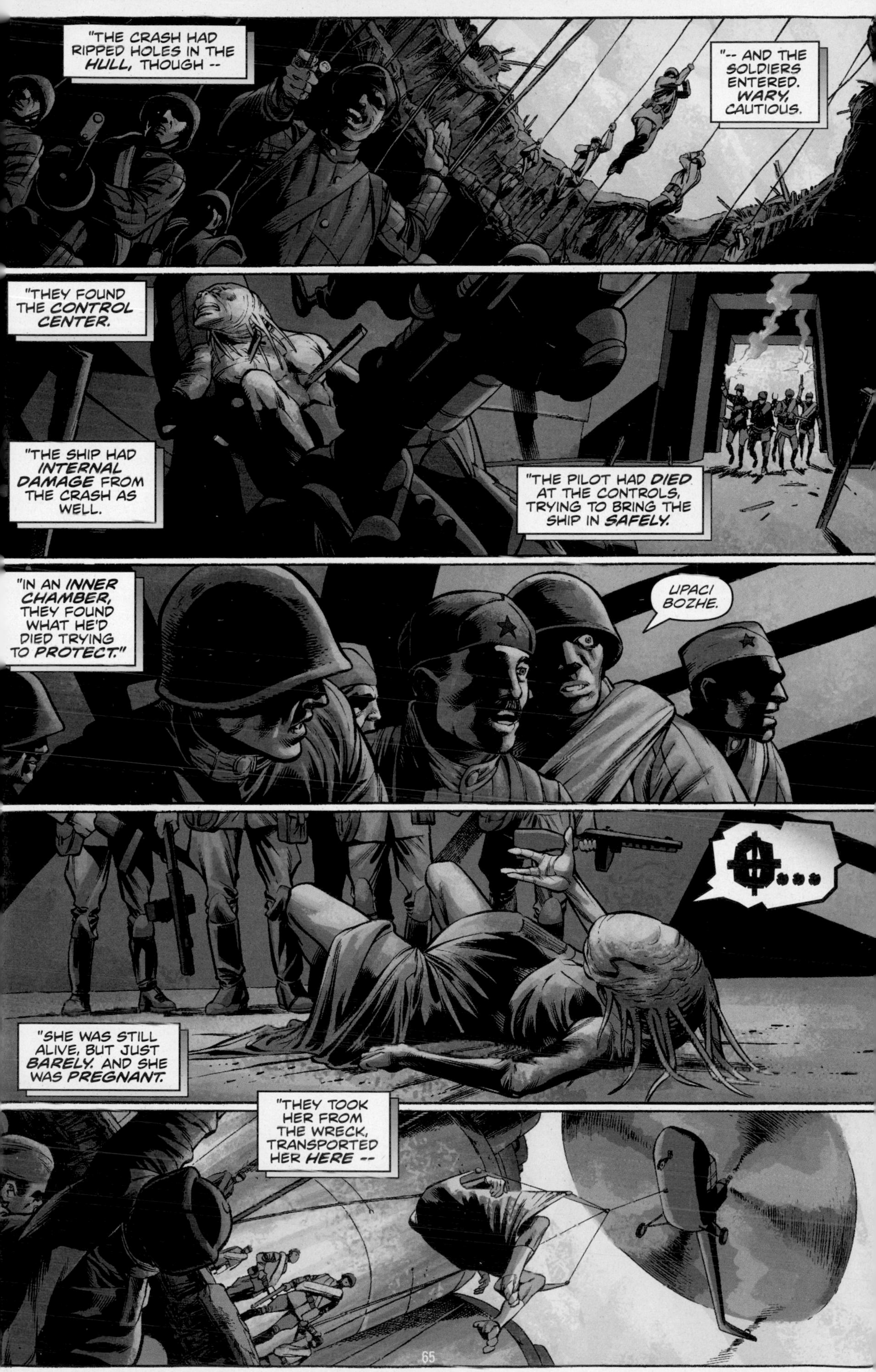
"THE CRASH HAD RIPPED HOLES IN THE *HULL*, THOUGH --
"-- AND THE SOLDIERS ENTERED. *WARY*, CAUTIOUS.
"THEY FOUND THE *CONTROL CENTER*.
"THE SHIP HAD *INTERNAL DAMAGE* FROM THE CRASH AS WELL.
"THE PILOT HAD *DIED* AT THE CONTROLS, TRYING TO BRING THE SHIP IN *SAFELY*.
"IN AN *INNER CHAMBER*, THEY FOUND WHAT HE'D DIED TRYING TO *PROTECT*."
UPACI BOZHE.
"SHE WAS STILL ALIVE, BUT JUST *BARELY*. AND SHE WAS *PREGNANT*.
"THEY TOOK HER FROM THE WRECK, TRANSPORTED HER *HERE* --

"ACCORDING TO THE REPORTS, THEY TRIED TO *SAVE* HER.

"BUT IN EARTH'S ATMOSPHERE, UNDER OUR *SUN*, HER SKIN WAS GROWING *HARDER*, HER MUSCULATURE MORE *DENSE*. THERE WERE COMPLICATIONS.

"WHETHER IT WAS THE SURGERY OR THE DEVELOPING *SUPER-POWERS*, SHE DID NOT SURVIVE.

"BUT HER *BABY* --"

ЦТ! - ЦТ!

THE *INFANT* BEGAN DEVELOPING SUPER-POWERS AS WELL. BUT *SLOWLY*, PERHAPS DUE TO HIS YOUTH.

THEY FOUND WAYS TO *RETARD* THEM, TO PREVENT HIM FROM ABSORBING *WHATEVER* IT WAS THAT MADE THE POWERS MANIFEST.

THEY KEPT HIM *SEDATED*, NEAR-COMATOSE. AND, SUPERMAN --

-- THEY *EXPERIMENTED* ON HIM. FOR *DECADES*.

SLOMIČU TE --

I hear her read off a litany of the experiments they performed on the baby alien.

Analyzing his organs, installing internal sensors, trying to duplicate his skin, to use his blood to create super-soldiers...

H-UHH!

66

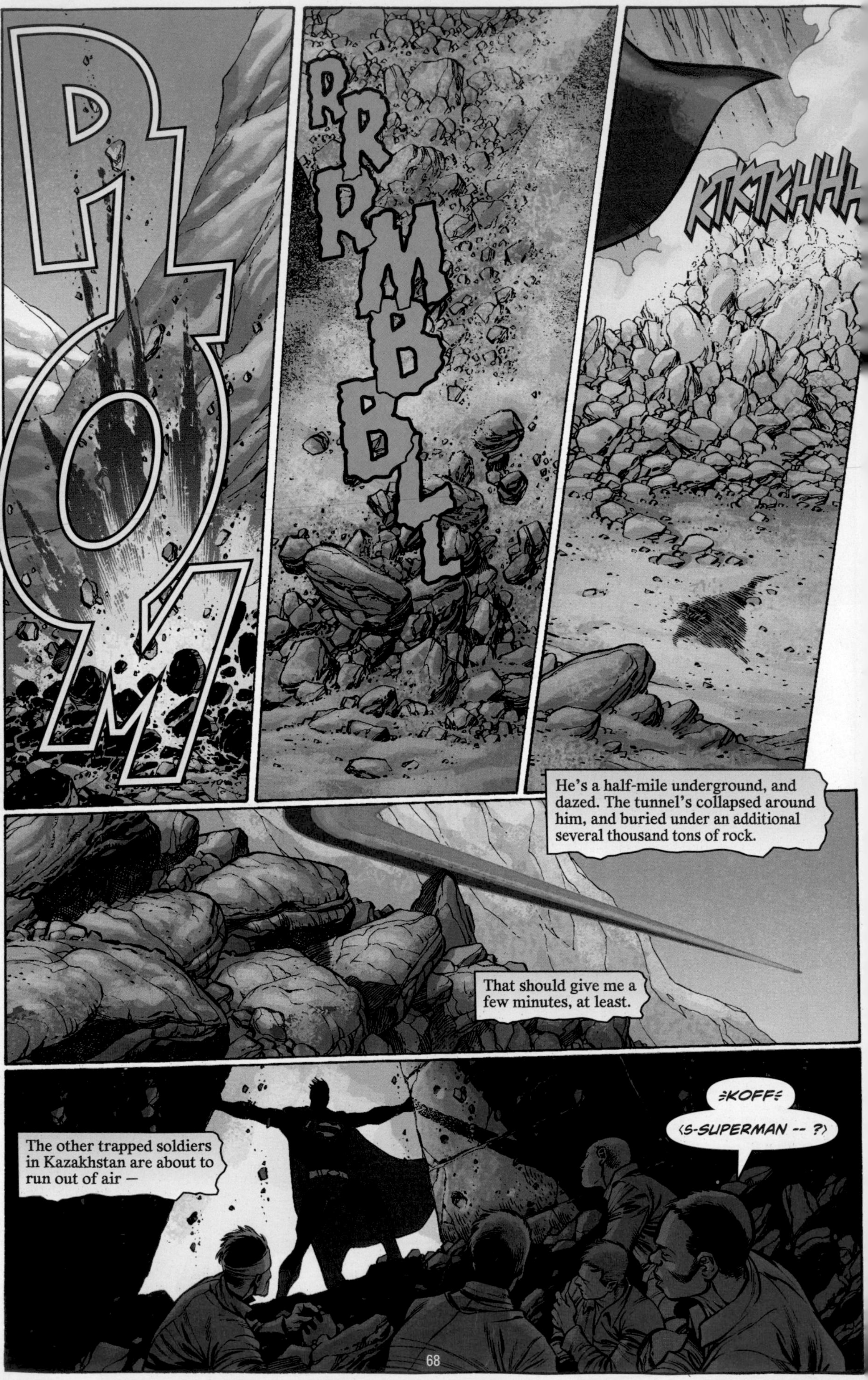
DOOM
RRRMBBLL
KKKKHHH
He's a half-mile underground, and dazed. The tunnel's collapsed around him, and buried under an additional several thousand tons of rock.
That should give me a few minutes, at least.
The other trapped soldiers in Kazakhstan are about to run out of air —
=KOFF=
‹S-SUPERMAN -- ?›

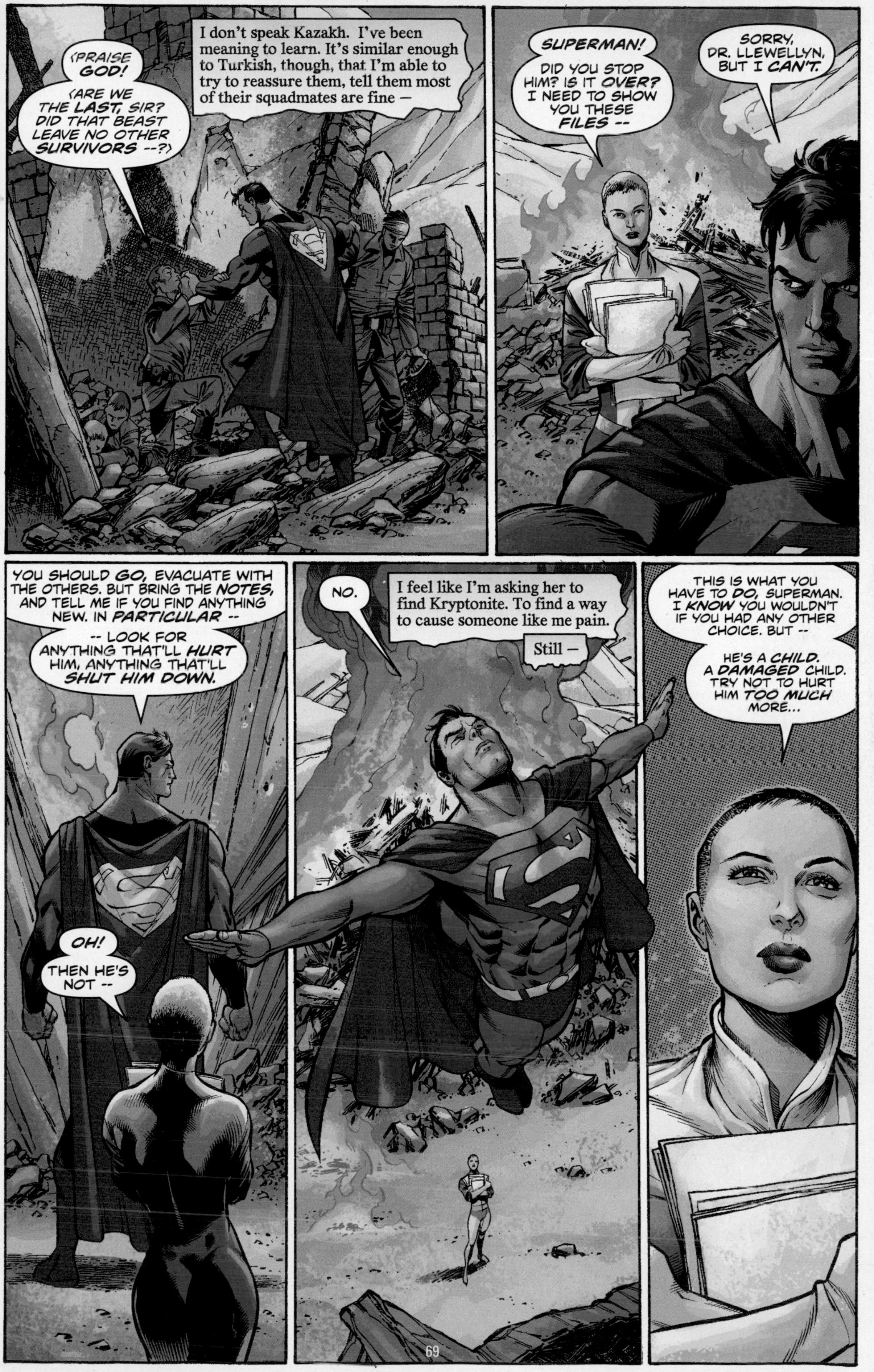

‹PRAISE GOD!
‹ARE WE THE LAST, SIR? DID THAT BEAST LEAVE NO OTHER SURVIVORS --?›
I don't speak Kazakh. I've been meaning to learn. It's similar enough to Turkish, though, that I'm able to try to reassure them, tell them most of their squadmates are fine —
SUPERMAN!
DID YOU STOP HIM? IS IT OVER? I NEED TO SHOW YOU THESE FILES --
SORRY, DR. LLEWELLYN, BUT I CAN'T.
YOU SHOULD GO, EVACUATE WITH THE OTHERS. BUT BRING THE NOTES, AND TELL ME IF YOU FIND ANYTHING NEW. IN PARTICULAR --
-- LOOK FOR ANYTHING THAT'LL HURT HIM, ANYTHING THAT'LL SHUT HIM DOWN.
OH!
THEN HE'S NOT --
NO.
I feel like I'm asking her to find Kryptonite. To find a way to cause someone like me pain.
Still —
THIS IS WHAT YOU HAVE TO DO, SUPERMAN. I KNOW YOU WOULDN'T IF YOU HAD ANY OTHER CHOICE. BUT --
HE'S A CHILD. A DAMAGED CHILD. TRY NOT TO HURT HIM TOO MUCH MORE...

YOU -- YOU -- I FEEL YOU -- SEE -- SEE THROUGH YOU --

He's got me in a telekinetic hold. And he's speaking English — I thought he'd started to, before.

I can feel his power, playing over me —

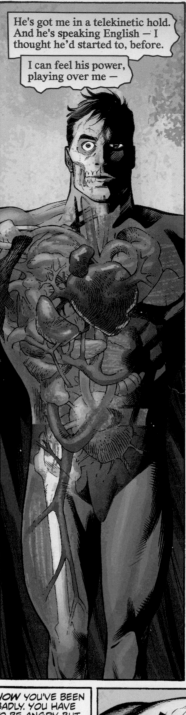

YOU -- NOT LIKE THEM. NOT MONSTER, NOT "HUMAN."

YOU -- OTHER. ALIEN. LIKE SUBJEKT. LIKE ME.

Callie was wrong. He's not a child.

He's an adult. An adult that was never socialized, never taught anything. He learned from what he was subjected to — cruelty and pain.

But if he can reason —

LISTEN. I KNOW YOU'VE BEEN TREATED BADLY. YOU HAVE REASON TO BE ANGRY. BUT IT DOESN'T HAVE TO GO ON LIKE THIS. THOSE MEN --

NO!! YOU ARE LIKE ME! AND YOU HELP THEM! HELP HUMANS AGAINST SUBJEKT --

HURT SUBJEKT MORE --

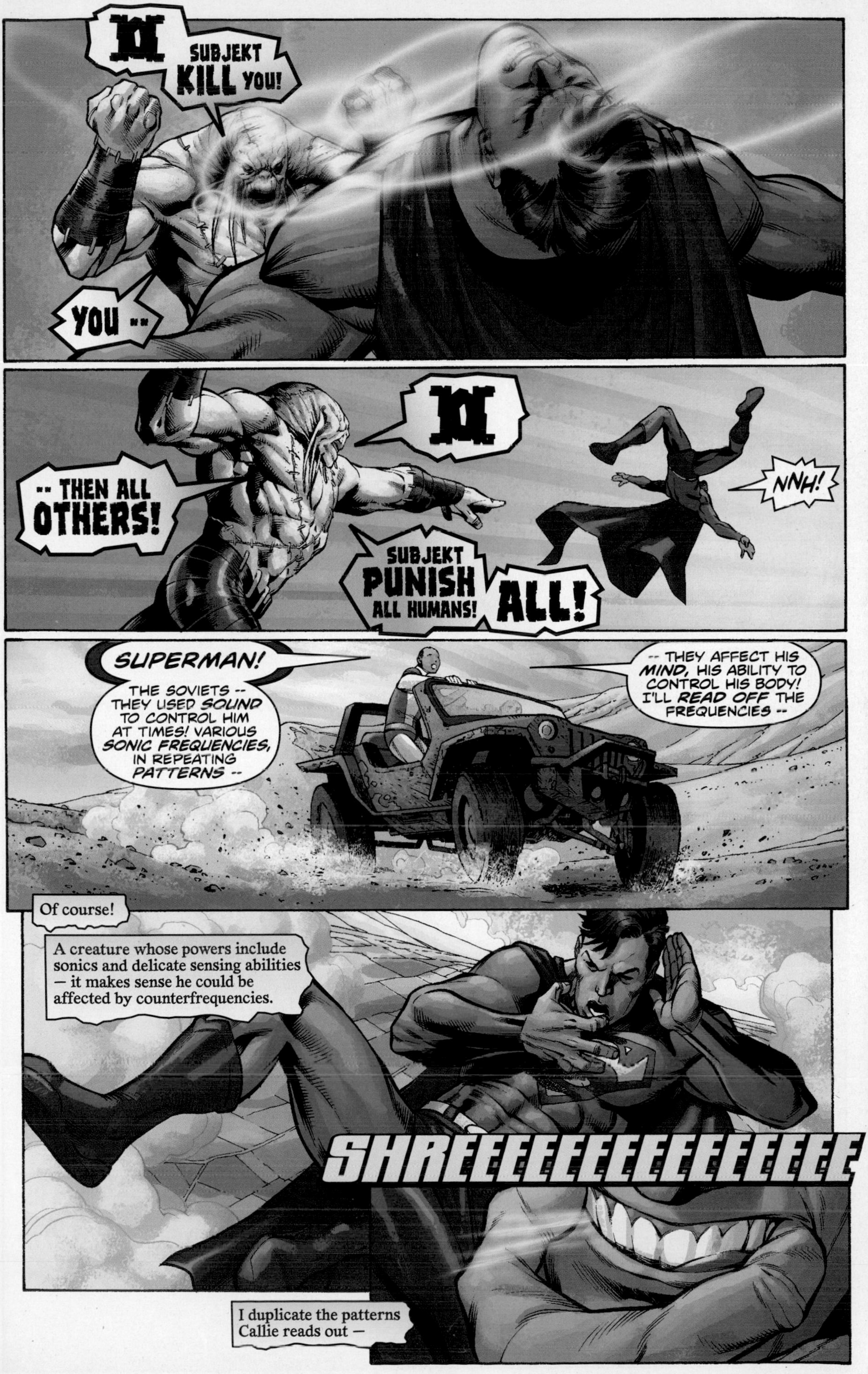

SUBJEKT KILL YOU!
YOU --
-- THEN ALL OTHERS!
SUBJEKT PUNISH ALL HUMANS!
ALL!
NNH!
SUPERMAN!
THE SOVIETS -- THEY USED SOUND TO CONTROL HIM AT TIMES! VARIOUS SONIC FREQUENCIES, IN REPEATING PATTERNS --
-- THEY AFFECT HIS MIND, HIS ABILITY TO CONTROL HIS BODY! I'LL READ OFF THE FREQUENCIES --
Of course!
A creature whose powers include sonics and delicate sensing abilities — it makes sense he could be affected by counterfrequencies.
SHREEEEEEEEEEEEEEEE
I duplicate the patterns Callie reads out —

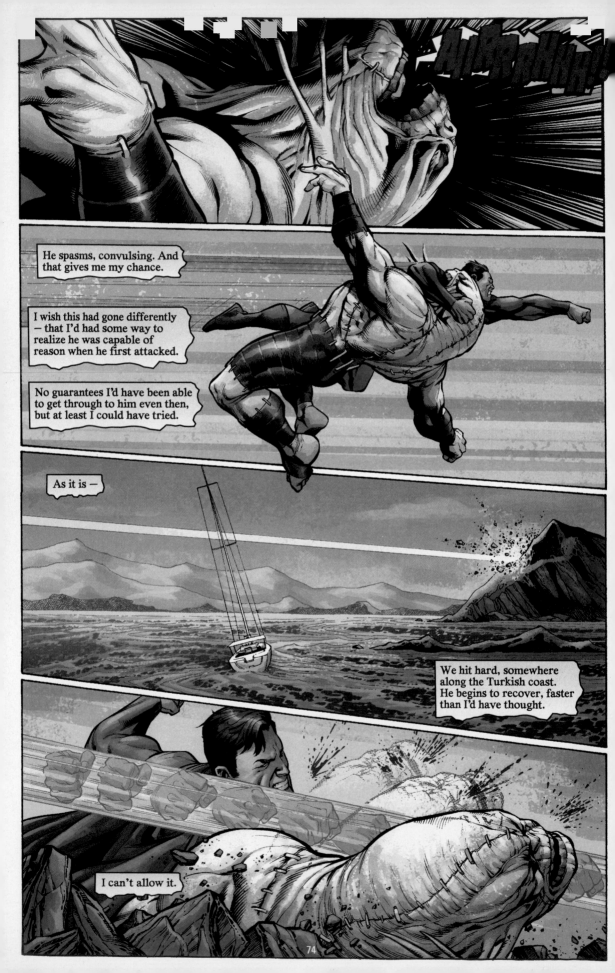

AERRHHH!

He spasms, convulsing. And that gives me my chance.

I wish this had gone differently — that I'd had some way to realize he was capable of reason when he first attacked.

No guarantees I'd have been able to get through to him even then, but at least I could have tried.

As it is —

We hit hard, somewhere along the Turkish coast. He begins to recover, faster than I'd have thought.

I can't allow it.

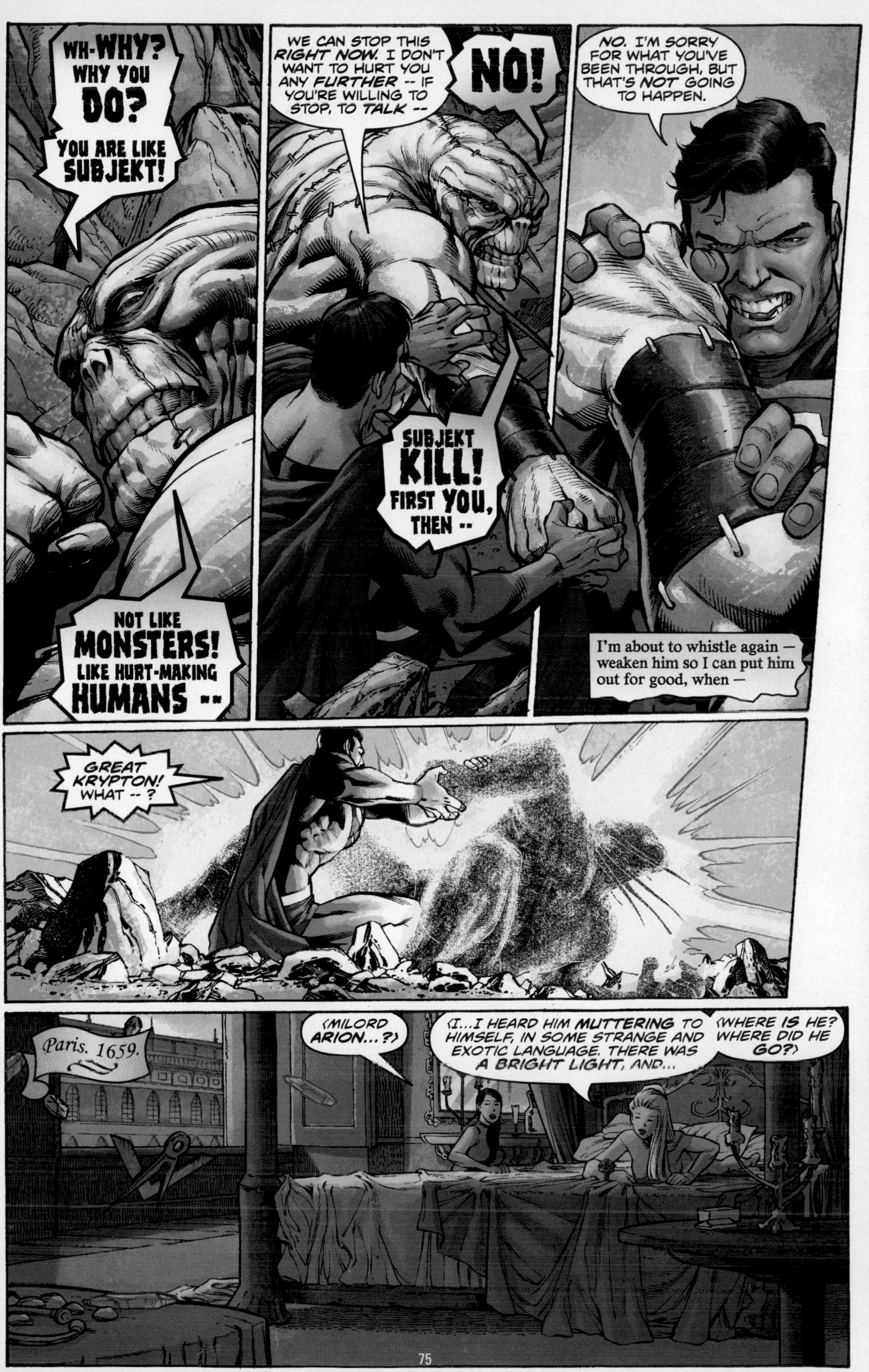

WH-WHY? WHY YOU DO? YOU ARE LIKE SUBJEKT!
NOT LIKE MONSTERS! LIKE HURT-MAKING HUMANS --
WE CAN STOP THIS RIGHT NOW. I DON'T WANT TO HURT YOU ANY FURTHER -- IF YOU'RE WILLING TO STOP, TO TALK --
NO!
SUBJEKT KILL! FIRST YOU, THEN --
NO. I'M SORRY FOR WHAT YOU'VE BEEN THROUGH, BUT THAT'S NOT GOING TO HAPPEN.
I'm about to whistle again — weaken him so I can put him out for good, when —
GREAT KRYPTON! WHAT -- ?
Paris. 1659.
‹MILORD ARION...?›
‹I...I HEARD HIM MUTTERING TO HIMSELF, IN SOME STRANGE AND EXOTIC LANGUAGE. THERE WAS A BRIGHT LIGHT, AND...
‹WHERE IS HE? WHERE DID HE GO?›

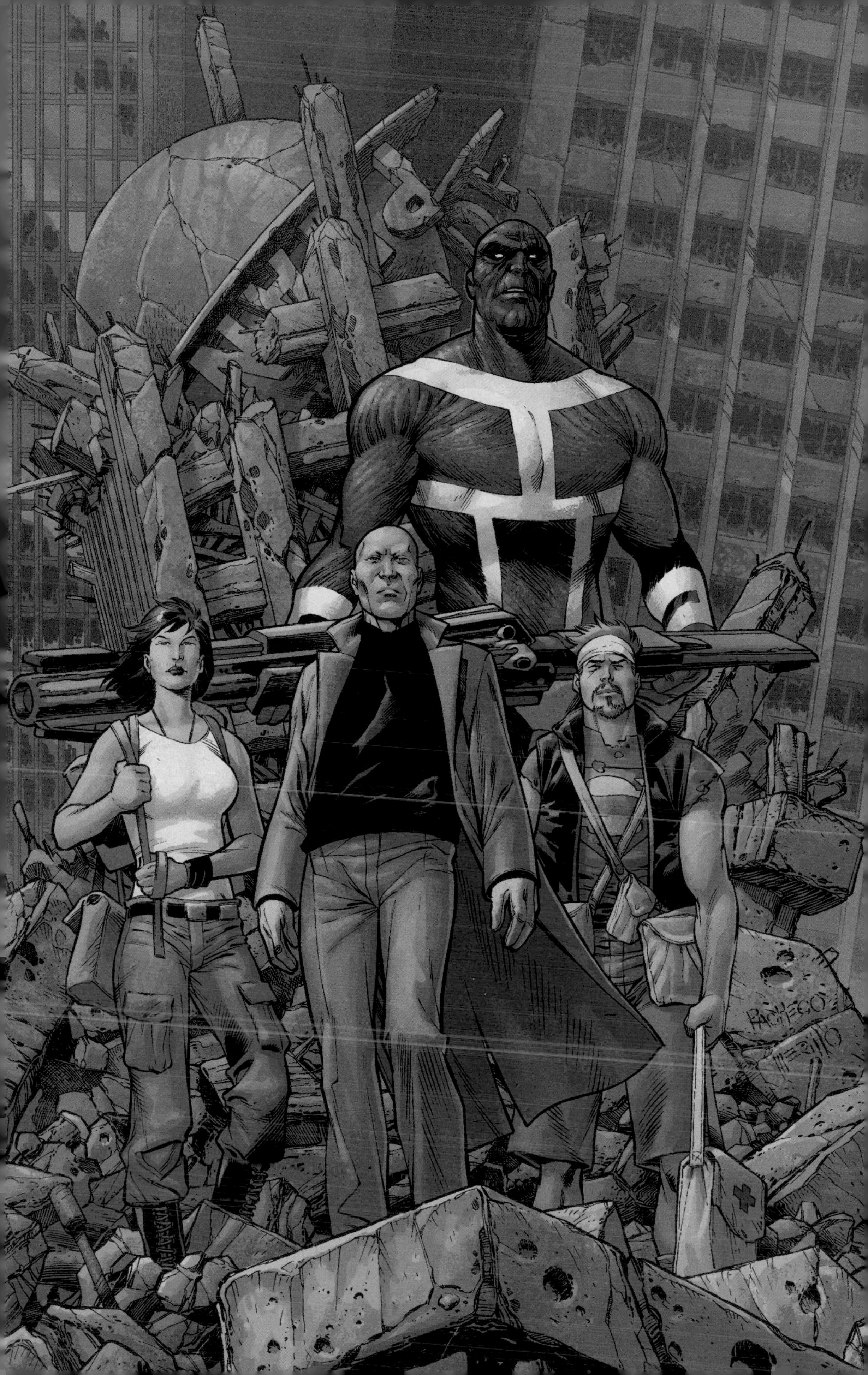
PACHECO

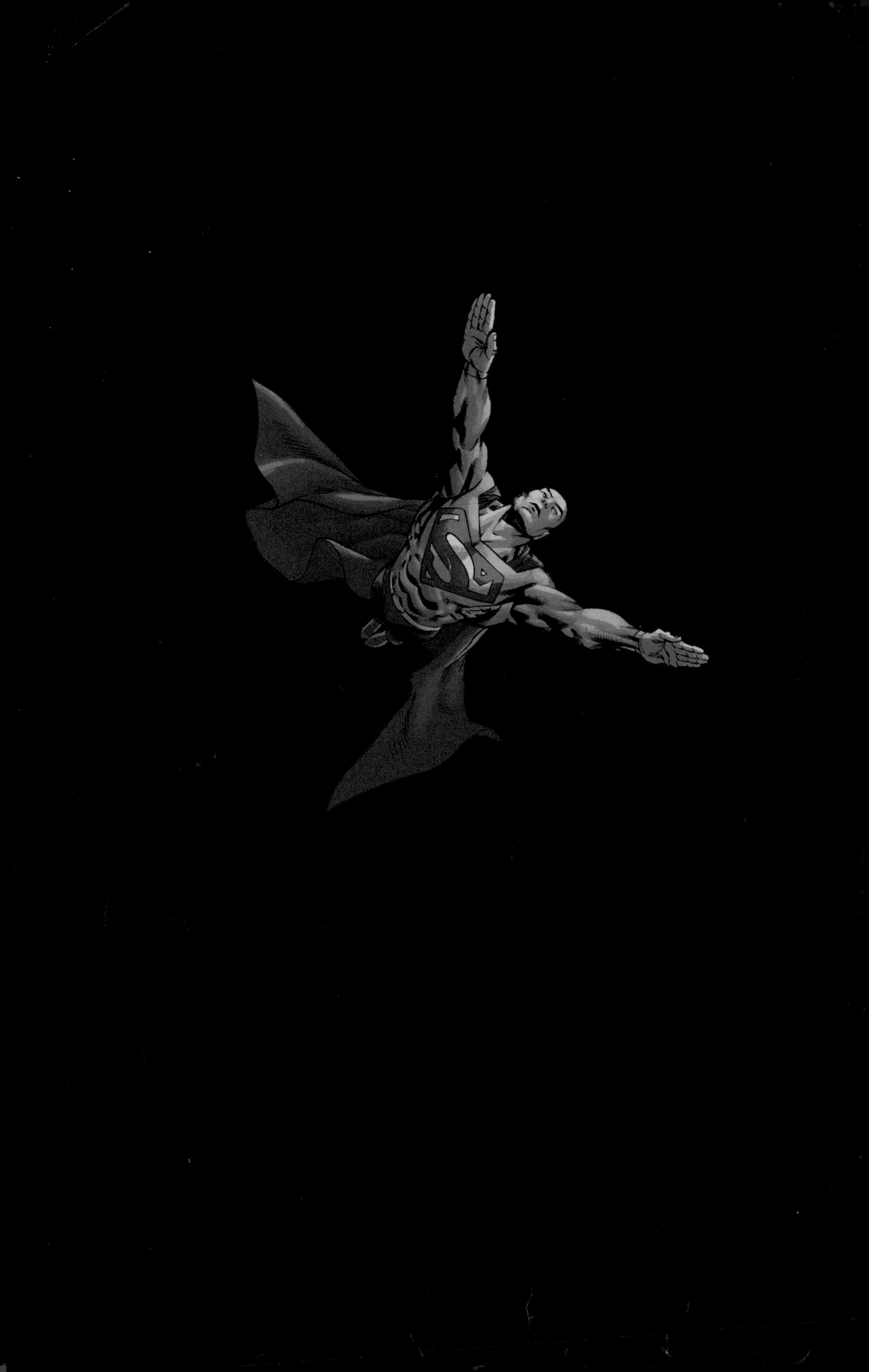

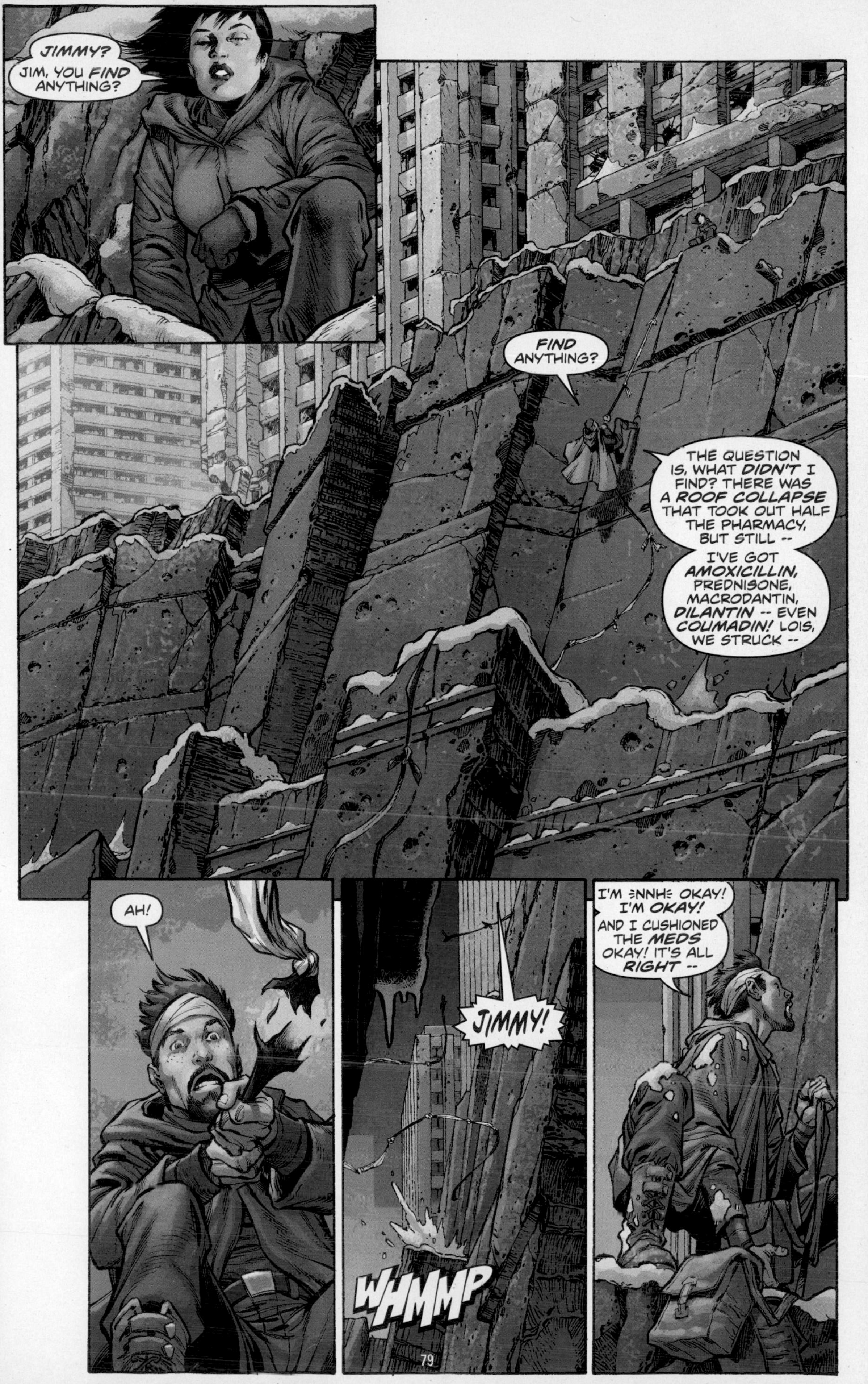
JIMMY?
JIM, YOU FIND ANYTHING?
FIND ANYTHING?
THE QUESTION IS, WHAT DIDN'T I FIND? THERE WAS A ROOF COLLAPSE THAT TOOK OUT HALF THE PHARMACY, BUT STILL --
I'VE GOT AMOXICILLIN, PREDNISONE, MACRODANTIN, DILANTIN -- EVEN COUMADIN! LOIS, WE STRUCK --
AH!
JIMMY!
WHMMP
I'M =NNH= OKAY! I'M OKAY! AND I CUSHIONED THE MEDS OKAY! IT'S ALL RIGHT --

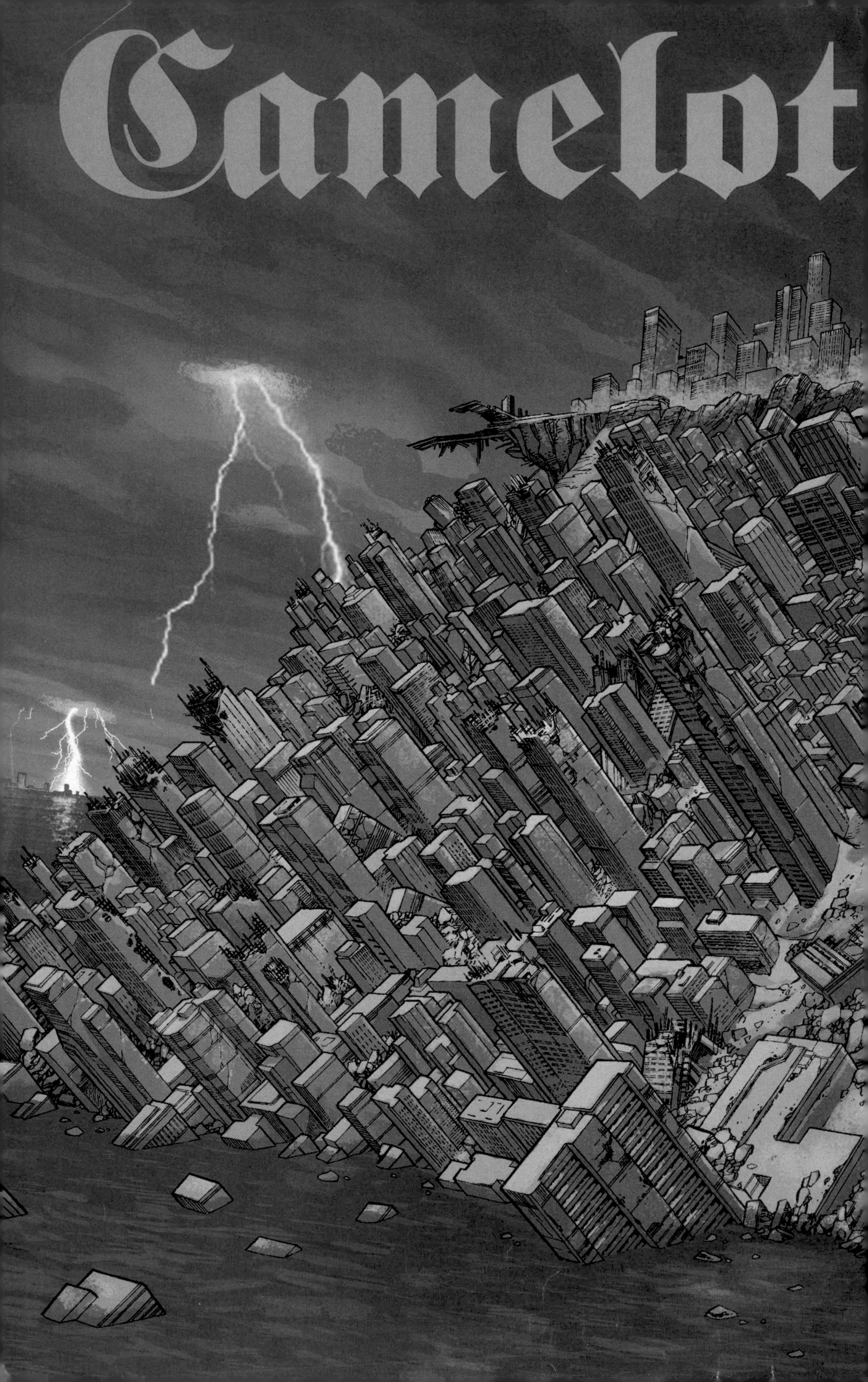
Camelot

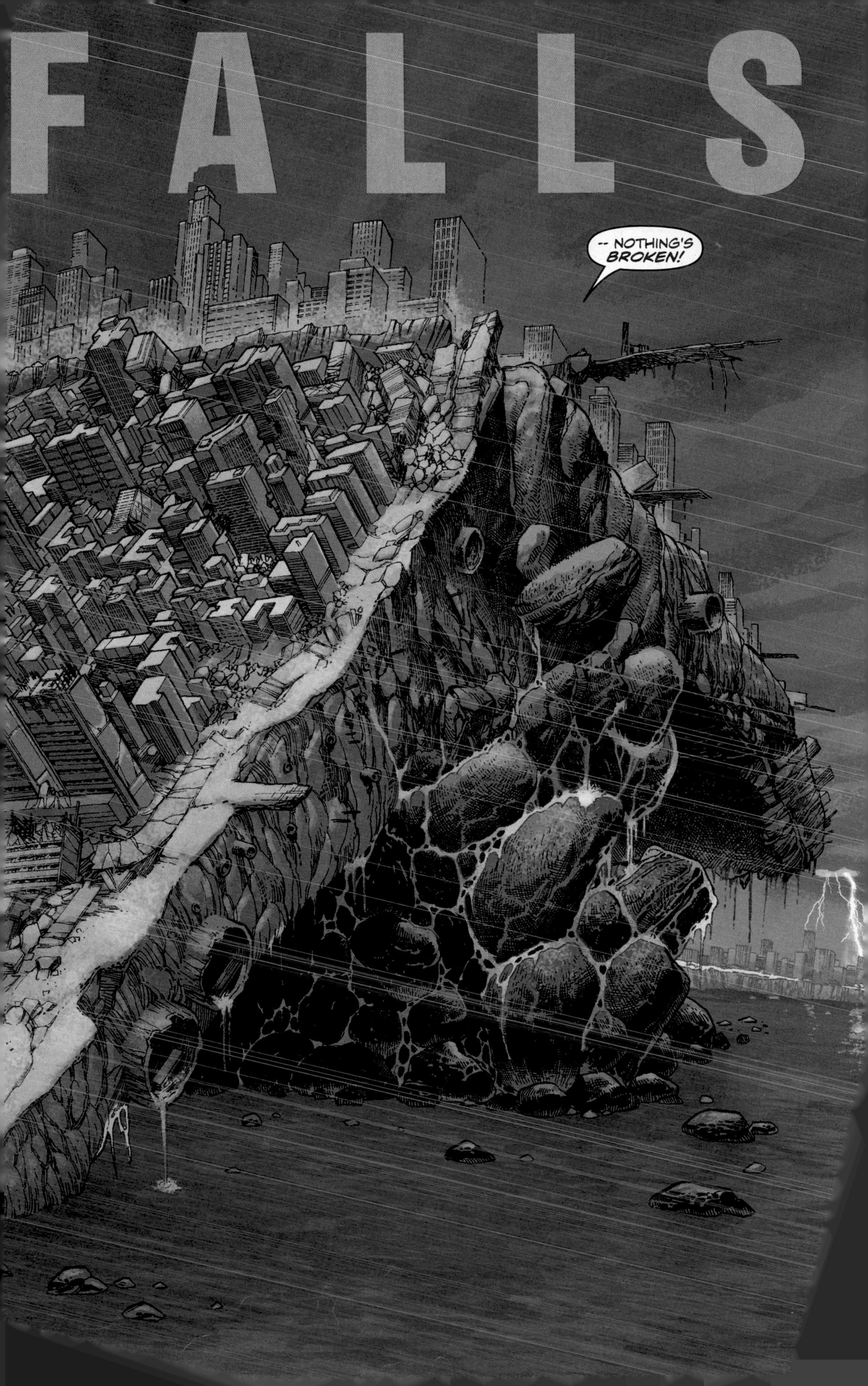
FALLS
-- NOTHING'S BROKEN!

August 3, 2014

Metropolis. Once — no, three times, all told — it floated above the eastern seaboard like a shining temple to technology and the future.

HUH. THEY WERE SUPPOSED TO *MEET* US HERE. ANY BETS LEX GOT CAUGHT UP REWIRING A.T.M.S INTO *ONE-MAN HOVERCRAFT* AGAIN?

Now we're just lucky parts of it are up high enough to discourage scavengers.

BE FAIR, JIM. THERE'S NO VIEW OF THE *SUN* TO MEASURE TIME, AND SINCE THE *WORLDWIDE PULSE*, MOST CLOCKS AND WATCHES DON'T --

YEAH, I'M JUST CRANKY 'CAUSE I LANDED ON MY *TAILBONE.*

PERRY'S OLD *POCKET WATCH* DOESN'T KEEP GREAT TIME ANY MORE, BUT AS FAR AS I CAN TELL, WE'RE ACTUALLY A LITTLE *EARLY,* FOR --

VTT

VTT

VTTT

GHOSTWOLVES! FOUR OF -- NNH!

DOWN, JIMMY!

AIHHH.

ZVAK

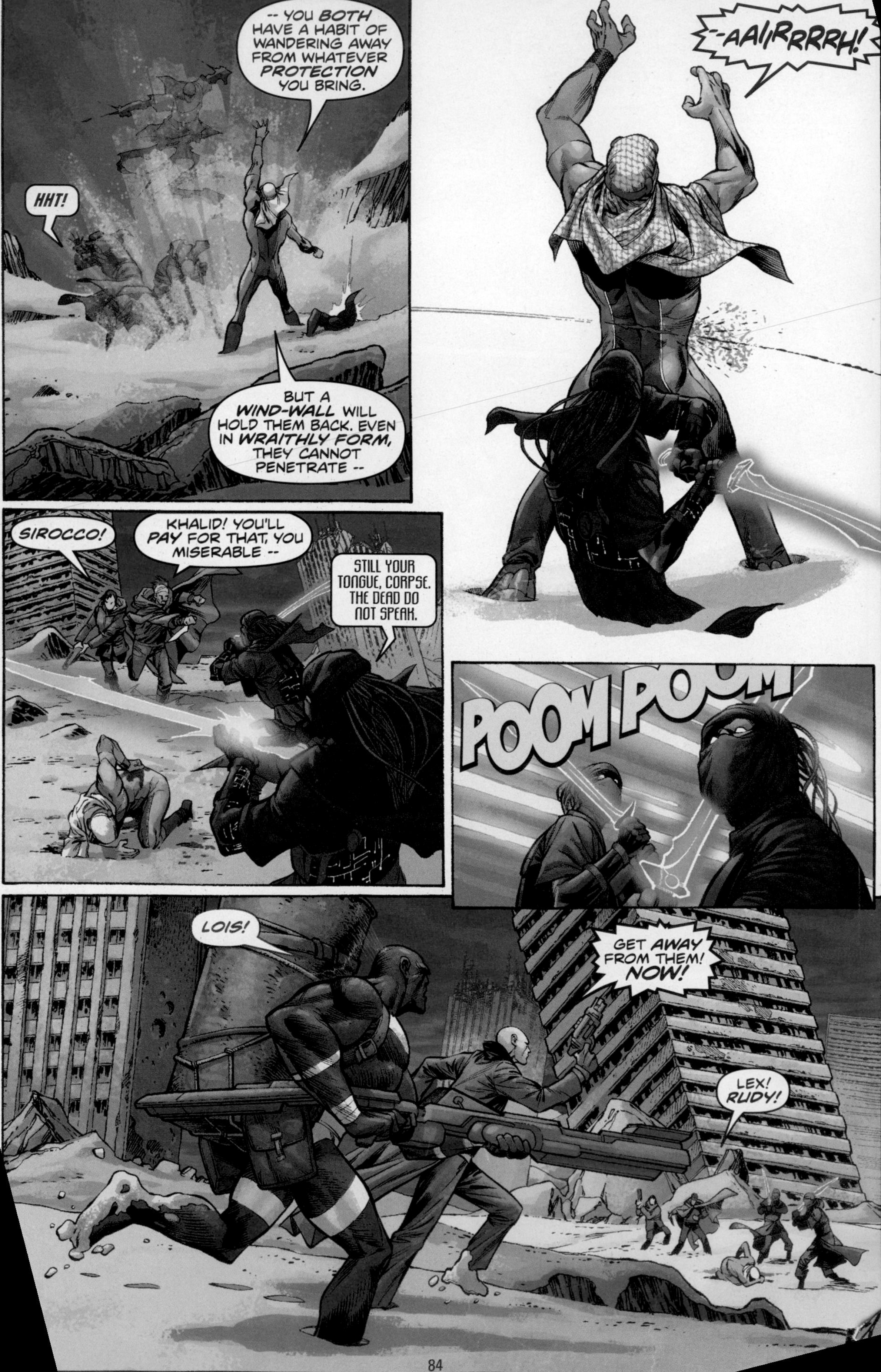

-- YOU BOTH HAVE A HABIT OF WANDERING AWAY FROM WHATEVER PROTECTION YOU BRING.
HHT!
BUT A WIND-WALL WILL HOLD THEM BACK. EVEN IN WRAITHLY FORM, THEY CANNOT PENETRATE --
--AAIIRRRRH!
SIROCCO!
KHALID! YOU'LL PAY FOR THAT, YOU MISERABLE --
STILL YOUR TONGUE, CORPSE. THE DEAD DO NOT SPEAK.
POOM POOM
LOIS!
GET AWAY FROM THEM! NOW!
LEX! RUDY!

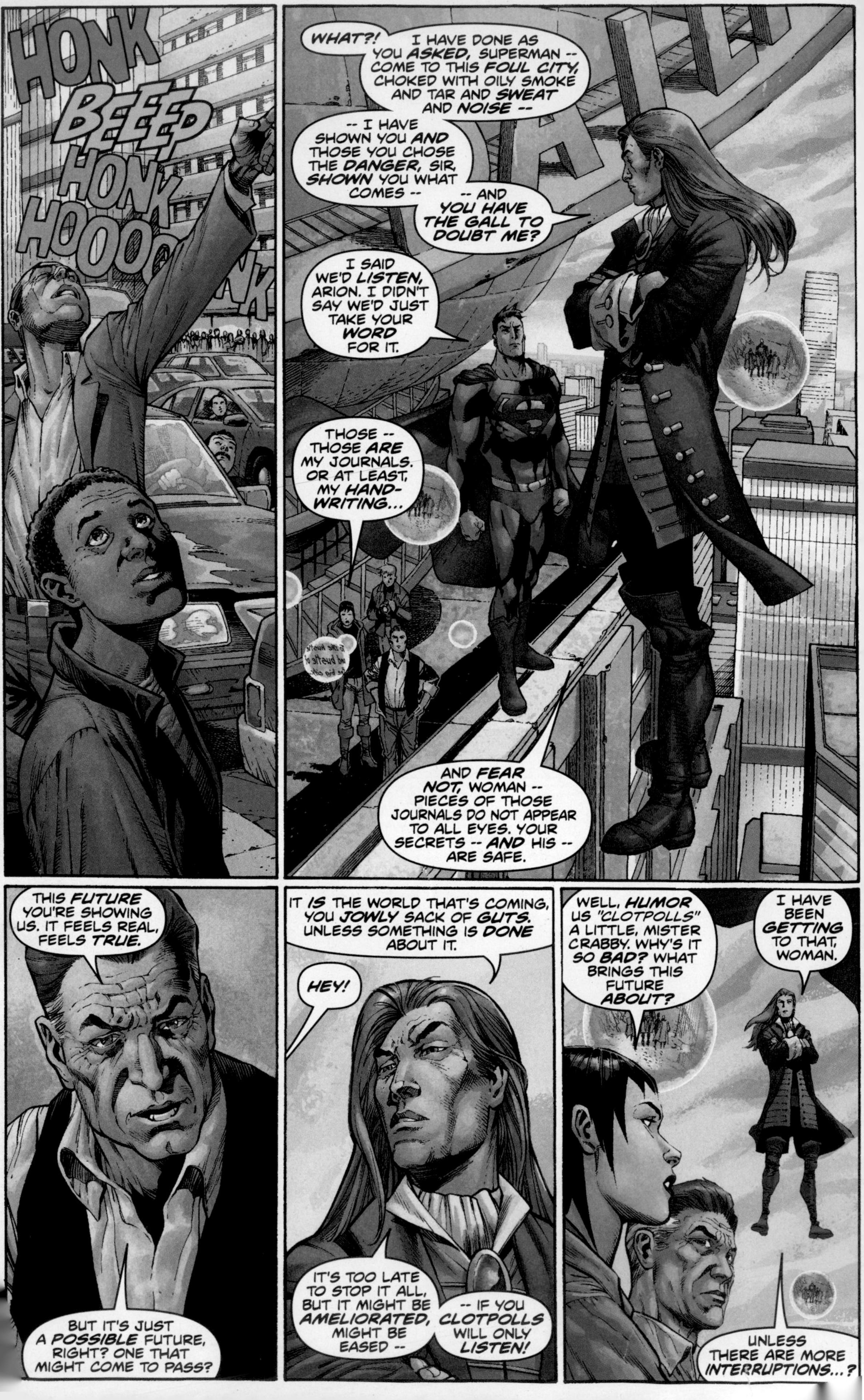
HONK
BEEEP
HONK
HOOOONK
WHAT?!
I HAVE DONE AS YOU ASKED, SUPERMAN -- COME TO THIS FOUL CITY, CHOKED WITH OILY SMOKE AND TAR AND SWEAT AND NOISE --
-- I HAVE SHOWN YOU AND THOSE YOU CHOSE THE DANGER, SIR, SHOWN YOU WHAT COMES --
-- AND YOU HAVE THE GALL TO DOUBT ME?
I SAID WE'D LISTEN, ARION. I DIDN'T SAY WE'D JUST TAKE YOUR WORD FOR IT.
THOSE -- THOSE ARE MY JOURNALS. OR AT LEAST, MY HAND-WRITING...
AND FEAR NOT, WOMAN -- PIECES OF THOSE JOURNALS DO NOT APPEAR TO ALL EYES. YOUR SECRETS -- AND HIS -- ARE SAFE.
THIS FUTURE YOU'RE SHOWING US. IT FEELS REAL, FEELS TRUE.
BUT IT'S JUST A POSSIBLE FUTURE, RIGHT? ONE THAT MIGHT COME TO PASS?
IT IS THE WORLD THAT'S COMING, YOU JOWLY SACK OF GUTS. UNLESS SOMETHING IS DONE ABOUT IT.
HEY!
IT'S TOO LATE TO STOP IT ALL, BUT IT MIGHT BE AMELIORATED, MIGHT BE EASED --
-- IF YOU CLOTPOLLS WILL ONLY LISTEN!
WELL, HUMOR US "CLOTPOLLS" A LITTLE, MISTER CRABBY. WHY'S IT SO BAD? WHAT BRINGS THIS FUTURE ABOUT?
I HAVE BEEN GETTING TO THAT, WOMAN.
UNLESS THERE ARE MORE INTERRUPTIONS...?

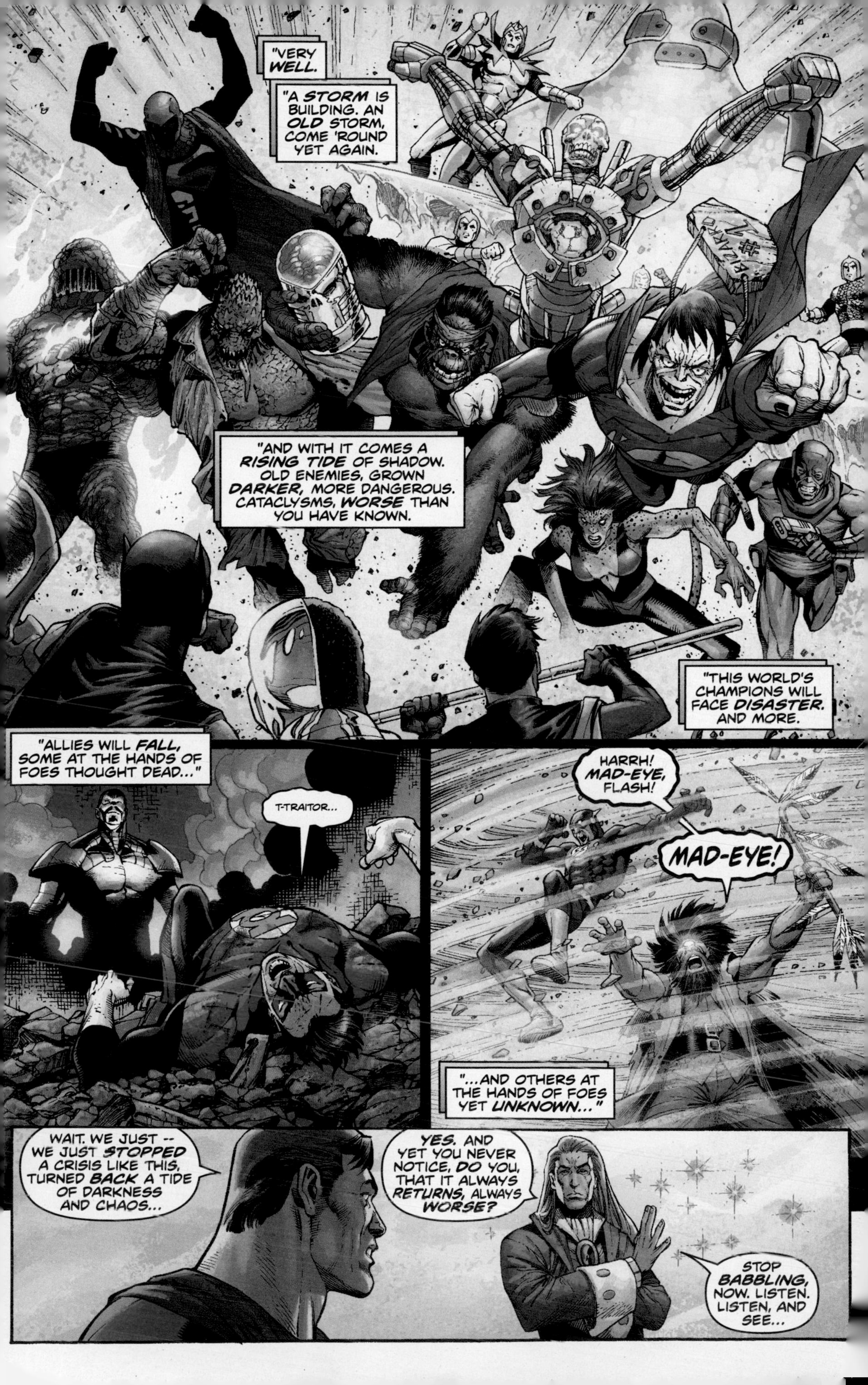
"VERY WELL.
"A STORM IS BUILDING. AN OLD STORM, COME 'ROUND YET AGAIN.
"AND WITH IT COMES A RISING TIDE OF SHADOW. OLD ENEMIES, GROWN DARKER, MORE DANGEROUS. CATACLYSMS, WORSE THAN YOU HAVE KNOWN.
"THIS WORLD'S CHAMPIONS WILL FACE DISASTER. AND MORE.
"ALLIES WILL FALL, SOME AT THE HANDS OF FOES THOUGHT DEAD..."
T-TRAITOR...
HARRH! MAD-EYE, FLASH!
MAD-EYE!
"...AND OTHERS AT THE HANDS OF FOES YET UNKNOWN..."
WAIT. WE JUST -- WE JUST STOPPED A CRISIS LIKE THIS, TURNED BACK A TIDE OF DARKNESS AND CHAOS...
YES. AND YET YOU NEVER NOTICE, DO YOU, THAT IT ALWAYS RETURNS, ALWAYS WORSE?
STOP BABBLING, NOW. LISTEN. LISTEN, AND SEE...

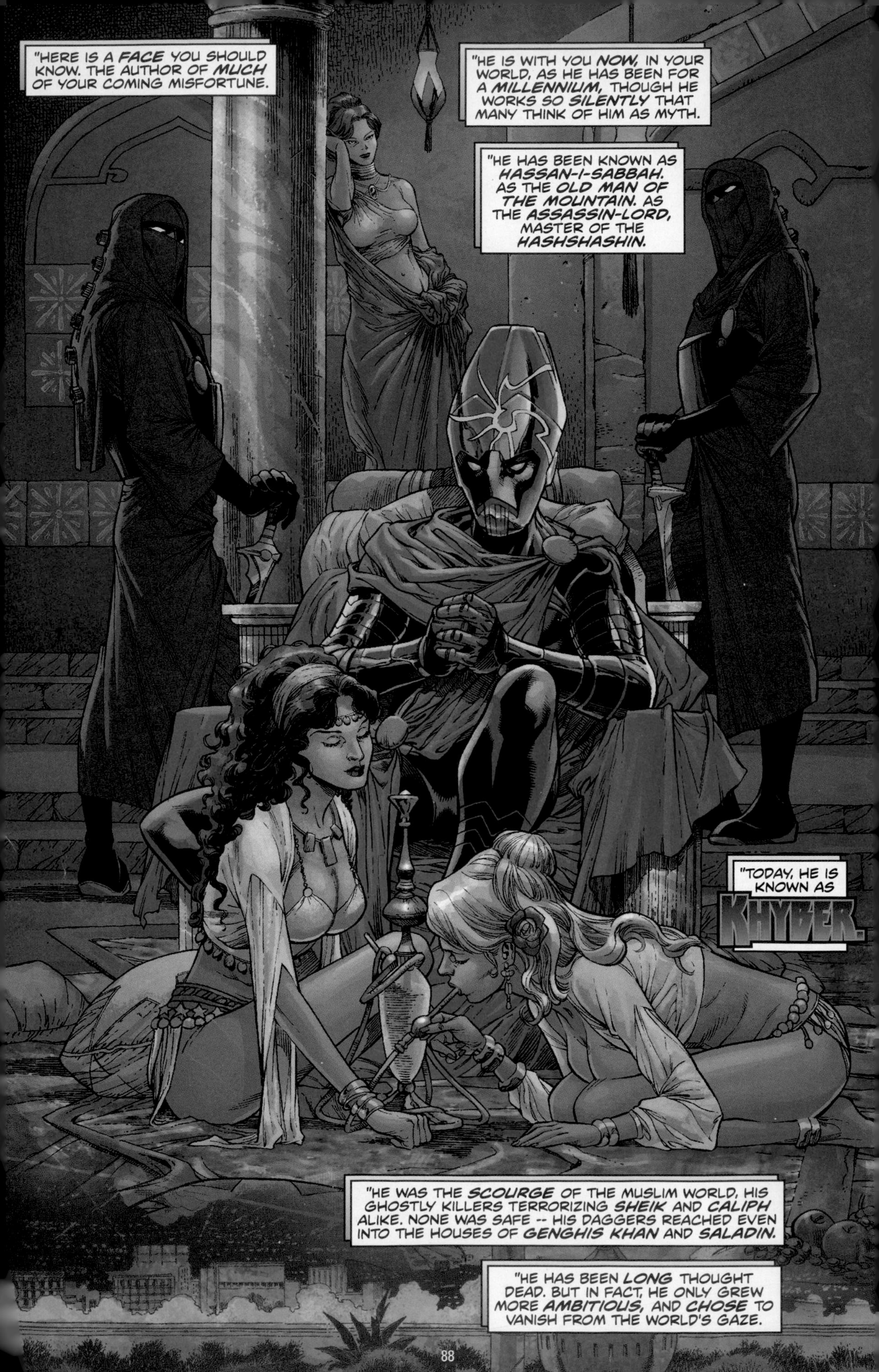
"HERE IS A FACE YOU SHOULD KNOW. THE AUTHOR OF MUCH OF YOUR COMING MISFORTUNE.
"HE IS WITH YOU NOW, IN YOUR WORLD, AS HE HAS BEEN FOR A MILLENNIUM, THOUGH HE WORKS SO SILENTLY THAT MANY THINK OF HIM AS MYTH.
"HE HAS BEEN KNOWN AS HASSAN-I-SABBAH. AS THE OLD MAN OF THE MOUNTAIN. AS THE ASSASSIN-LORD, MASTER OF THE HASHSHASHIN.
"TODAY, HE IS KNOWN AS
KHYBER.
"HE WAS THE SCOURGE OF THE MUSLIM WORLD, HIS GHOSTLY KILLERS TERRORIZING SHEIK AND CALIPH ALIKE. NONE WAS SAFE -- HIS DAGGERS REACHED EVEN INTO THE HOUSES OF GENGHIS KHAN AND SALADIN.
"HE HAS BEEN LONG THOUGHT DEAD. BUT IN FACT, HE ONLY GREW MORE AMBITIOUS, AND CHOSE TO VANISH FROM THE WORLD'S GAZE.

"HE WORKS IN *SECRET* IN YEARS TO COME, AS IS HIS PREFERENCE..."

"...USING THE CONFLICT BETWEEN MUSLIM EXTREMISM AND THE WEST TO *MASK* MANY OF HIS ACTIVITIES, AS HE HAS ALREADY DONE SO OFTEN.

"WHEN HIS PLANS ARE *RIPE*, HE MAKES ALLIANCES..."

THE NORTH ATLANTIC? *ALL OF* IT? THROW IN THE *ARCTIC*, KHYBER, AND YOU'VE GOT A DEAL. I'VE GOT *INTERESTS* UNDER THE ICECAP.

DONE. STEP FORWARD, ASSEGAI. I WILL TREAT WITH YOU NEXT.

"...AND BEGINS, STILL MOVING IN SECRET, TO *DESTABILIZE* THE MORE POWERFUL NATIONS OF THE WORLD."

-- ROCKED BY THE *VIOLENT EXPLOSION* TODAY AT 10 DOWNING STREET, WHICH CLAIMED THE LIVES OF --

"IN TIME, HOWEVER, HE *OVERREACHES*, AS AMBITIOUS MEN DO. HE SEEKS TO RECRUIT THOSE *PROUD* AND *POWERFUL* ENOUGH TO REJECT HIM."

SO BE IT, TETH-ADAM. I HAD THOUGHT YOU WOULD SEE VALUE IN THE OLD WAYS. YOU WILL NOT PAY THE PRICE FOR YOUR FOLLY ALONE.

YOU ARE A *MADMAN*. I WILL *EXPOSE* YOU TO THE WORLD. AND I WILL SEE YOU *BROKEN* AND BROUGHT *LOW*.

"BY THIS TIME, HE HAS A *NETWORK* OF ALLIES, AND *UNSEEN* INFLUENCE FAR BEYOND. A FEW *WHISPERED WORDS*, A FEW TUGGED *STRINGS*..."

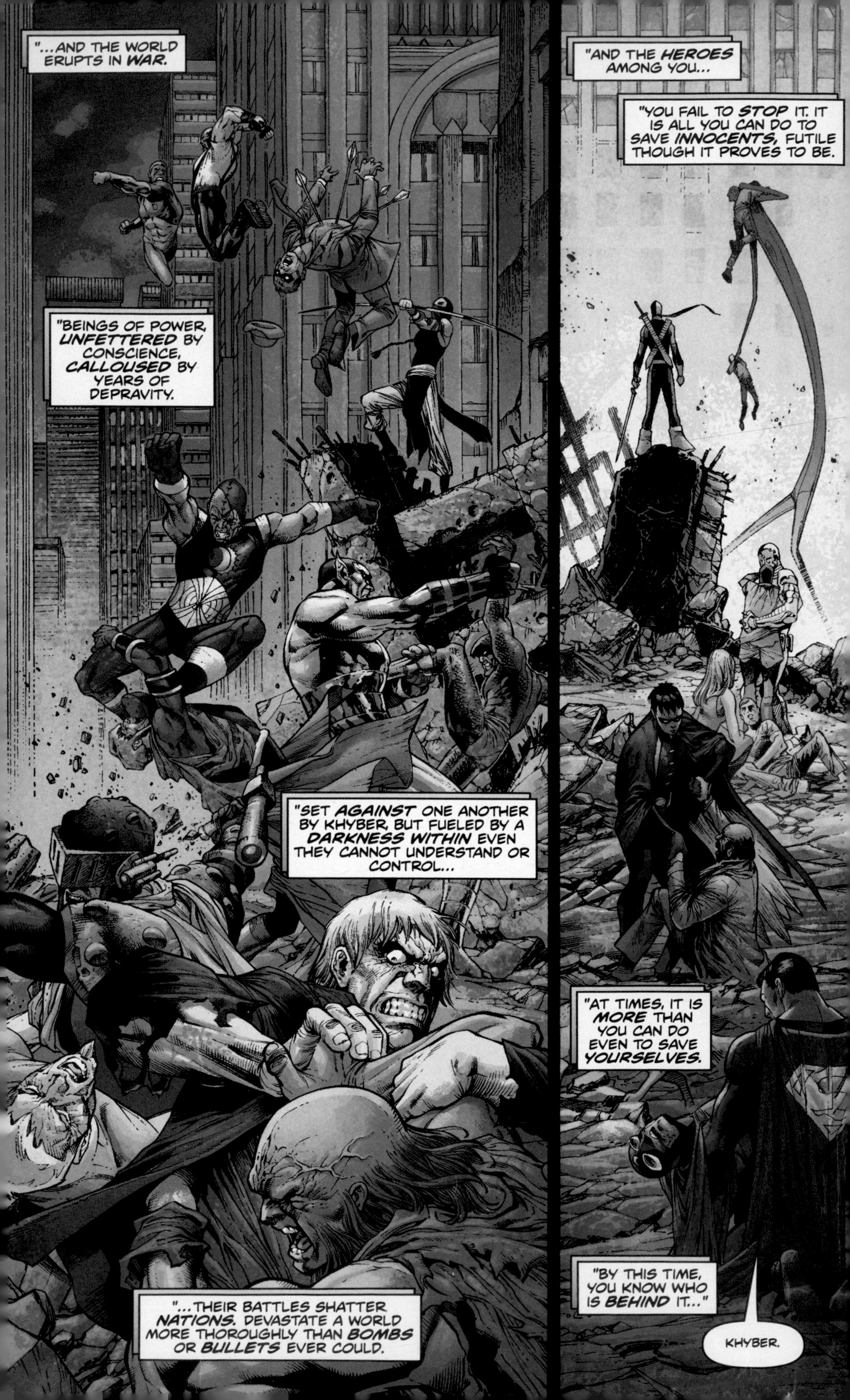
"...AND THE WORLD ERUPTS IN WAR.
"BEINGS OF POWER, UNFETTERED BY CONSCIENCE, CALLOUSED BY YEARS OF DEPRAVITY.
"SET AGAINST ONE ANOTHER BY KHYBER, BUT FUELED BY A DARKNESS WITHIN EVEN THEY CANNOT UNDERSTAND OR CONTROL...
"...THEIR BATTLES SHATTER NATIONS. DEVASTATE A WORLD MORE THOROUGHLY THAN BOMBS OR BULLETS EVER COULD.
"AND THE HEROES AMONG YOU...
"YOU FAIL TO STOP IT. IT IS ALL YOU CAN DO TO SAVE INNOCENTS, FUTILE THOUGH IT PROVES TO BE.
"AT TIMES, IT IS MORE THAN YOU CAN DO EVEN TO SAVE YOURSELVES.
"BY THIS TIME, YOU KNOW WHO IS BEHIND IT..."
KHYBER.

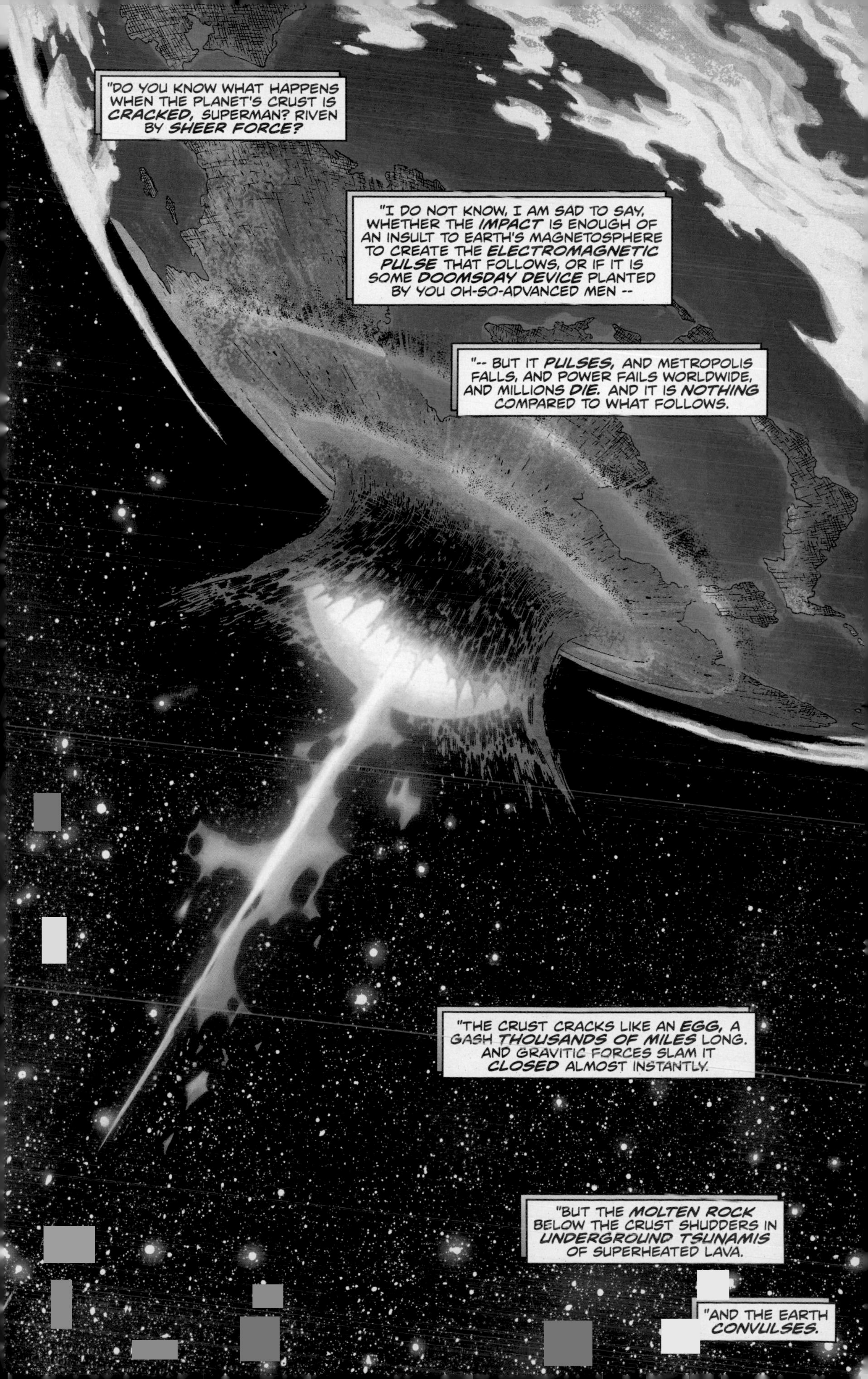
"DO YOU KNOW WHAT HAPPENS WHEN THE PLANET'S CRUST IS CRACKED, SUPERMAN? RIVEN BY SHEER FORCE?
"I DO NOT KNOW, I AM SAD TO SAY, WHETHER THE IMPACT IS ENOUGH OF AN INSULT TO EARTH'S MAGNETOSPHERE TO CREATE THE ELECTROMAGNETIC PULSE THAT FOLLOWS, OR IF IT IS SOME DOOMSDAY DEVICE PLANTED BY YOU OH-SO-ADVANCED MEN --
"-- BUT IT PULSES, AND METROPOLIS FALLS, AND POWER FAILS WORLDWIDE, AND MILLIONS DIE. AND IT IS NOTHING COMPARED TO WHAT FOLLOWS.
"THE CRUST CRACKS LIKE AN EGG, A GASH THOUSANDS OF MILES LONG. AND GRAVITIC FORCES SLAM IT CLOSED ALMOST INSTANTLY.
"BUT THE MOLTEN ROCK BELOW THE CRUST SHUDDERS IN UNDERGROUND TSUNAMIS OF SUPERHEATED LAVA.
"AND THE EARTH CONVULSES.

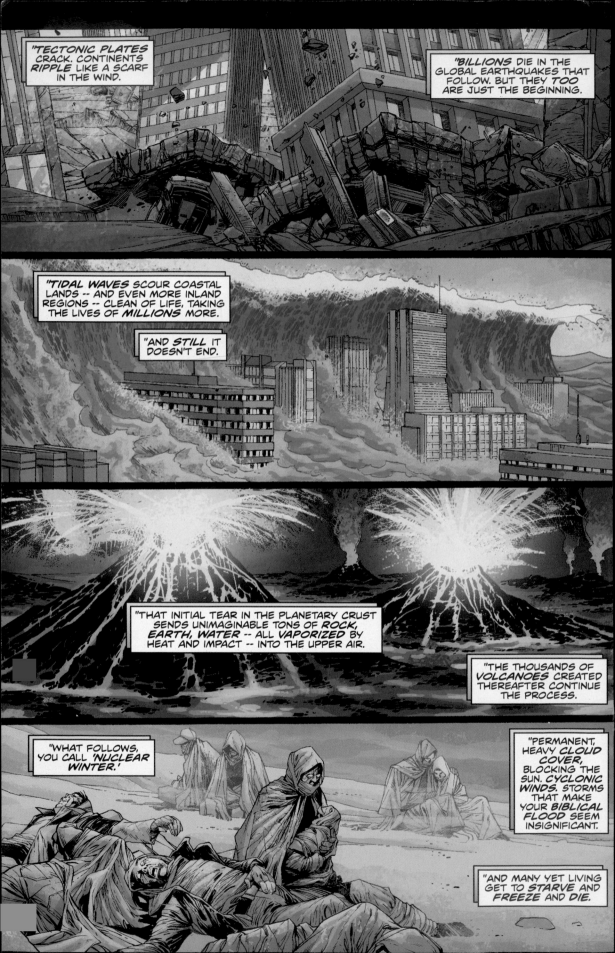

"KHYBER'S ALLIES AND SLAVES SEEK TO *CONSOLIDATE* THE WORLD UNDER HIS *REIGN*, AND OTHERS SEEK MERELY TO *SEIZE* WHAT THEY CAN."

"THOUGH PARTS OF THE WORLD ARE MORE *CONTESTED-OVER* THAN OTHERS."

"AND *STILL* YOU FOOLS FIGHT, OVER THE SCRAPS THAT REMAIN."

ZAK

WH -- ?

ZAK

ZAK

ZAK

ZAKK

LOOK, CHILDREN! LOOK!

OUR OWN *HIGHLY-REALISTIC, FULLY-DETAILED* PLAYSET, JAM-PACKED WITH ALL THE *ACCESSORIES* ANY INQUISITIVE YOUNG MIND COULD W--

I'LL TELL YOU THIS *ONCE,* TOYMAN: METROPOLIS IS *OFF-LIMITS.*

ITS PITIFUL FEW ARE UNDER *MY* PROTECTION. HERE, CIVILIZATION *STANDS.* AND *FROM* HERE, IT WILL SPREAD. THE AGE OF REASON *LIVES,* AND *LEX LUTHOR* IS ITS CHAMPION.

SPREAD THE *WORD.*

"BUT FEW MEN OF POWER ARE AS *HIGH-MINDED* EVEN AS LUTHOR, AND THE BROKEN WORLD IS *TORN* BETWEEN THEM."

"OCEAN MASTER TAKES THE *NORTH ATLANTIC,* AS PROMISED, AND WARS ON ALL OTHERS BENEATH THE SEA."

"*KOBRA* TAKES AS MUCH OF ASIA AS HE CAN PRY FROM KHYBER. THE *ATOMIC SKULL* IS GRANTED THE ANDES. THE CURIOUSLY-NAMED *MISTER BIG* BUILDS AN EMPIRE CENTERED ON LOS ANGELES."

"AND THEY *FIGHT* AND WAR AND *BLEED,* AND INNOCENTS DIE. AND ONE BY ONE, THEY *FALL* TO KHYBER..."

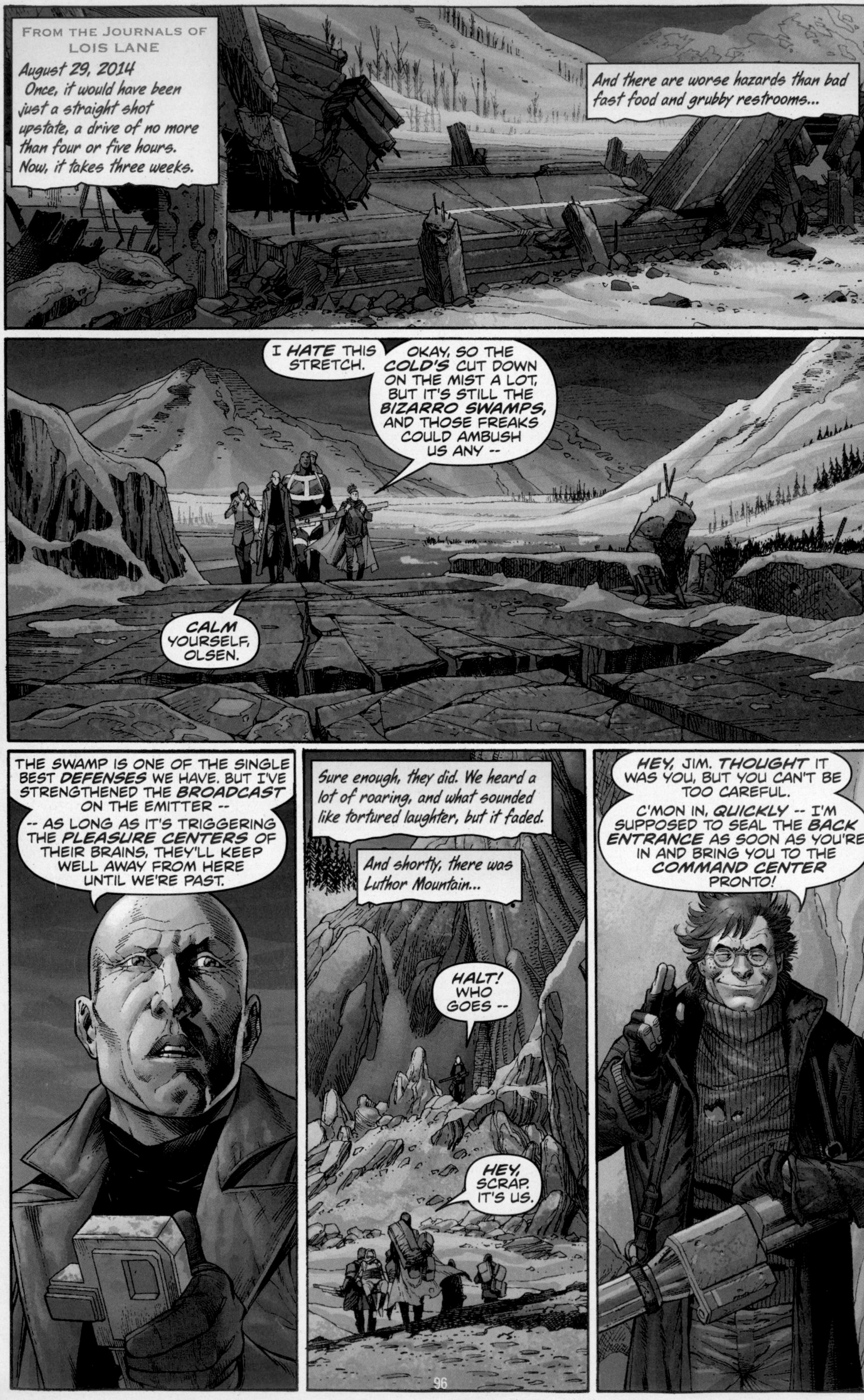

FROM THE JOURNALS OF LOIS LANE
August 29, 2014
Once, it would have been just a straight shot upstate, a drive of no more than four or five hours. Now, it takes three weeks.
And there are worse hazards than bad fast food and grubby restrooms...
I HATE THIS STRETCH.
OKAY, SO THE COLD'S CUT DOWN ON THE MIST A LOT, BUT IT'S STILL THE BIZARRO SWAMPS, AND THOSE FREAKS COULD AMBUSH US ANY --
CALM YOURSELF, OLSEN.
THE SWAMP IS ONE OF THE SINGLE BEST DEFENSES WE HAVE. BUT I'VE STRENGTHENED THE BROADCAST ON THE EMITTER --
-- AS LONG AS IT'S TRIGGERING THE PLEASURE CENTERS OF THEIR BRAINS, THEY'LL KEEP WELL AWAY FROM HERE UNTIL WE'RE PAST.
Sure enough, they did. We heard a lot of roaring, and what sounded like tortured laughter, but it faded.
And shortly, there was Luthor Mountain...
HALT! WHO GOES --
HEY, SCRAP. IT'S US.
HEY, JIM. THOUGHT IT WAS YOU, BUT YOU CAN'T BE TOO CAREFUL.
C'MON IN, QUICKLY -- I'M SUPPOSED TO SEAL THE BACK ENTRANCE AS SOON AS YOU'RE IN AND BRING YOU TO THE COMMAND CENTER PRONTO!

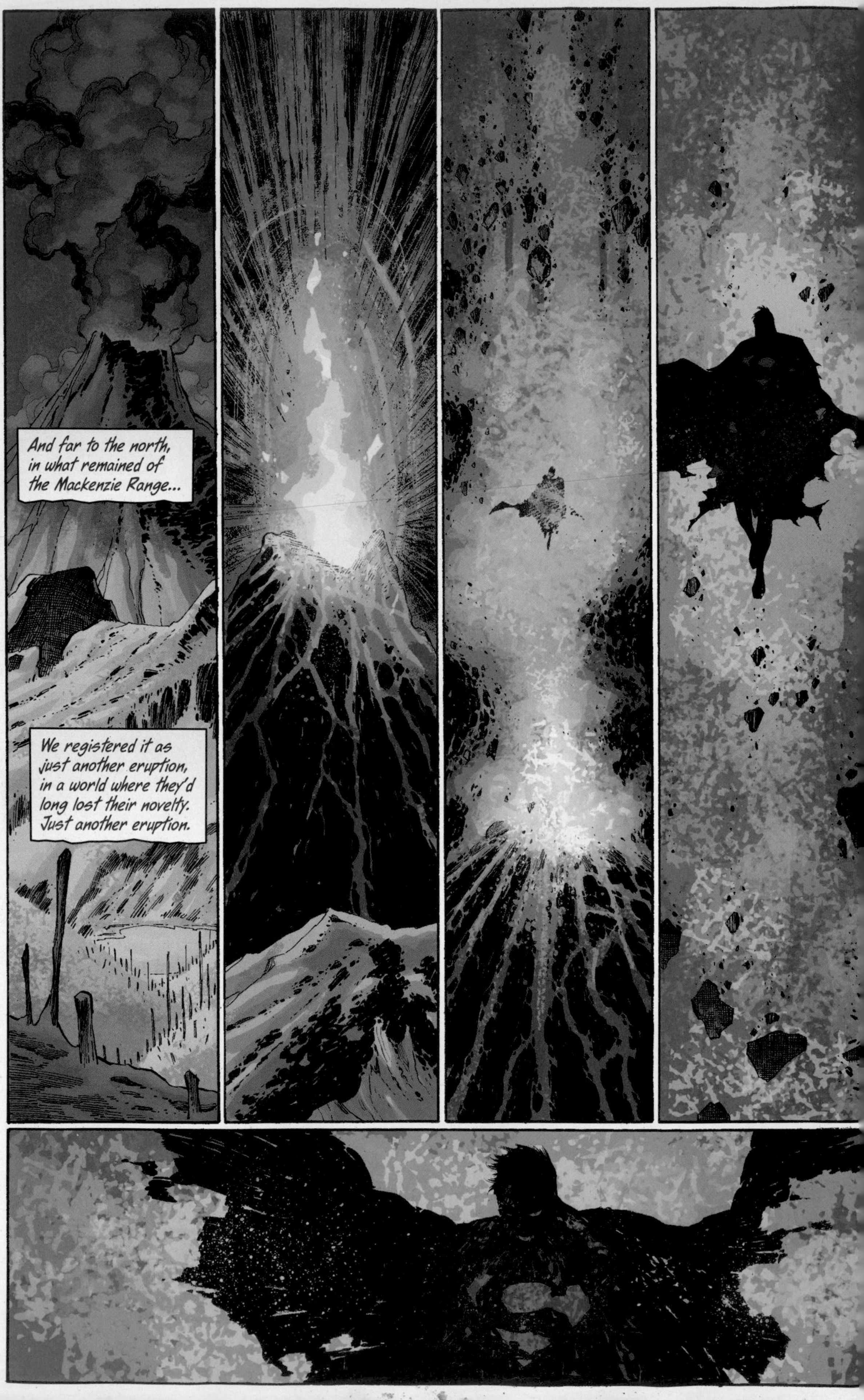
And far to the north, in what remained of the Mackenzie Range...
We registered it as just another eruption, in a world where they'd long lost their novelty. Just another eruption.

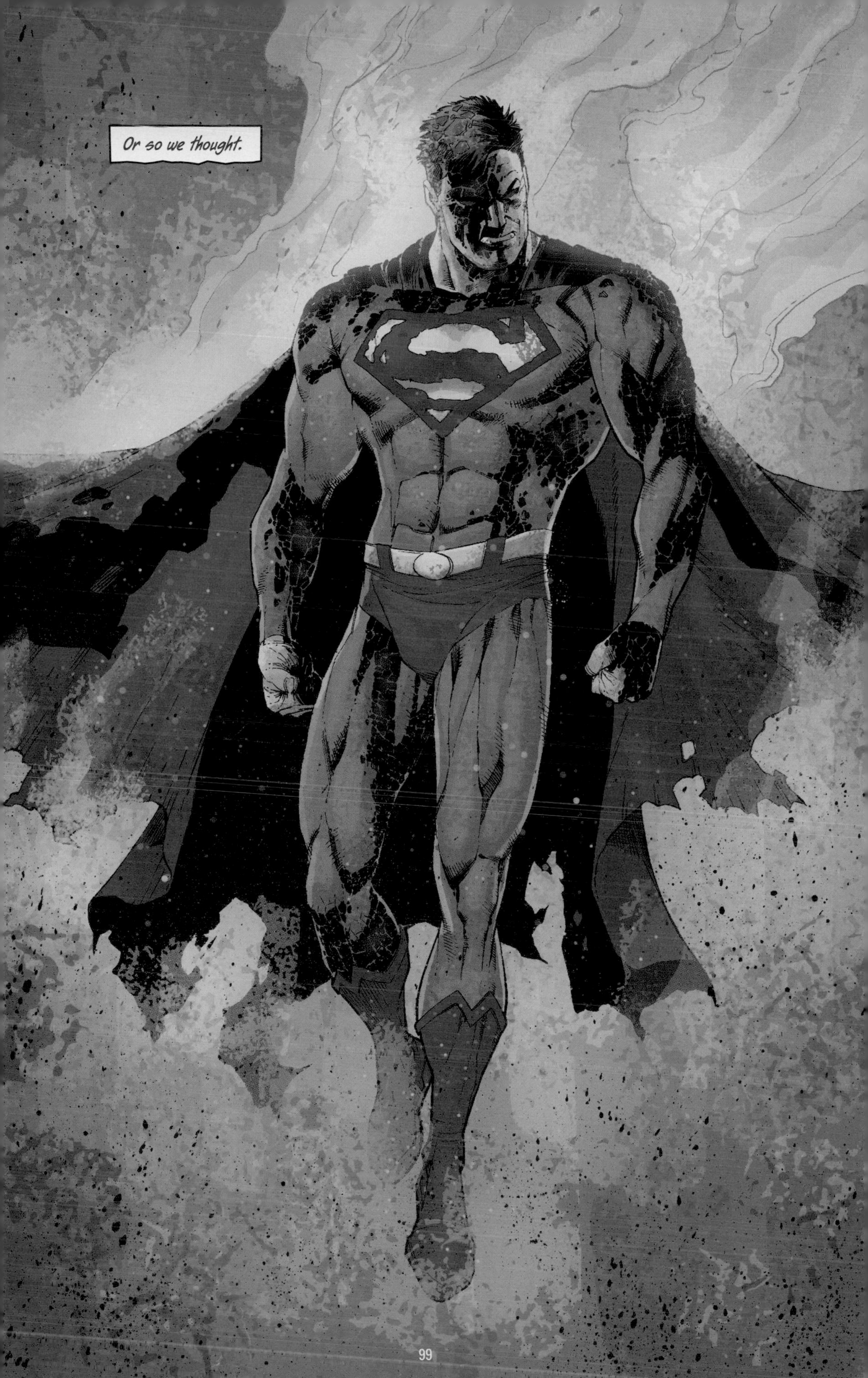
Or so we thought.

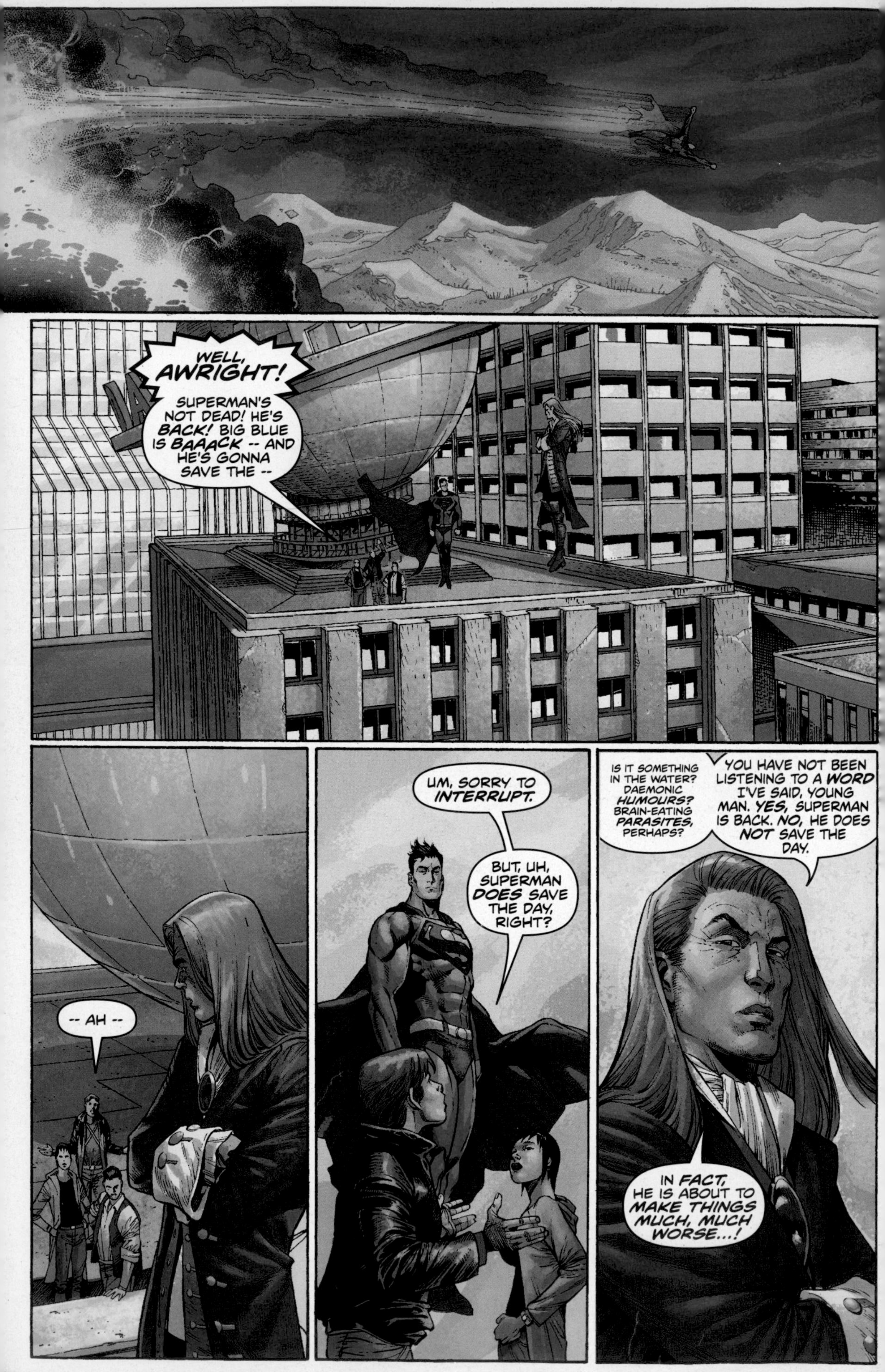

WELL, AWRIGHT!
SUPERMAN'S NOT DEAD! HE'S BACK! BIG BLUE IS BAAACK -- AND HE'S GONNA SAVE THE --
-- AH --
UM, SORRY TO INTERRUPT.
BUT, UH, SUPERMAN DOES SAVE THE DAY, RIGHT?
IS IT SOMETHING IN THE WATER? DAEMONIC HUMOURS? BRAIN-EATING PARASITES, PERHAPS?
YOU HAVE NOT BEEN LISTENING TO A WORD I'VE SAID, YOUNG MAN. YES, SUPERMAN IS BACK. NO, HE DOES NOT SAVE THE DAY.
IN FACT, HE IS ABOUT TO MAKE THINGS MUCH, MUCH WORSE...!

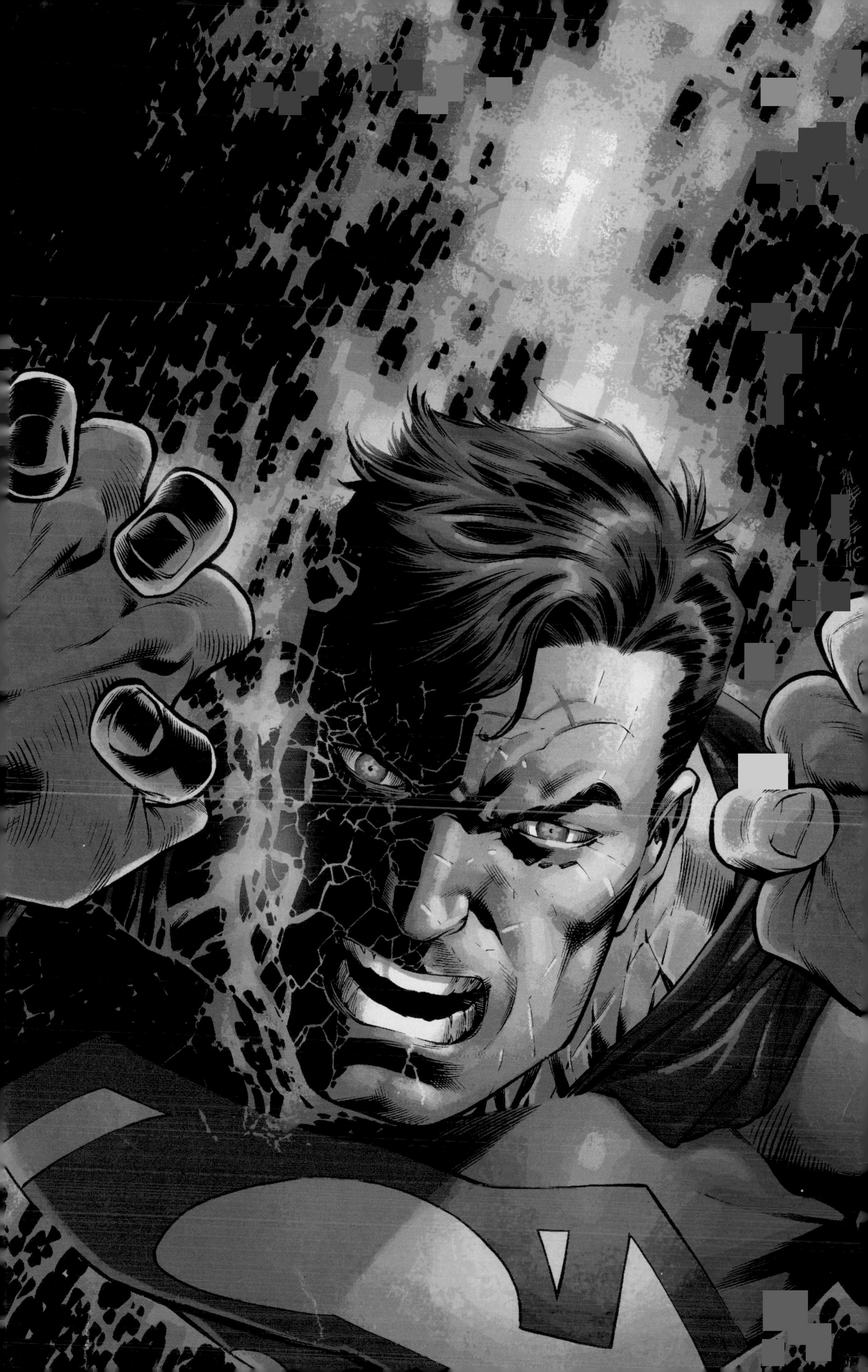

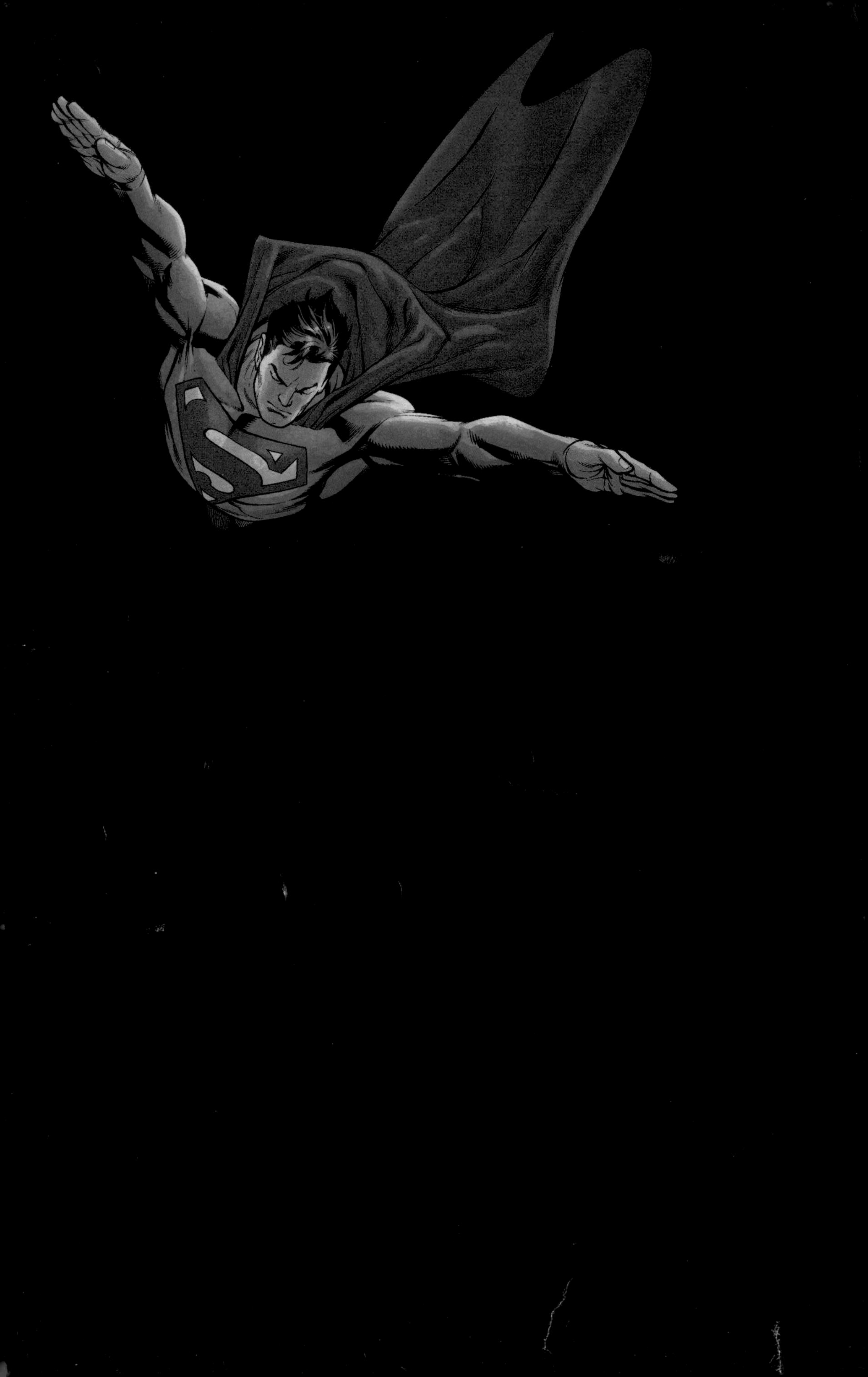

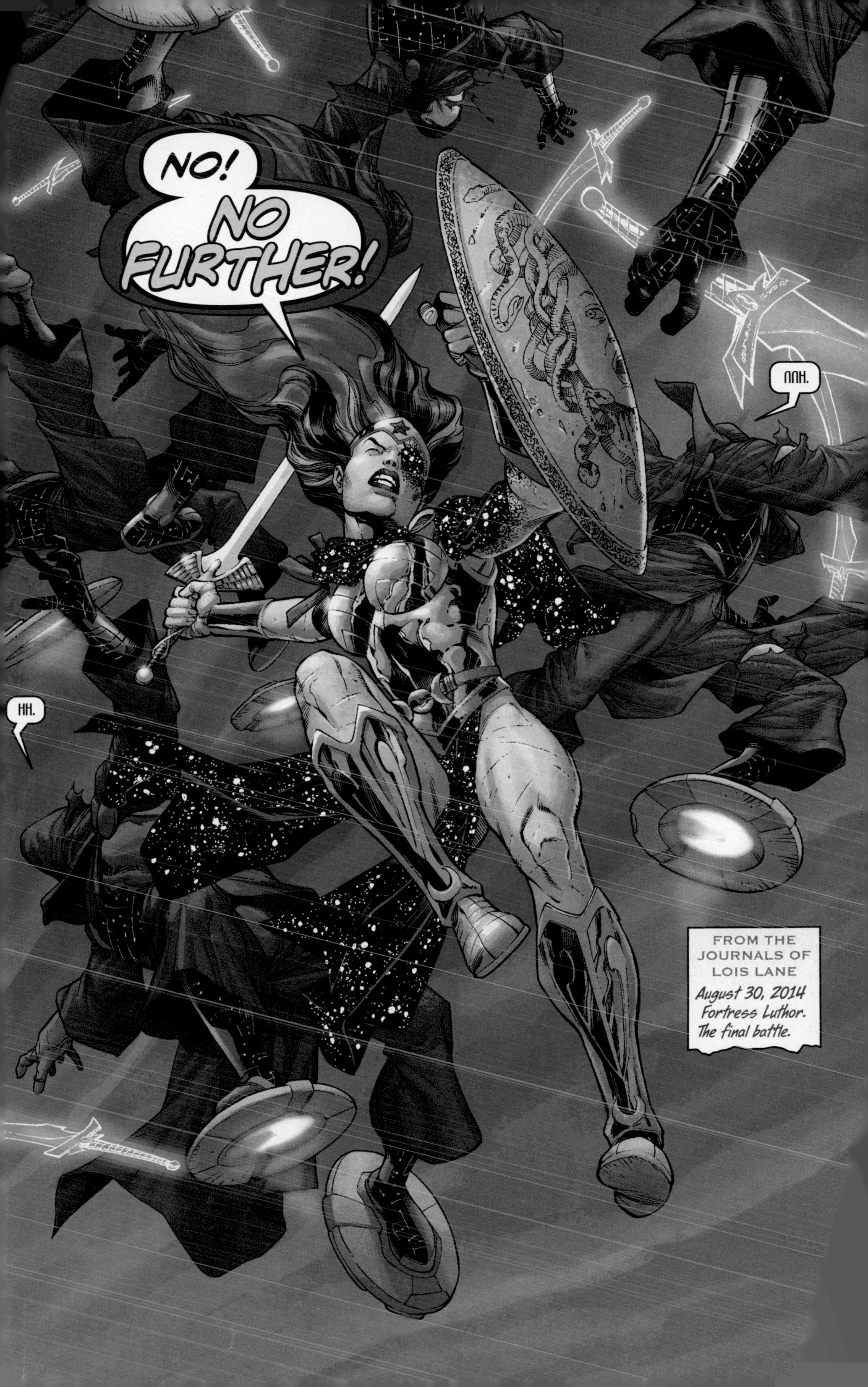
NO! NO FURTHER!
NNH.
HH.
FROM THE JOURNALS OF LOIS LANE
August 30, 2014
Fortress Luthor.
The final battle.

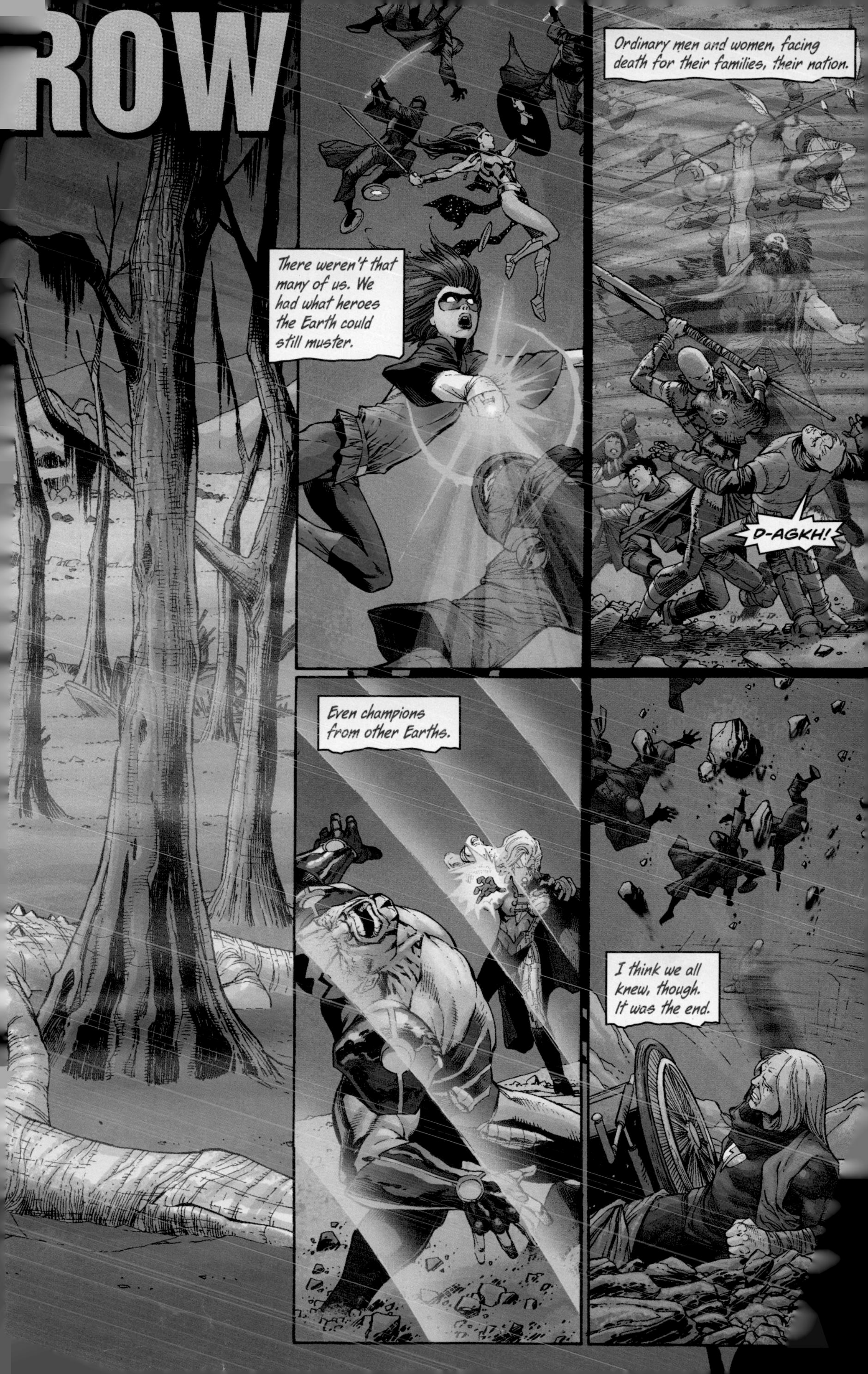
ROW
There weren't that many of us. We had what heroes the Earth could still muster.
Ordinary men and women, facing death for their families, their nation.
D-AGKH!
Even champions from other Earths.
I think we all knew, though. It was the end.

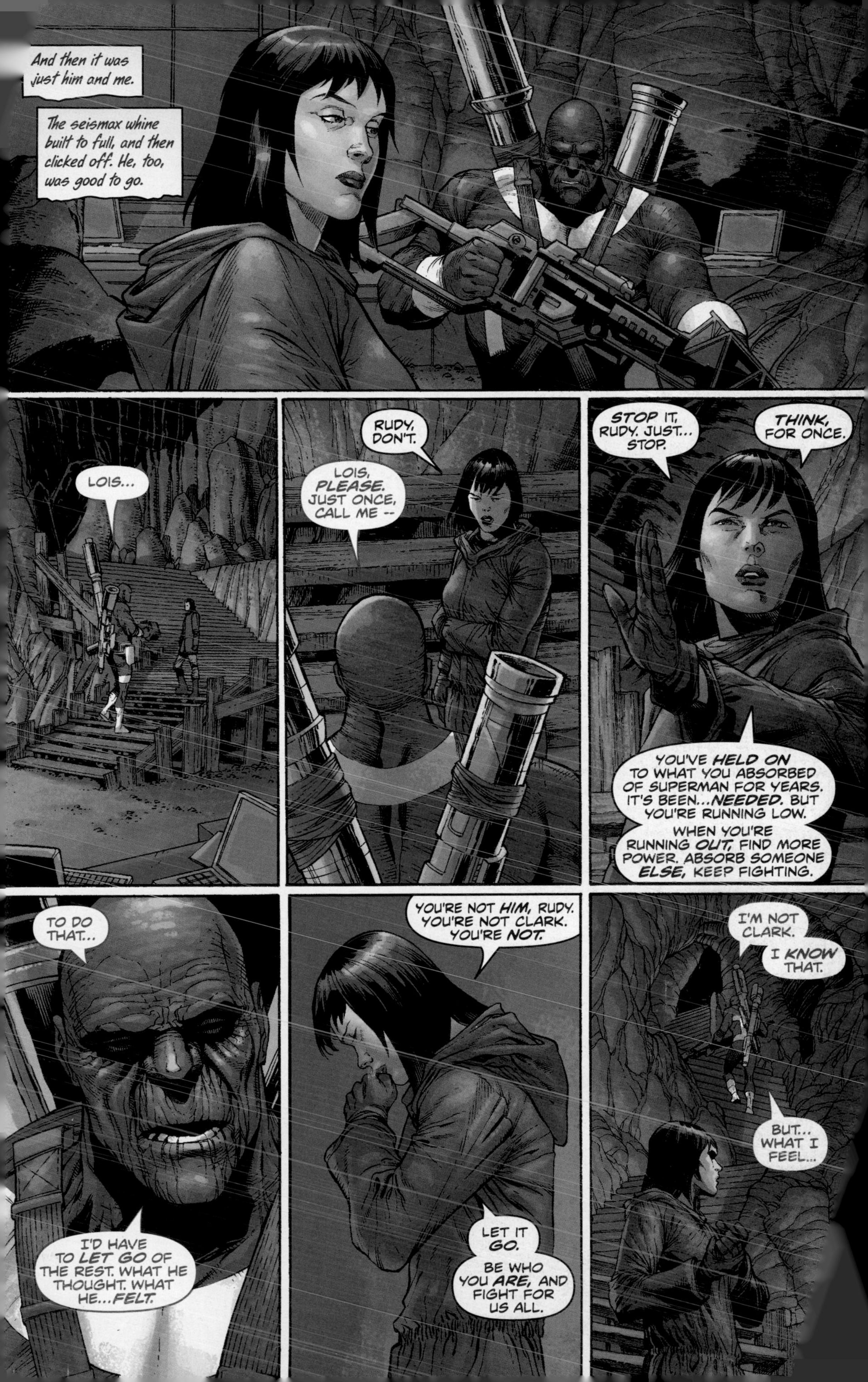
And then it was just him and me.
The seismax whine built to full, and then clicked off. He, too, was good to go.
LOIS...
RUDY, DON'T.
LOIS, PLEASE. JUST ONCE, CALL ME --
STOP IT, RUDY. JUST... STOP.
THINK, FOR ONCE.
YOU'VE HELD ON TO WHAT YOU ABSORBED OF SUPERMAN FOR YEARS. IT'S BEEN...NEEDED. BUT YOU'RE RUNNING LOW.
WHEN YOU'RE RUNNING OUT, FIND MORE POWER. ABSORB SOMEONE ELSE, KEEP FIGHTING.
TO DO THAT...
I'D HAVE TO LET GO OF THE REST. WHAT HE THOUGHT. WHAT HE...FELT.
YOU'RE NOT HIM, RUDY. YOU'RE NOT CLARK. YOU'RE NOT.
LET IT GO.
BE WHO YOU ARE, AND FIGHT FOR US ALL.
I'M NOT CLARK.
I KNOW THAT.
BUT... WHAT I FEEL...

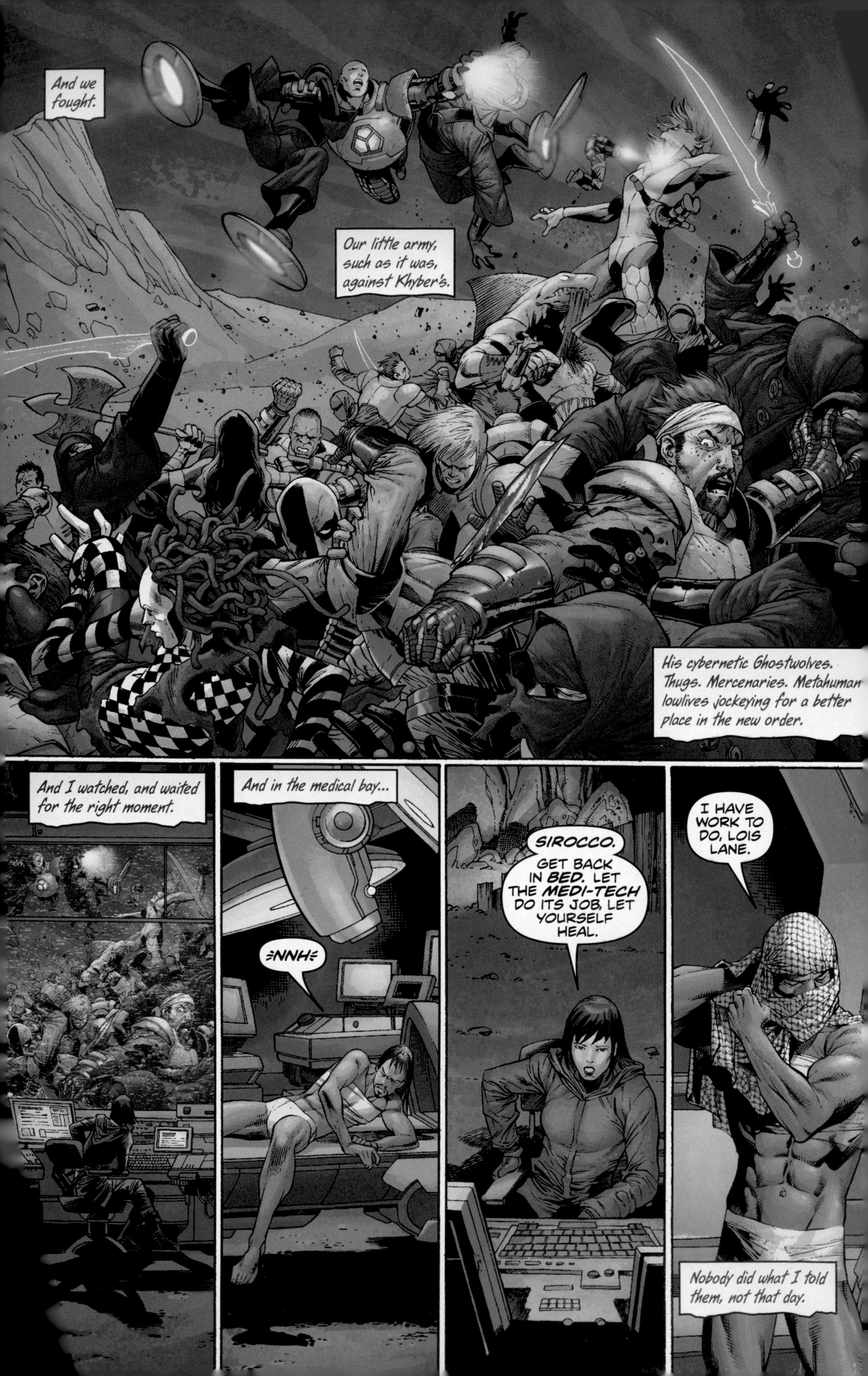

And we fought.
Our little army, such as it was, against Khyber's.
His cybernetic Ghostwolves. Thugs. Mercenaries. Metahuman lowlives jockeying for a better place in the new order.
And I watched, and waited for the right moment.
And in the medical bay...
NNH
SIROCCO.
GET BACK IN BED. LET THE MEDI-TECH DO ITS JOB, LET YOURSELF HEAL.
I HAVE WORK TO DO, LOIS LANE.
Nobody did what I told them, not that day.

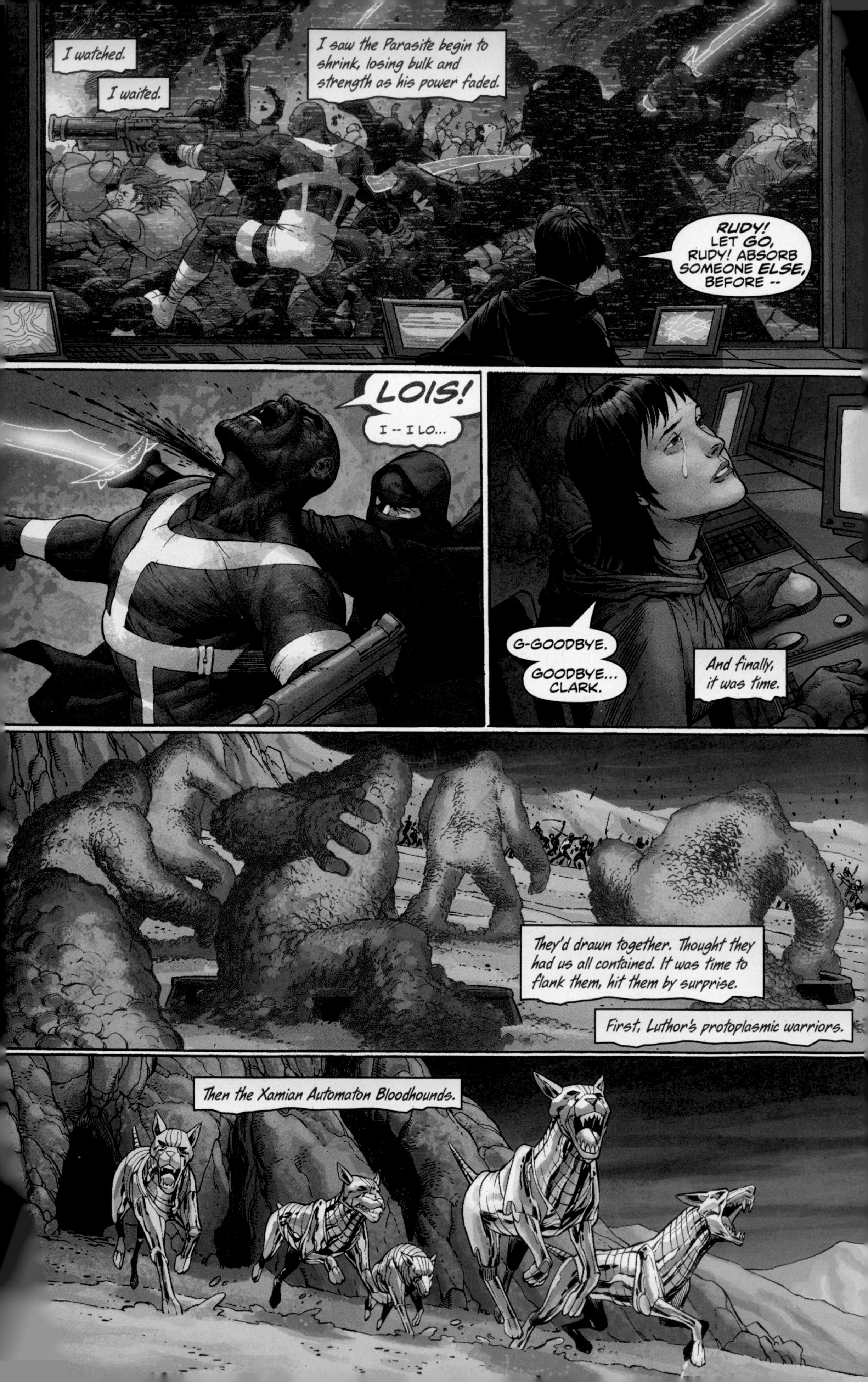
I watched.
I waited.
I saw the Parasite begin to shrink, losing bulk and strength as his power faded.
RUDY! LET GO, RUDY! ABSORB SOMEONE ELSE, BEFORE --
LOIS!
I -- I LO...
G-GOODBYE.
GOODBYE... CLARK.
And finally, it was time.
They'd drawn together. Thought they had us all contained. It was time to flank them, hit them by surprise.
First, Luthor's protoplasmic warriors.
Then the Xamian Automaton Bloodhounds.

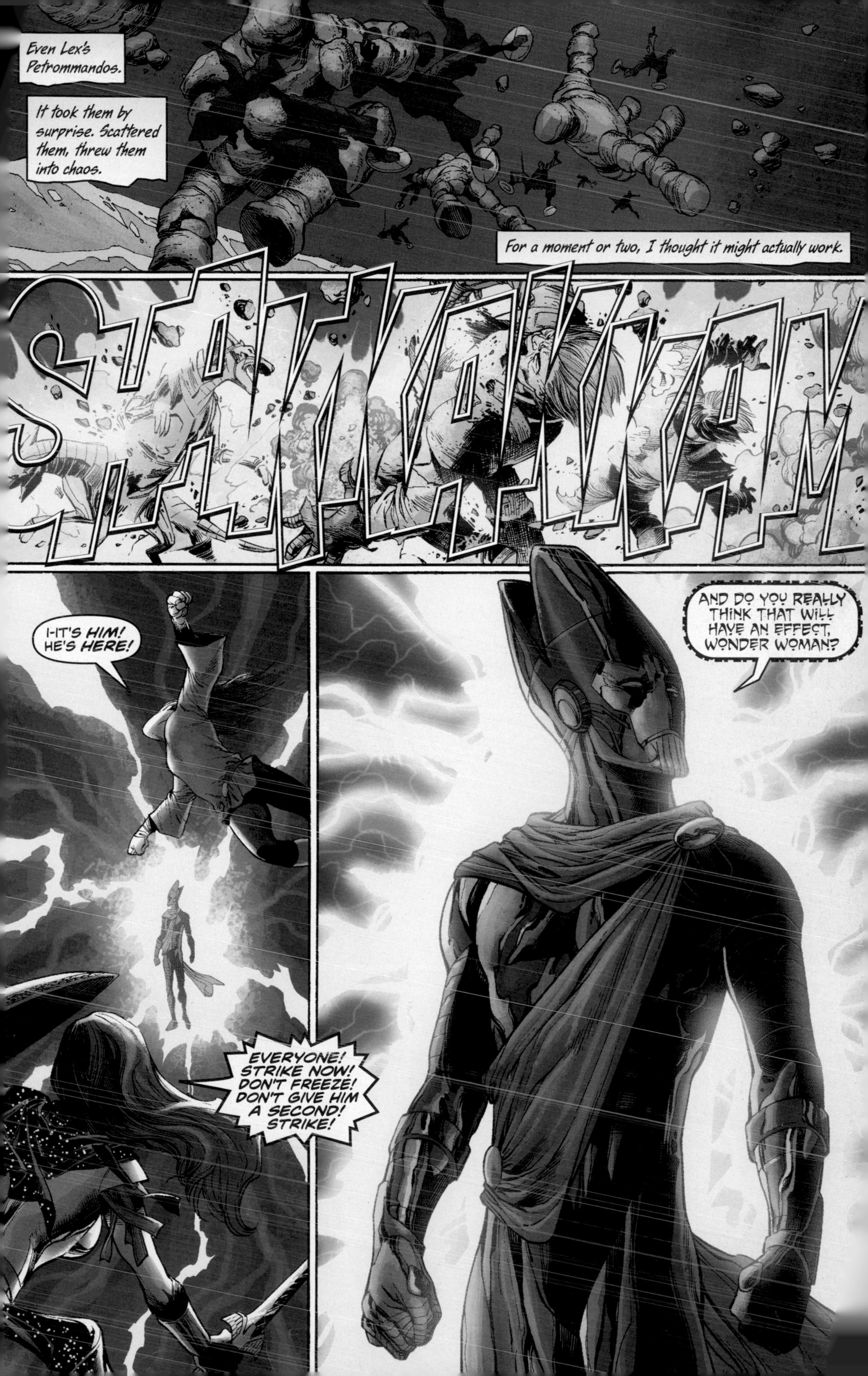
Even Lex's Petrommandos.
It took them by surprise. Scattered them, threw them into chaos.
For a moment or two, I thought it might actually work.
I-IT'S HIM! HE'S HERE!
EVERYONE! STRIKE NOW! DON'T FREEZE! DON'T GIVE HIM A SECOND! STRIKE!
AND DO YOU REALLY THINK THAT WILL HAVE AN EFFECT, WONDER WOMAN?

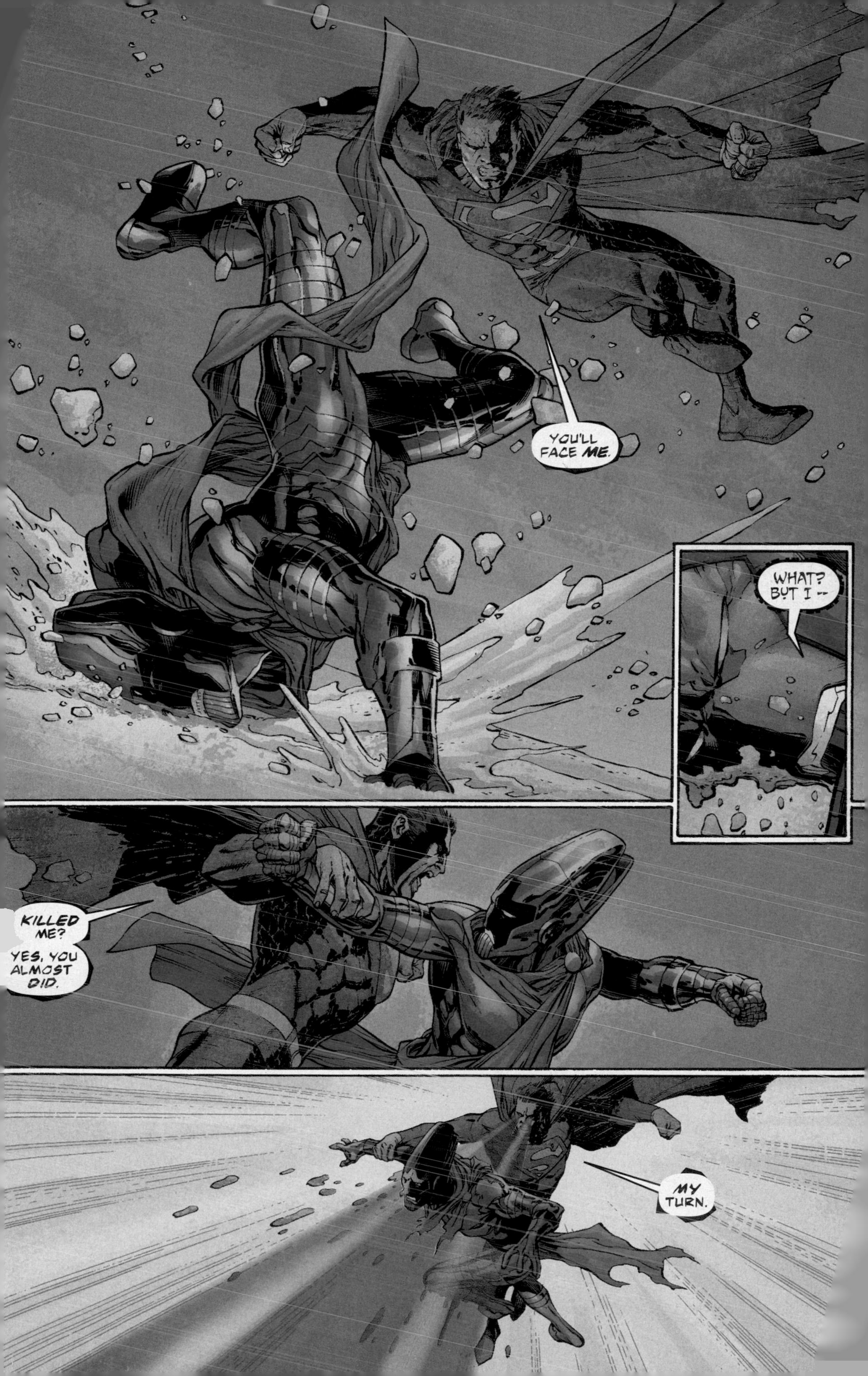
YOU'LL FACE ME.
WHAT? BUT I --
KILLED ME?
YES, YOU ALMOST DID.
MY TURN.

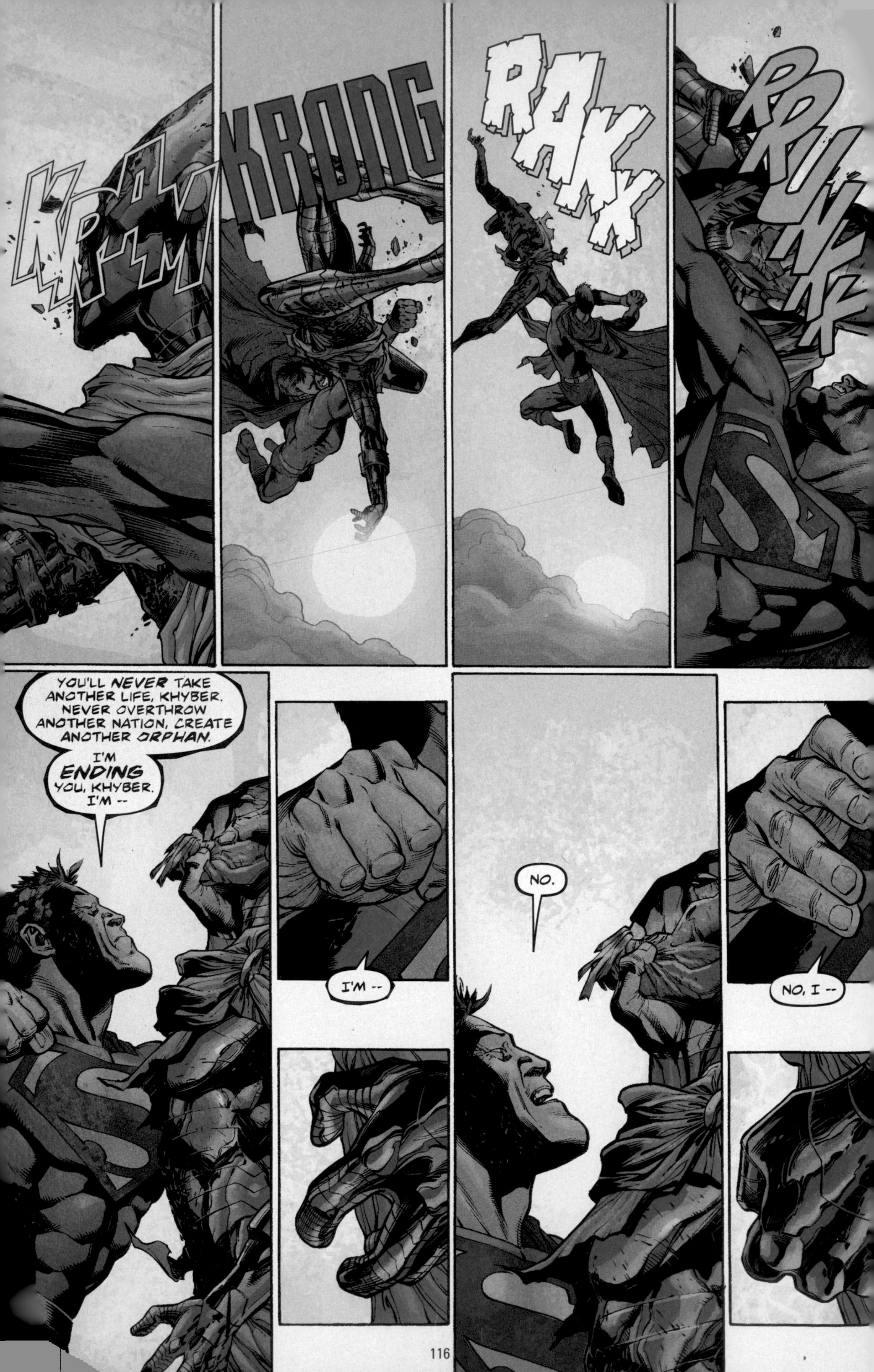

KRAM
KRONG
RAKK
RONK
YOU'LL NEVER TAKE ANOTHER LIFE, KHYBER. NEVER OVERTHROW ANOTHER NATION, CREATE ANOTHER ORPHAN.
I'M ENDING YOU, KHYBER. I'M --
I'M --
NO.
NO, I --

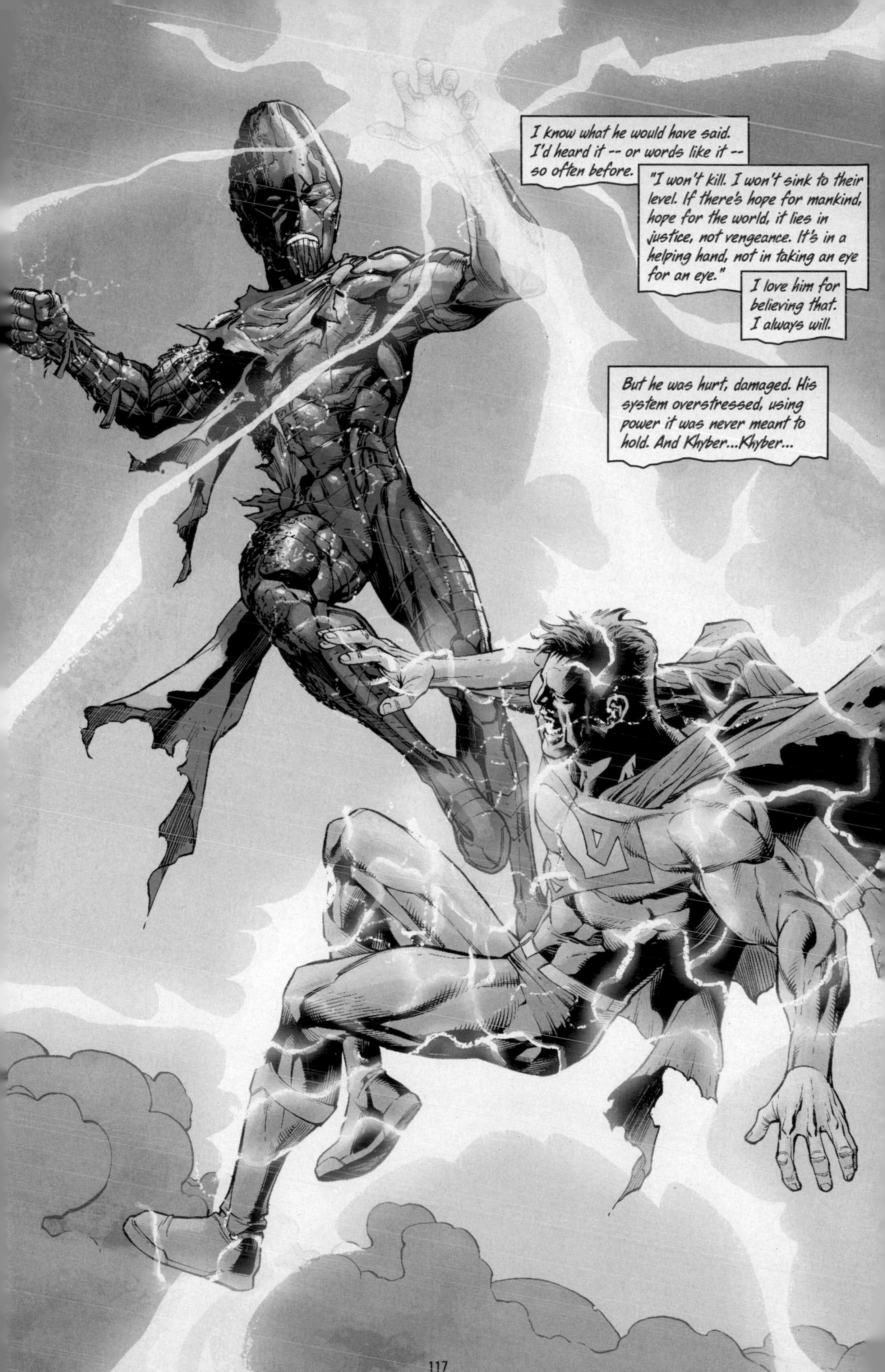
I know what he would have said. I'd heard it -- or words like it -- so often before.
"I won't kill. I won't sink to their level. If there's hope for mankind, hope for the world, it lies in justice, not vengeance. It's in a helping hand, not in taking an eye for an eye."
I love him for believing that. I always will.
But he was hurt, damaged. His system overstressed, using power it was never meant to hold. And Khyber...Khyber...

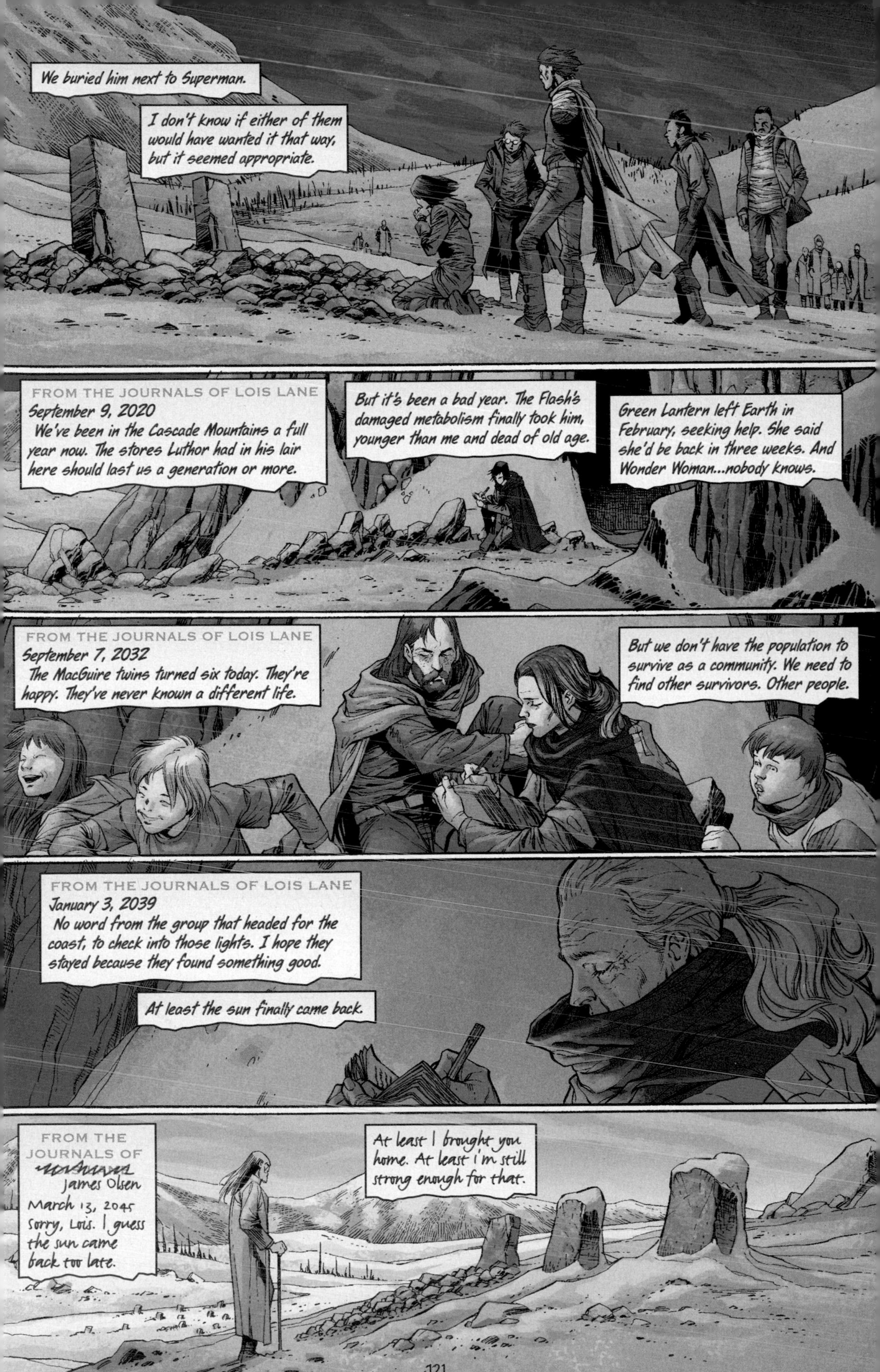
We buried him next to Superman.
I don't know if either of them would have wanted it that way, but it seemed appropriate.
FROM THE JOURNALS OF LOIS LANE
September 9, 2020
We've been in the Cascade Mountains a full year now. The stores Luthor had in his lair here should last us a generation or more.
But it's been a bad year. The Flash's damaged metabolism finally took him, younger than me and dead of old age.
Green Lantern left Earth in February, seeking help. She said she'd be back in three weeks. And Wonder Woman...nobody knows.
FROM THE JOURNALS OF LOIS LANE
September 7, 2032
The MacGuire twins turned six today. They're happy. They've never known a different life.
But we don't have the population to survive as a community. We need to find other survivors. Other people.
FROM THE JOURNALS OF LOIS LANE
January 3, 2039
No word from the group that headed for the coast, to check into those lights. I hope they stayed because they found something good.
At least the sun finally came back.
FROM THE JOURNALS OF
James Olsen
March 13, 2045
Sorry, Lois. I guess the sun came back too late.
At least I brought you home. At least I'm still strong enough for that.

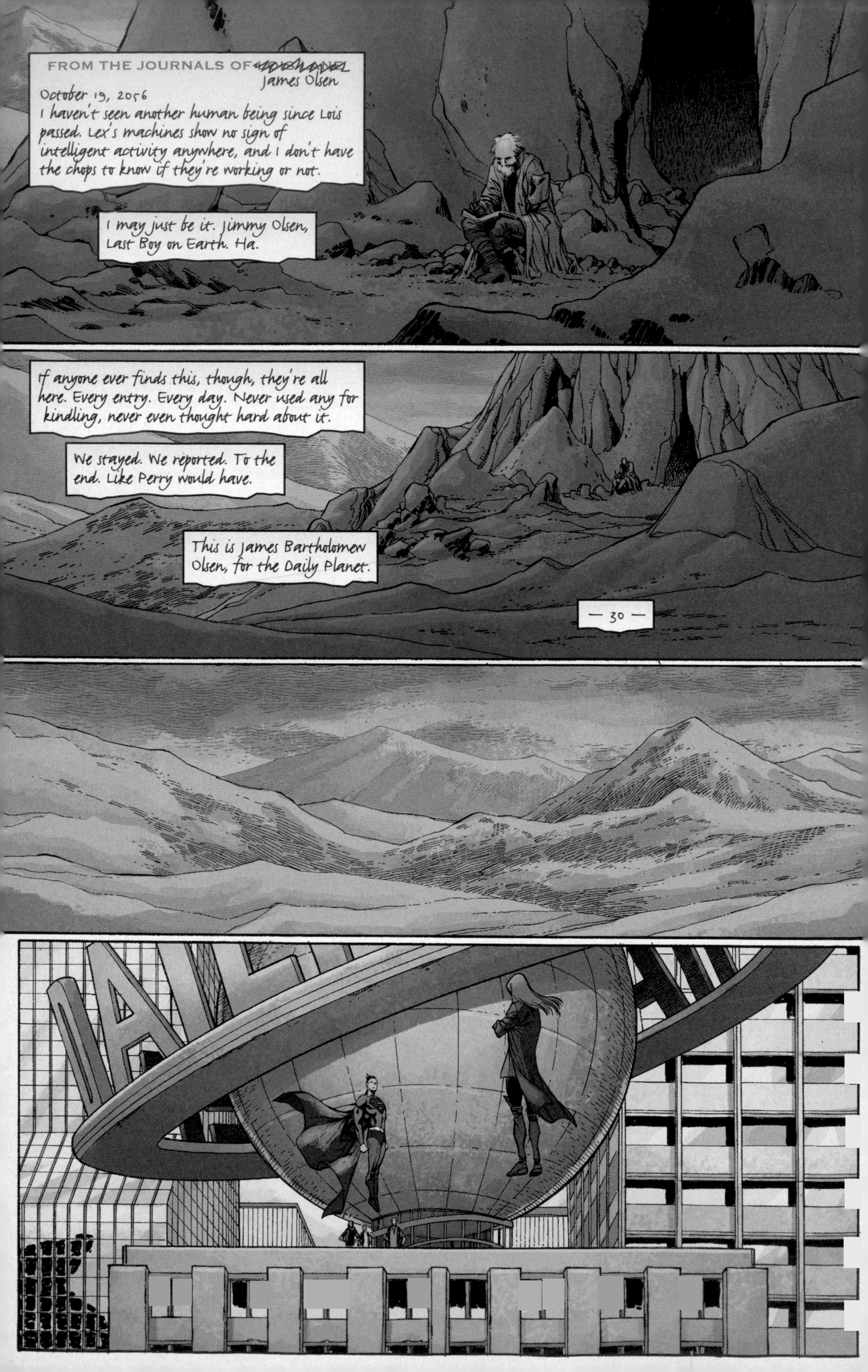
FROM THE JOURNALS OF James Olsen
October 19, 2056
I haven't seen another human being since Lois passed. Lex's machines show no sign of intelligent activity anywhere, and I don't have the chops to know if they're working or not.
I may just be it. Jimmy Olsen, Last Boy on Earth. Ha.
If anyone ever finds this, though, they're all here. Every entry. Every day. Never used any for kindling, never even thought hard about it.
We stayed. We reported. To the end. Like Perry would have.
This is James Bartholomew Olsen, for the Daily Planet.
— 30 —

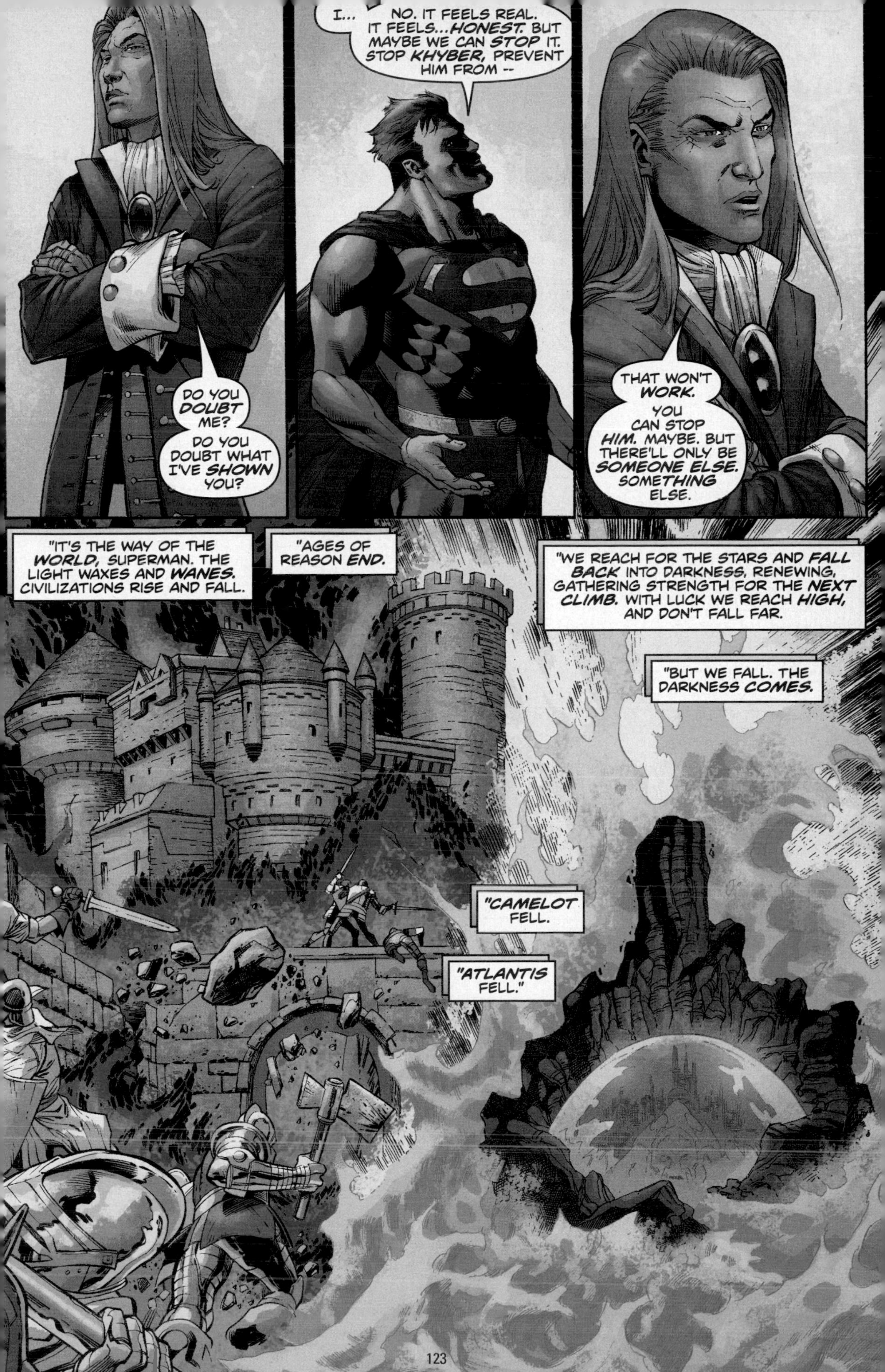
I...
NO. IT FEELS REAL. IT FEELS...HONEST. BUT MAYBE WE CAN STOP IT. STOP KHYBER, PREVENT HIM FROM --
DO YOU DOUBT ME?
DO YOU DOUBT WHAT I'VE SHOWN YOU?
THAT WON'T WORK.
YOU CAN STOP HIM. MAYBE. BUT THERE'LL ONLY BE SOMEONE ELSE. SOMETHING ELSE.
"IT'S THE WAY OF THE WORLD, SUPERMAN. THE LIGHT WAXES AND WANES. CIVILIZATIONS RISE AND FALL.
"AGES OF REASON END.
"WE REACH FOR THE STARS AND FALL BACK INTO DARKNESS, RENEWING, GATHERING STRENGTH FOR THE NEXT CLIMB. WITH LUCK WE REACH HIGH, AND DON'T FALL FAR.
"BUT WE FALL. THE DARKNESS COMES.
"CAMELOT FELL.
"ATLANTIS FELL."

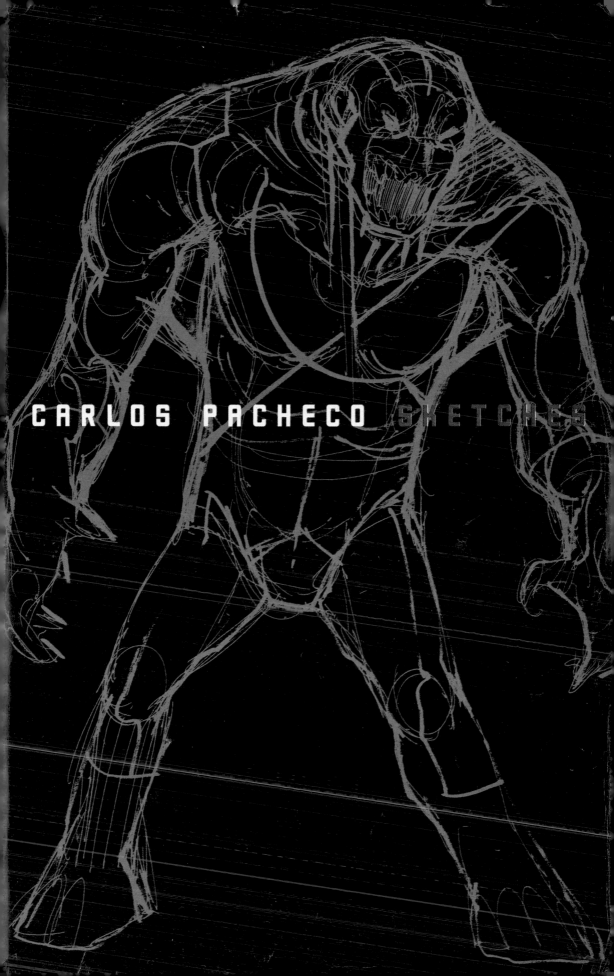

CARLOS PACHECO SKETCHES

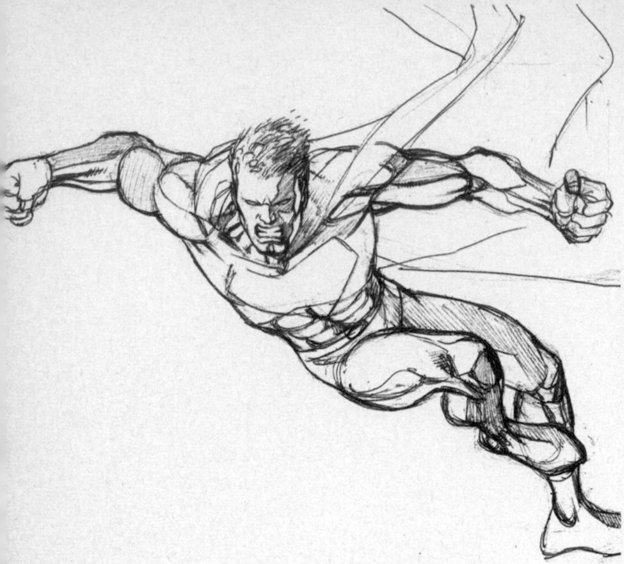

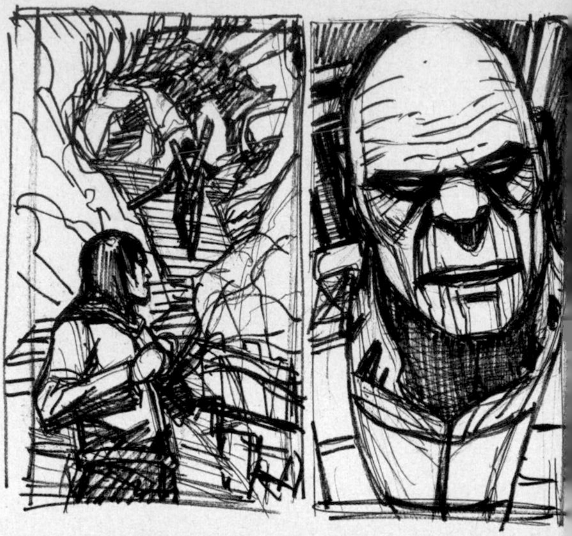

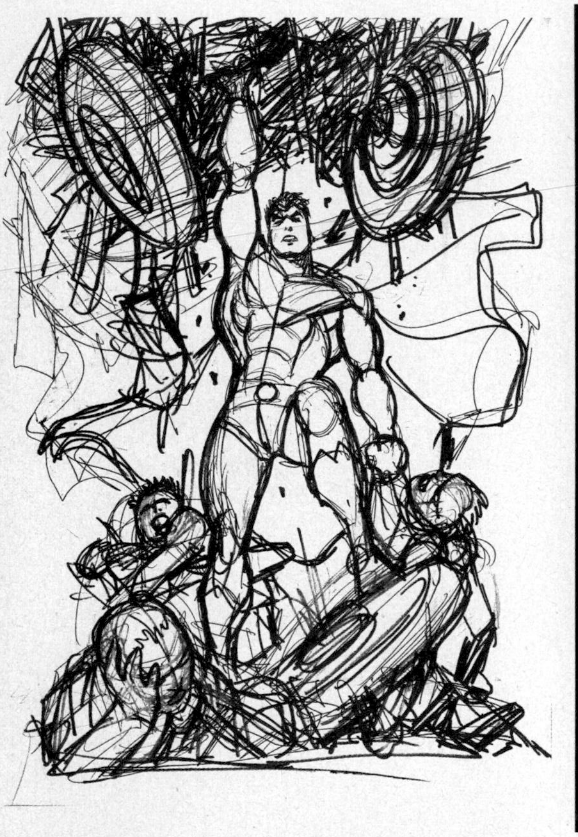

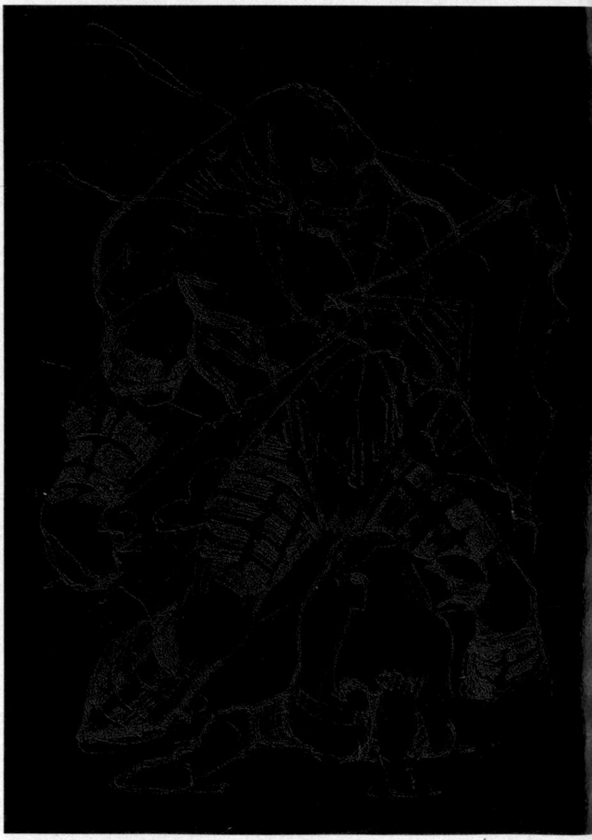

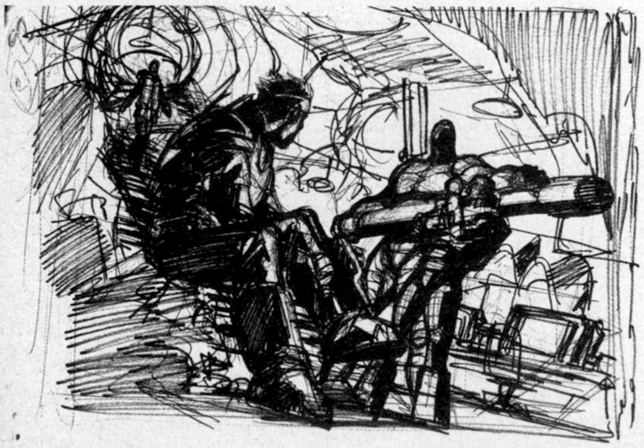

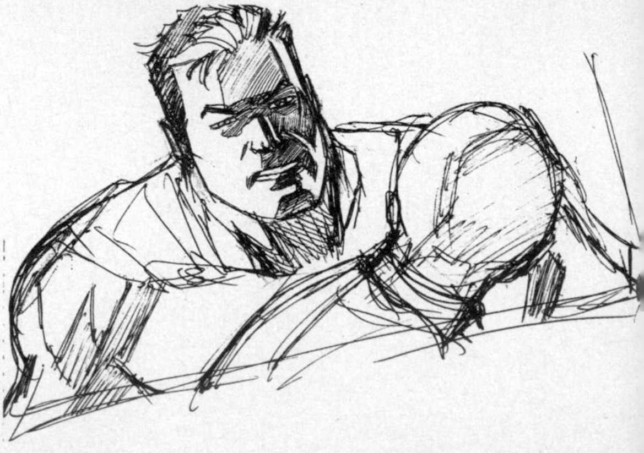

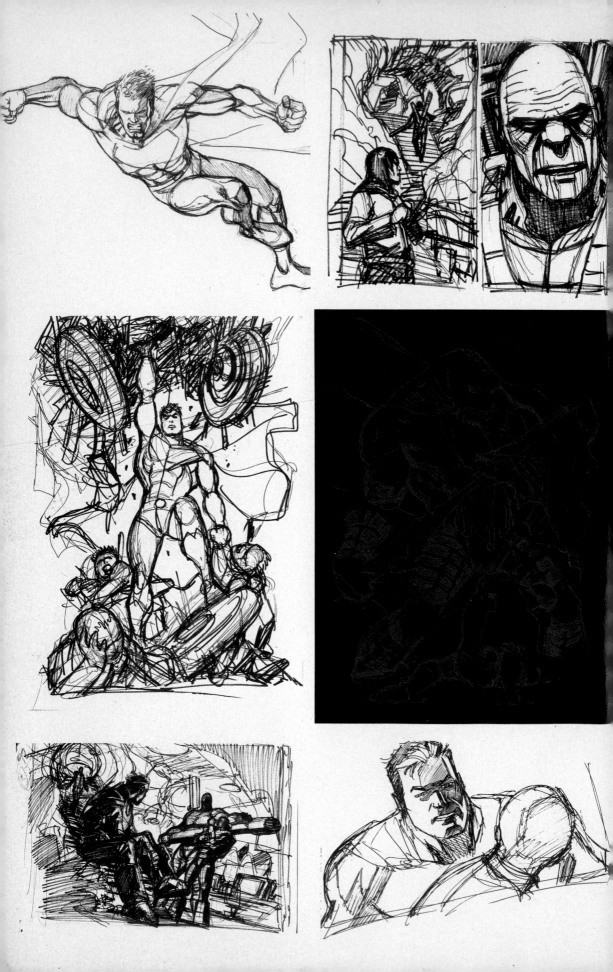

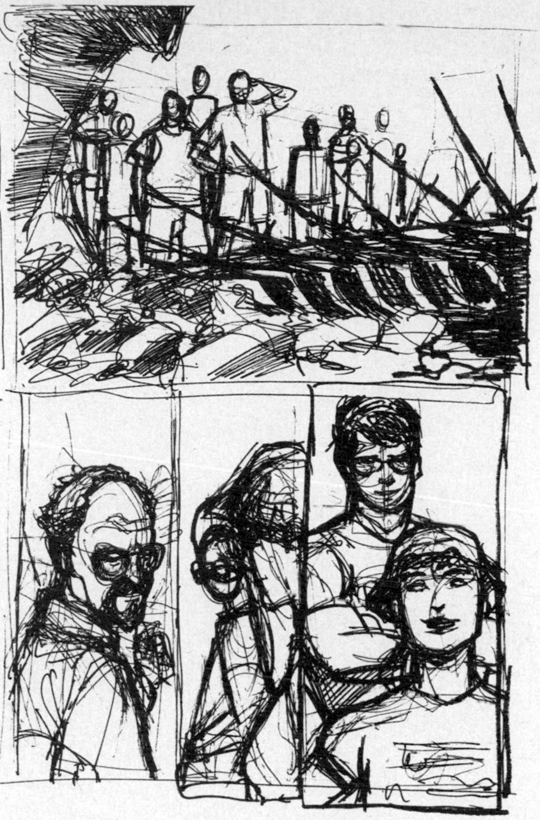

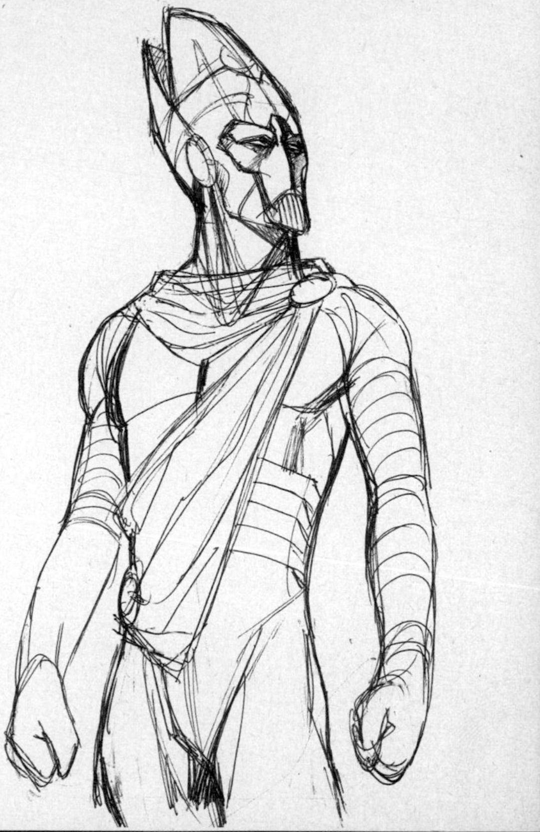

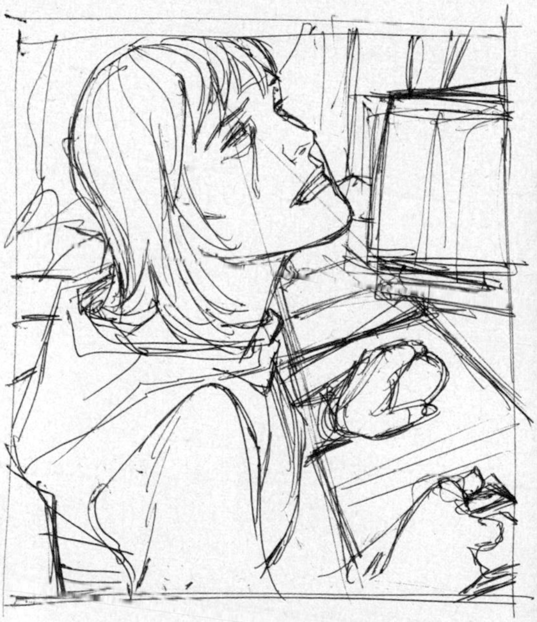

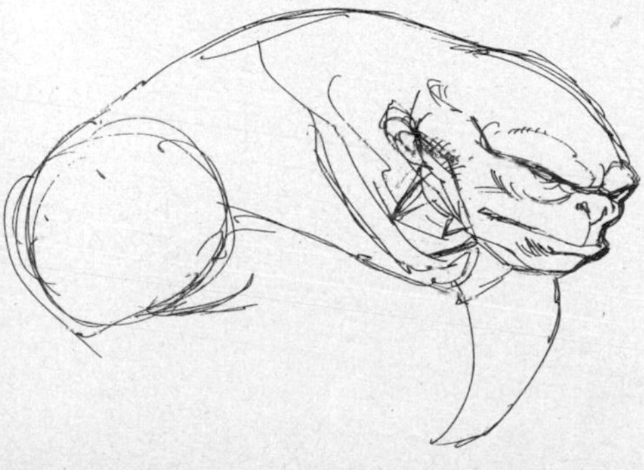

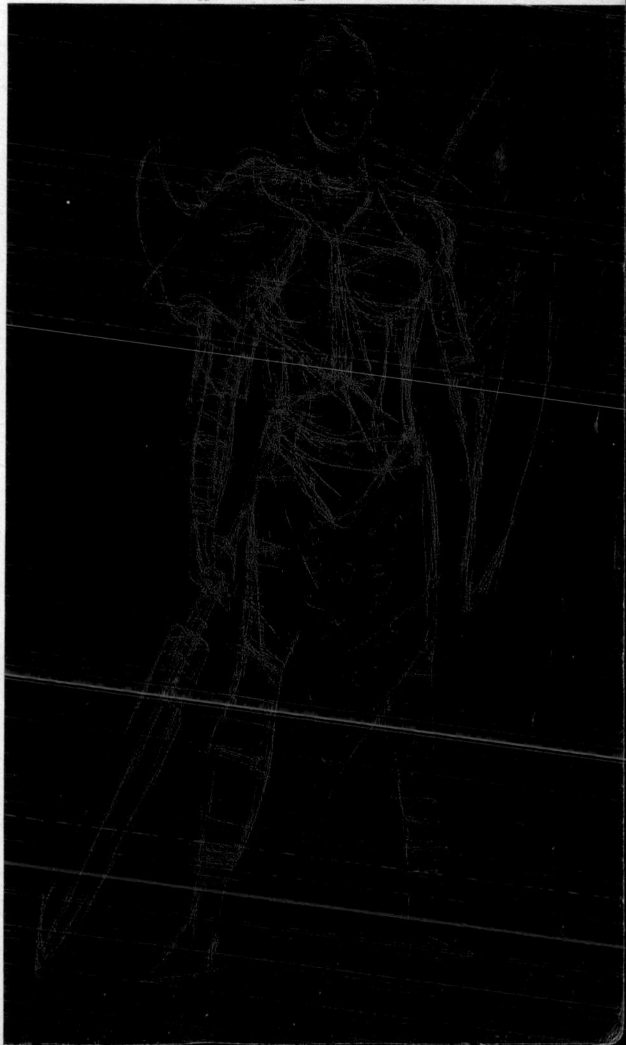

READ MORE OF THE MAN OF STEEL'S ADVENTURES IN THESE COLLECTIONS FROM DC COMICS:

SUPERMAN

BRIAN AZZARELLO JIM LEE SCOTT WILLIAMS
FOR TOMORROW
VOLUME ONE

SUPERMAN FOR TOMORROW VOLUME 1

Brian Azzarello, Jim Lee and Scott Williams tell the epic tale of a cataclysmic event that strikes the Earth, affecting millions – including those closest to the Man of Steel.

"A BIG HERO NEEDS A BIG STORY, AND THIS TEAM DOESN'T DISAPPOINT."
— THE WASHINGTON POST

SUPERMAN THE MAN OF STEEL VOLUME 1

JOHN BYRNE DICK GIORDANO
SUPERMAN
THE MAN OF STEEL

JOHN BYRNE
DICK GIORDANO

SUPERMAN FOR ALL SEASONS

Superman
For All Seasons
Jeph Loeb
Tim Sale
with Bjarne Hansen

JEPH LOEB
TIM SALE

THE DEATH OF SUPERMAN

THE BEST-SELLING GRAPHIC NOVEL OF ALL TIME!
THE DEATH OF
SUPERMAN
Dan JURGENS
Jerry ORDWAY
Louise SIMONSON
Roger STERN
Jon BOGDANOVE
Tom GRUMMETT
Jackson GUICE
Brett BREEDING
Rick BURCHETT
Doug HAZLEWOOD
Dennis JANKE
Denis RODIER

DAN JURGENS
JERRY ORDWAY
JACKSON GUICE

SEARCH THE GRAPHIC NOVELS SECTION OF

www.DCCOMICS.com

FOR ART AND INFORMATION ON ALL OF OUR BOOKS!

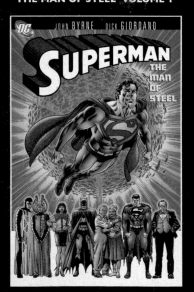

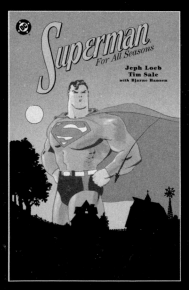

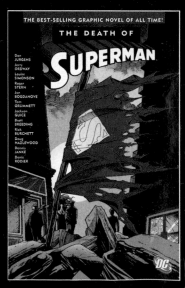